Wildlife in North Carolina

Wildlife in North Carolina

EDITED BY JIM DEAN & LAWRENCE S. EARLEY

Ken Taylor

The University of North Carolina Press / Chapel Hill & London

© 1987 The University of North Carolina Press

All rights reserved

Manufactured in the United States of America

Library of Congress Cataloging-in-Publication Data

Wildlife in North Carolina.

Articles and pictures from the magazine

Wildlife in North Carolina.

1. Natural history—North Carolina.   2. Nature

conservation—North Carolina.   3. North Carolina—

Description and travel.   I. Dean, Jim.   II. Earley,

Lawrence S.   III. Wildlife in North Carolina.

QH105.N8W55   1987   508.756   87-5858

ISBN 0-8078-1751-1

Contents

Introduction / vii

PART ONE: Sporting Heritage

Old Times on Currituck / 3
H. H. Brimley

Currituck's Historic Sporting Clubs / 9
Lawrence S. Earley

Core Sound Memoir / 16
*Julian Hamilton, Jr., as told to Lawrence S. Earley
and Ted Dossett*

Some North Carolina Decoys and Their Makers / 21
James S. Lewis, Jr.

Traditional Boats of North Carolina / 28
Mark Taylor

Johannes Plott's Famous Hunting Dogs / 36
Curtis Wooten

I'm a Bear Hunter / 41
Clyde Huntsinger, as told to Lawrence S. Earley

PART TWO: Flora and Fauna

Stalking the Old-Time Apples / 49
Doug Elliott

Willie and Me and the Two-Moon "Turkles" / 56
Paul Koepke

Those Incredible Hummingbirds / 59
Jane Rohling

Magnificent Monarchs / 65
Harry Ellis

Our Wild Orchids / 72
Doug Elliott

Discovering the World of Spiders / 79
Harry Ellis

The Ultimate Survivor / 85
Doug Elliott

PART THREE: Special Places

A Quest for Wilderness / 91
George Ellison

Following the French Broad / 102
Jay Davies

Discovering Stone Mountain / 108
Terry Shankle

Rambling the Uwharries / 116
Jane Rohling

Two Days in John Green's Swamp / 124
Lawrence S. Earley

Mattamuskeet Memories / 131
Jim Dean

Saving Nags Head Woods / 138
Michael Godfrey

PART FOUR: Hunting and Fishing

The Perfect Bird Hunt / 147
Mike Gaddis

Three Score and Three with Whitetails / 151
Charles Elliott

Brackish Water Bass / 158
Joel Arrington

Into Big Timber Creek / 163
Stewart Hardison

Two Different Ducks / 168
Joel Arrington

Gigging and Swatting / 173
Curtis Wooten

A History of Blues / 177
Joel Arrington

Ten to One / 186
Rod Amundson

Thirty-five Acres Was the World / 188
Mike Gaddis

A Country Store Gourmet / 191
Jim Dean

Epilogue / 195

Publication History / 197

Contributors / 199

OUR NATURAL HERITAGE

Ship of Frogs / 14
Death of a Turtle / 34
Cutting the Tree / 54
Everything but the Squeal / 70
Where the Wind Comes From / 100
Fishing for Ice Age Trout / 114
A Kinship in Stone / 122
The Expendable Bobwhite / 156
Calendar Art and the Sacrificial Bass / 166
Fly Fishing for Grouse / 184

Introduction

On a given day in North Carolina, a fisherman may be mending a net on a remote island along the coast as a mountaineer splits oak shingles in the shadow of the Appalachians. Waterfowl hunters crouch in a Currituck blind and watch a distant "smoke" of ducks, while a bear hunter in Madison County cocks his head to listen to the dogs as they work their way through a laurel "hell." A city housewife stops at her window to watch two hummingbirds quarreling over the rights to a syrup feeder, as hikers pause along a wilderness trail to photograph wild orchids. An alligator pokes its snout through a bed of floating duckweed in an eastern swamp at the same moment that a fly-fisherman in the Smokies lands a native brook trout. Or perhaps a surfer at Hatteras is catching the perfect curl just as a canoeist on a Piedmont river picks the wrong chute and pays an icy price for the mistake.

It's an amazingly diverse place, this 33-million-acre state we call home, a land of such rich natural resources and outdoor traditions that not even a monthly magazine could exhaust all the potential throughout its 50 years of existence. As the official publication of the North Carolina Wildlife Resources Commission, *Wildlife in North Carolina* has explored these resources and traditions, and the book you are holding consists of articles that have appeared in the magazine at some time during this period. They, of course, are merely "windows" that open onto North Carolina's wildlife and sporting heritage.

There is much to see and appreciate. Yet, whether you are a longtime native of North Carolina or a newcomer, we hope to give you at least a sampling of this astonishing diversity. Stretching longitudinally like a lazy hound, our borders encompass one of the most extensive barrier island and estuarine systems in the world. Moving west from the Atlantic, those borders enclose the Piedmont plateau and eventually gather in the highest mountains east of the Mississippi River.

Because North Carolina also lies between the Deep South and the far North in latitude, its landscape is a natural crossroads for many species of plants and animals. A climate that may range from subtropical along the south coast to near Arctic on the peaks of the tallest mountains further enhances this incredible diversity.

Longtime readers of *Wildlife in North Carolina* should find some old favorites in this book—features, photographs, and artwork reprinted, for the most part, from issues that have appeared since the magazine adopted a largely full-color format. Though many of the photos and artwork that appeared throughout our earlier history are long gone, and the articles dated, we've added bits and pieces of this early material to preserve our links to the past. Even so, it has been no easy task to decide what to print and what to leave out. The list was initially narrowed to 200 articles, then 70, then 40, and finally the last painful cuts were made to reach a consensus between the editors and the publisher. The book, therefore, is divided into four categories—sporting heritage, flora and fauna, special places, and hunting and fishing. These categories do not cover all subjects treated by the magazine, nor do these articles represent what we feel to be the "best of *Wildlife in North Carolina*." Many features were left out simply because they did not fit the theme of the book. Also, although the magazine has published many hard-hitting environmental articles over the years, some of them are now dated.

North Carolina, of course, has changed greatly since our first issue, much of that change reflecting an increasing urbanization and industrialization along with a loss of rural flavor and uncharted wilderness. Perhaps this change has been inevitable, and some would argue that it is for the better. Yet, those of us who have witnessed the loss of a favorite jumping-off spot, or paid a sad visit to an old swimming hole long since dammed or polluted, would remain unconvinced.

The good news, however, is that North Carolina still has an opportunity to benefit greatly from the stewardship of its citizens. If we recognize the beauty around us and the value of our natural resources and sporting traditions, we can find ways to make certain they are part of our future. If we understand the biological dynamics of our wildlife, we can sustain or even improve its chance for lasting prosperity.

These are not idle hopes. In this decade, we have seen some promising beginnings. Unlikely coalitions of environmentalists and developers have combined to protect sensitive natural areas. Industrial giants and conservation organizations have joined forces to save valuable wetlands. Hunters and fishermen have greatly enhanced populations of white-tailed deer, wild turkeys, and other game species. Nonsportsmen and sportsmen have worked hand-in-hand to protect nongame species and help restore threatened or endangered species such as bald eagles, peregrine falcons, and brown pelicans.

This, then, is not simply an introduction to some of North Carolina's more interesting and enchanting places, or a nostalgic look at sporting traditions. Nor is it merely an introduction to some of the more fascinating creatures that share our part of the world. It's all of those things, to be sure, but perhaps it can be more. Our hope is to also inspire a greater cooperative effort from all North Carolinians to appreciate, understand, and enhance the natural qualities that make this state unique.

We all have a stake in this, and our ultimate goals are remarkably similar. Stated simply, these are things we celebrate. These are things we want to keep.

The Editors

PART ONE
Sporting Heritage

"Feeding Largemouth Bass," courtesy of artist, Duane Raver

"Collector's Choice," courtesy of artist, Joe Seme

Old Times on Currituck

H. H. BRIMLEY

My first direct knowledge of Currituck Sound was in February 1884. Reaching Currituck was not easy in those days, as that section of the state then possessed no railway facilities. By rail to Norfolk was the first lap; thence by steamer up the Elizabeth River, through the Albemarle and Chesapeake canal and North River into Currituck Sound. The canal was again entered at the south end of Coinjock Bay, my getting-off place being the settlement of Coinjock. From there, across Church Island to the Midyette place on the sound was by oxcart.

My business there was to collect and preserve specimens of waterfowl for exhibition at the State Exposition that was to be held during the whole of the following October at the old State Fair Grounds near Raleigh.

My headquarters being situated about the center of the market-hunting industry, most of the specimens secured were purchased from the professional gunners. But I did some personal collecting on bluebird days when the market hunters would not bother to go out. I would borrow a battery they used for hunting and would pick up a few specimens that way.

The gas boat was unknown in those days, all boat movement being by sail or man power. The sailboats were known as "canoes." They were large dugouts, roomy enough for five or six horses or head of cattle. The canoes were used by the duck hunters to carry their batteries to and from the shooting grounds, with the stand of decoys occupying one or more skiffs and towed by the canoe.

These crafts were built by dowelling together three dugout pieces, with an inside framing that helped fasten the three units to tight, waterproof joints. They were heavy crafts but safe and seaworthy, their sail plan being the more or less standardized spritsail and jib rig, perhaps the most handy and convenient rig ever used on a comparatively small sailboat. The skiffs were never rowed or paddled, as the shallow waters of the sound made poling a much more efficient method of propulsion.

There were ducks and geese on the sound in those days. One afternoon I tried to roughly count the number of Canada geese in a straggling line of flocks that was crossing Church Island for their night's resting place in Coinjock Bay. My estimate was well above the 10,000 mark. From my viewpoint, that flight represented only a small part of the myriads frequenting the sound both north and south.

My host, Uncle Ned Midyette, owned four batteries and employed the gunners to man them, two men constituting the crew of each. He also employed a boy to do odd jobs around the house. The boy's first duty every morning—as soon as it was light enough to distinguish objects—was to take his gun and inspect several miles of shoreline to pick up crippled ducks that had swum ashore during the night. It was a well-known habit of ducks to come ashore when wounded.

One day, when the boy was hauling wood with the oxcart, he asked me if I wanted an eagle or two. When I replied in the affirmative, he told me that he had just driven his cart directly beneath a pair of white-

North Carolina Museum of Natural Sciences

The fabled marshes of Currituck Sound held many hunting establishments. One of them, Whalehead, was built in 1925 as the private lodge of Edward Collins Knight, Jr., a wealthy Northerner.

headed (bald) eagles perched in medium-sized pines a little way back in the woods, and that they took no notice of his outfit. If I could go with him, he felt quite sure that he could take me directly under them, the rest being up to me. So I slipped a couple of heavy loads in my gun and we started for the woods. I was sitting on the bottom boards of the cart with my legs hanging over at the rear end, all ready for a quick slide out when we were under the birds. He did his part all right, but when I slid out of the cart almost directly under the eagles, expecting to get one with each barrel, my foot slipped and I made a clean miss on both! Since then I have often wondered what sort of a tale the boy told his fellow employees about the poor marksmanship of the city feller

who couldn't hit as big an object as an eagle when it was almost sitting on his head! But I did kill an eagle before I left—while after ducks.

The following are the approximate prices the gunners were getting for their fowl, cash on the spot by the regular buyers, all prices per pair except as otherwise noted: canvasback, one dollar; redhead, fifty cents; "common duck," thirty cents; small ducks, such as teal, ruddy, and bufflehead, twenty-five cents, with four ducks constituting a pair! Canada geese brought fifty cents each.

At that time, of course, no refrigeration facilities were available, though a small amount of icing may have been done. The usual method, however, was to allow the fowl to hang up over night to cool off. The

next morning they were packed in barrels and shipped to Norfolk by steamer.

One night a very interesting visitor made a call at the house, another of the Midyettes, I think. He was quite an old man, but an interesting talker. Among other things, he mentioned the fact that he remembered the first "karasene" that was ever seen on Currituck. It came from a wreck, I think he said, but I fail to recall whether they burned whale oil or candles before the invasion of kerosene. When asked if he had noticed any decrease in the number of fowl frequenting the sound, he said that he thought the geese were not as plentiful as in years gone by. Further questioning brought out the statement that he made his best bag of geese a number of years back, on

North Carolina Museum of Natural Sciences

Hunters sometimes put out as many as five hundred decoys to draw ducks and geese. This hunter has grouped a large goose rig.

a snowy day, when he and his two sons killed 103 using "flint and steel" guns. Considering the speaker's apparent age, one might believe that the episode he recounted could have happened back in the 1840s, when the percussion gun was rapidly replacing the flintlock. However, I saw a flintlock in actual use a year later (in 1885) when a boy living near Cherry Point, Craven County, was seen taking such a weapon with him early one morning on a quest for ducks in Hancock's Creek. This was the only time I ever saw a gun of this type in actual use.

Batteries have been outlawed for a number of years now, and it may be of interest—particularly to the younger generation—to describe an old-time battery and its outfit as used on Currituck Sound in the 1880s.

Another name for the device was "sink box," which is far more descriptive than the name commonly used, which means hardly anything in this connection. The box itself was a coffin-shaped affair, of such dimensions as to afford a fairly close fit, both in length and width, for an average-sized man lying on his back. Its depth was such that no part of the occupant could be seen when the box was viewed from the side.

A small pillow or cushion was used by the hunter to raise his head to put his eyes on a level with the rims of the box. At this same level, a rigid deck some three feet wide was attached on all four sides. It sloped slightly down toward the water, with a particularly long extension at the head end. Flexible floating wings attached to all four sides of the fixed

deck would rise and fall with the motion of the surface water, tending to keep the water from running up the fixed deck and so into the box. An added precaution against this most uncomfortable possibility was the use of two strips of sheet lead an inch or two wide. The strips were tacked along their inner edges, so that they could be turned slightly by their outer edges whenever the surface became rough enough to warrant such procedure. When finished, the whole upper surface of the complete battery was painted a flat slaty gray, which made it almost invisible a short distance away.

At its best, a battery was always a clumsy affair and awkward to handle, and setting one out and taking it up again on a cold, windy day was no job for weaklings. It was securely

Poplar Branch Landing was a favorite jumping-off place to Currituck's clubs and its shooting grounds. Many hunting guides still dock their boats here, negotiating the way to hunting blinds before light and in bone-cutting cold.

anchored by the head, with a dragging anchor of lighter weight out over the tail end, the latter to prevent too much swinging sidewise.

An average "stand" for a single battery was possibly 150 decoys. I have seen much larger stands used as well as many not so large. The decoys would be best arranged by concentrating the bulk of the decoys at about right angles to the box, on the left side of the occupant. For a left-handed gunner, the arrangement would be reversed. The remainder of the decoys would gradually taper off in width and be more widely scattered downwind from the larger concentration near the battery.

Movable ballast was used to sink the battery to its most effective level in the water, the ballast consisting of cast-iron decoys weighing about twenty-five pounds each. The number of iron ducks used was variable, perhaps ten being an average. They were painted in keeping with the wooden decoys, and each iron decoy was fastened with a stout line to one of its wooden brethren, so that, if the weather should turn rough enough to threaten water in the box, some of the iron ducks could be slid overboard and thus raise the battery to a safer level.

The professional gunners, and some experienced amateurs, would take two guns with them in the box. The 32-inch barrels made it easier to rest the muzzles on the footboard, which should always be done for reasons of safety. The guns usually used by the market gunners were double-barreled 10-gauge weapons, with 32-inch barrels and hammers.

Automatics and repeaters came along at a later date.

I have tried this method of shooting on a number of occasions but have nearly always had better shooting from a blind, though the battery was a deadly method of taking waterfowl when practiced by experienced professionals. There is a Chesapeake Bay record of more than 500 ducks killed in one day's shooting by a market hunter using two guns in his battery. On Currituck, bags of 100 a day from a battery were not rare enough to get one's name in the paper. A now-deceased friend of mine, a crack shot on ducks, substituting for a market hunter at his request, once averaged about 130 a day for three successive days, and that was well within the present century.

North Carolina Museum of Natural Sciences

A typical Currituck blind is a construction of marsh grass and weeds, with a few wooden boards to stand on.

I never saw or heard anything to make me believe that "punt" guns had ever been in general use on Currituck Sound, at least in comparatively recent years, as they had been in some parts of Chesapeake Bay. But, some years later, the State Museum was given the choice of purchasing one or both of two guns of this type from a resident of Currituck County. We secured the better of the two, which is now on display in the museum. Our specimen is a flintlock, weighing nearly one hundred pounds. The barrel is eight feet long, with a bore of one and a half inches. The standard load for this weapon would have been about one pound of shot driven by an ounce and a half to two ounces of black powder. Larger swivel guns, breechloaders, were used in later years,

some of them being handsomely finished pieces to be used with nitro powders. So far as I can learn, no gun of this more modern type ever found its way to Currituck.

I have often heard of crow roosts, but never saw one, though I am confident that a very heavily populated roost of this character was in existence at the time of my first visit, situated on the Banks in a northeasterly direction from Church Island. Every afternoon when I happened to be out-of-doors, vast numbers of crows were seen crossing the sound in the direction indicated. From about an hour before sunset until dusk the flight was fairly steady though, of course, by no means regular. There must have been many thousands of crows congregating for the night somewhere in the region

indicated, but it was a long way off and, with the transportation facilities what they were, no attempt was made to ascertain the facts.

It goes almost without saying that a majority of the inhabitants of the shores of the sound made most of their winter's income directly or indirectly from the commercial hunting of wildfowl. During the summer months many of the market hunters shifted to fishing, black bass and white perch being their main objectives. About that time, or a few years later, the commercial catch of black bass alone from that region reached a total of about half a million pounds annually, which is quite a lot of bass!

On one of those bluebird days, the weather felt so much like a day in late spring that I experimented

The legendary hunting at Currituck Sound drew hunters from all over the country, inspiring the production of push poles, skiffs, decoys, and other native industries.

with a swim in the sound. But you can bet your last dollar that I didn't stay in the water very long!

There were—and are—no brant on Currituck, this small species of goose being strictly a saltwater bird with us. But snow geese and whistling swan were plentiful, though in somewhat restricted areas, these geese feeding almost exclusively on the east side of the sound, and mainly on-land, as they now do on Pea Island.

It should also be remembered that in those remote days Lake Mattamuskeet was used but little by wildfowl, due to the absence of suitable food therein. It was in no sense a competitor with Currituck Sound then, Mattamuskeet having only come into its own as a great congregating spot for swan, geese, and ducks since it has been partly drained and the water level kept low.

I had my first taste of young swan, baked, on that trip, and later had a young swan sent me on several occasions for use on the home table. I need not caution my readers not to strain their teeth on an *old* swan, as such a feat has long been contrary to the law—and never has been highly recommended!

Currituck's Historic Sporting Clubs

LAWRENCE S. EARLEY

The night before, we had been eating oysters in Elizabeth City and trying to explain to Maughan Hull why we hadn't gotten to the Swan Island Club that day, or to any of the other historic hunting clubs out in Currituck Sound.

"The ice was too thick out of Tull's Bay," Jim Clark was saying.

"My skiff could have made it," Maughan said.

"We went up number eight, but the milfoil choked my prop."

"I know my skiff could have made it."

Jim didn't push his point. That's why the next day, in a skiff with ice runners, we were cutting through the February ice in Tull's Bay again, our prop slinging nuggets across the frozen surface. The cold wind knifed through our clothes and burnt our faces but the sky was a deep blue and when a cloud of black ducks erupted from the marsh off to our left we whooped in amazement. Then the ice thickened and we slowed to a crawl. To make headway we were forced to ram the ice like a man putting his shoulder to a locked door. After one high-speed attack had stranded us on top of the ice, it was obvious that our quest was futile. We would not see the clubhouses that day either. As we sat there glumly, the floes tipped rhythmically in our wake, setting up an eerie whistling. In the distance, Swan Island sat unreachable across Currituck's crusted expanse.

Currituck is remote, there's no getting around that. And if its ice and iron skies and sudden squalls can still put a crimp in your plans today, think of the obstacles it offered nineteenth-century travelers. But about the midpoint of the last century, there they were, hundreds of sportsmen from New York, Boston, and points farther north, jostling for position in Currituck Sound. They had to come hundreds of miles by rail, by boat, and even by oxcart to reach Poplar Landing, or Van Slyck's Landing, as it was then called, even before pitting themselves against the sound. Why, then, did their pulses race whenever they contemplated the desolate reaches of Currituck?

Currituck's secret was out, that's why, and it was about to bring the clubhouses to its marshes and signal the onset of its golden age of hunting. In the early nineteenth century, only the native fishermen and hunters who prowled its waters knew of the hundreds of thousands of waterfowl that swarmed into Currituck each winter. The waterfowl had increased when the New Currituck Inlet, the last inlet to the sea, closed in 1828. A flourishing oyster and saltwater fishing industry ended with this disaster, but in the sound's freshened waters wild celery and other favorite wildfowl foods began to grow. This food attracted enormous numbers of birds, especially the canvasback and redhead ducks. The thunder of their wings over the sound was music to the ears of Currituck's natives, for there was a growing market up north for these birds.

By the middle of the nineteenth century, rumors of the birds' abundance had crept northward. A few New Yorkers and Bostonians, hearing of the incredible rafts of waterfowl in Back Bay and Currituck Sound, pushed their way to Poplar Landing to check for themselves.

The Swan Island clubhouse sits four-square and solid on the island that gave it its name. Two others burned before this one was built in 1914. One of the largest clubs, Swan Island purchased more than 9,000 acres of island, beach, and marsh. In a Currituck fog the brass bell was handy to guide the hunters home.

Others stumbled into Currituck by accident, like the Harvard-educated sportsmen from Long Island, New York, who sailed for Florida in 1872 in their schooner *Anonyana*. Seeking shelter from a gale, they entered Currituck and ran aground off Swan Island. They must have been astonished at what they saw for they returned to their beached schooner several winters following, until they built the first of three clubhouses that have stood on that island.

However they came, these sportsmen struck for fair when they hit Currituck, and their reports made it sound like a waterfowler's Comstock Lode. In the decades after the Civil War, wealthy northerners flooded Currituck like the wind-driven tides, buying thousands of acres of beach, island, and marsh for prices as low as ten and fifty cents an acre. By the 1880s nothing was left. One traveler wrote with some dismay, "There is not a foot of this ground in the whole territory that is not owned, registered by title-deeds, recorded in the archives, and watched over as if it sheltered a gold mine."

Here and there in the marshes the clubs began to spring up. The Currituck Shooting Club, founded in 1857, was the first of the clubs and it built a clubhouse before the Civil War. The phenomenon of clubs needs some explanation. Almost all of the land was acquired by syndicates of sportsmen rather than individual sportsmen, a fact that reflects equally the social backgrounds of the club members and the social nature of duck hunting. With club shares costing from $1,000 to $5,000 and more, the ordinary pot hunter or market hunter was not likely to belong to one of these clubs. The members were among that restless breed of Gilded Age entrepreneurs—railroad men and steel men—who shot deer in the Adirondacks and ducks in Chesapeake Bay, Back Bay, and Currituck Sound. Their model was the English aristocracy and they called themselves sportsmen. Robert Roosevelt, an outdoor writer of the day, defined a sportsman as one who "pursues his game for pleasure; does not aspire to follow the grander animals of the chase; makes no profit of his success . . . ; shoots invariably on the wing; and never takes a mean advantage of

Of all the clubs, the Currituck Shooting Club (left) was and still is the most famous. Its clubhouse is over one hundred years old and has been placed on the National Register of Historic Places. The Pine Island Club (below) sits on the site of the former Palmer Island Club.

Photographs by Lawrence S. Earley

bird or man." Of course this didn't prevent some from shooting buffalo out West from private railroad cars, but, if shooting waterfowl on the wing was your pleasure, why not shoot in style, in the hearty male atmosphere of your social peers? Hunting clubs provided a way to rough it without having to leave your brandy behind.

There were about eight major membership clubs in Currituck Sound in the nineteenth century. From the northernmost point to the southernmost, there was Currituck Sound Club near the Virginia border, also called the Martin's Point Club (now the Currituck Gunning and Fishing Club); the Swan Island Club; the Monkey Island Club; the Narrows Island Club; the Lighthouse Club; the Currituck Shooting Club; and the Palmer Island Club (now the Pine Island Club). There were other clubs, and smaller lodges took in hunters, but, if a sportsman wanted to shoot at Currituck's prime points, he had best belong to one of these eight clubs.

The shooting differed from club to club. At the Currituck Shooting Club or the Pine Island Club you could expect a fine show of canvasbacks. Farther north, diving ducks were less numerous but there were plenty of shovelers and blue-wing teal at the Swan Island Club, and its sea meadows had the best bay-bird shooting on the East Coast. No matter where he was, a decent shot in those days often bagged anywhere from twenty-five to fifty fowl a day.

The clubhouses themselves, with one exception, perhaps, were all simple affairs. They usually contained several small bedrooms with wood stoves to be fired up by the guides in the predawn hours, a kitchen, a dining room, and a larger common room where the hunters would gather in the evenings and thaw frozen hands in front of a blazing fire. Whalehead was the exception. Completed in 1925, on the site of the Lighthouse Club, Whalehead is the only clubhouse that could be called palatial. Inside, the rooms are generously proportioned, the floors are made of cork, and there are magnificent mahogany door frames coiling with carved Art Nouveau motifs. The Tiffany light fixtures have been put away.

In comparison, the other clubhouses had lower architectural profiles. Even the legendary Currituck Shooting Club next door to Whalehead masks its astronomical initiation fees within a modest exterior of Cape Cod shingles. Still, a sportsman's needs were well attended to at his club, and he could certainly expect to dine well after a day's shooting. One dinner recorded for posterity, and, perhaps, not entirely untypical, featured a first course of diamondback terrapin followed by an entire butter-basted canvasback with side dishes of shore birds on toast. Champagne, fetched from the wine cellar, accompanied the meal; cigars and brandies ended it.

You might think that Yankee bon vivants flashing greenbacks would have provoked the hard-pressed Currituckians. But it doesn't seem to have been the case. During the Civil War, of course, Northerners prudently stayed at home. And though Confederate patriots reportedly stripped the Currituck Shooting Club of its goods and sold them as spoils of war, the clubhouse, according to one account, was left intact.

Most conflicts seemed to have been about shooting rights. When a club acquired over 9,000 acres of beach and marsh, hard feelings might be excused from natives who had once shot all over the sound. Poaching became a problem for the clubs, requiring a variety of remedies, some legal and some not. In the 1880s, the Narrows Island Club installed iron pipes in waters adjacent to the club in order to bar access to club marshes, but in 1888 the North Carolina Supreme Court ordered the pipes removed. Marsh guards earned a livelihood at all the clubs, but perhaps the most unusual step against poachers was taken by the Swan Island Club whose members mounted a pivoting rifle on the roof of the clubhouse.

The era of gentleman sporting ended in the 1920s, but many of Currituck's clubhouses have survived into the 1980s. The Currituck Shooting Club is the only one to escape nineteenth-century fires and storms—its clubhouse is over a hundred years old—and it is the only club still functioning as a membership club. The others have been purchased by individuals or corporations, or have been deeded to conservation groups. The Nature Conservancy has acquired both the Swan Island Club and the Monkey Island Club for use as wildlife refuges. In 1978, Earl Slick of Winston-Salem deeded most of the Pine Island Club to the National Audubon Society.

Still trim and tidy, just a little down at the heels, the hunting clubs of Currituck Sound occupy a special niche in North Carolina history. Their primary purpose historically was to serve their well-to-do members, but they have served Currituck and the state well. For years they have helped stimulate the economic life of a remote and depressed area

Lawrence S. Earley

Edward Collins Knight, Jr., reportedly built Whalehead in 1925 when his wife was refused membership in other Currituck clubs. Whalehead has been placed on the National Register of Historic Places.

by hiring not only marsh guards, but guides, cooks, and managers for the off-season. Club members needed decoys, skiffs, push poles, and blinds, and these needs kept afloat a variety of native industries. More important, the clubs have anchored the Currituck Outer Banks against the restless tide of commercial development that has changed the face of much of North Carolina's coast.

A half-million wild ducks, geese, and swans still winter in North Carolina each year. Many of them will fly over and around Currituck's old hunting clubs and settle in their marshes as they have for the past hundred years and more. Out in the sound on a late winter's afternoon, rafted coots scatter at your boat's approach. Snow geese feed in the cornfields skirting the mainland shore.

The scene has a certain Currier & Ives quality about it. But unlike the scenes of waving Christmas revelers in the horse-drawn sleighs memorialized on Currier & Ives prints, there's something more enduring about the sentinel clubhouses in the remote marshes of Currituck County. The age of hunting that they recall has long ended, but still caught in these old buildings is an impulse as constant as the tides: to

seek the wild places and to see meaning in the flight of the wild duck.

Editors' Note: In 1983, a large portion of the North Carolina Nature Conservancy's holdings at Swan Island and Monkey Island was set aside to form the Currituck National Wildlife Refuge, which is administered by the U.S. Fish and Wildlife Service. In 1984, the new refuge was increased, taking almost all the acreage originally owned by the Conservancy. In July 1984, a grant from the U.S. Department of Commerce was used to purchase a portion of the Monkey Island tract for use as a component of the North Carolina National Estuarine Sanctuary.

Ship of Frogs

The old cigar box had not been opened since I was a child, yet, when I saw it in the attic, I knew it still contained magic. Inside, I found some of the things that had been important to me more than thirty years ago. There was a beanshooter (you might call it a slingshot), a powerful magnifying glass, a dried turtle shell, a small rubberband-powered speargun, a deck of playing cards with fish species on the back, a tube of BBs, a broken pocketknife, fish hooks, a tiny, but functional bow and arrow, and a raccoon's foot.

There were also marbles, an old coin or two, a Crackerjacks' prize, and a number of other items, but the most prized possessions were those toys that had introduced me to the adventure and mystery of the natural world.

Like most kids, I was both protector and terrorist. I bought turtles at the dimestore, peeled the pink paint from their shells, and nurtured them to health, yet I spent hours trying to develop that rubberband speargun into an effective weapon for the huge bullfrogs that lived in the ditch in front of the house.

I used the magnifying glass to study countless bugs, marvel at the colored scales in a butterfly wing, or watch ants milk aphids. But I confess I also sizzled a few ants by directing the sun's rays on them. An injured bird was a special project requiring popsicle stick splints and eyedropper feedings, yet I would hunt sparrows with an air rifle until I ran out of BBs.

The typical kid practices a mixture of stewardship and harvest, a blend that I suspect is entirely natural. I think of my friend, a noted entomologist, who confided that his lifelong fascination with insects began when he fed ants to ant lions in the sandy soil under a shed in his backyard. His special interest now is rare insects.

"I was absolutely charmed by the life around me, by the variety and the violence," he says now. "What was merely an interest has grown into a career, and feeding ants to ant lions may well have been the impetus for it. I can tell you this, I learned early that sentiment does not exist in the natural world I studied. But most of all, I developed a lasting curiosity about things, and it is just as intense today as it was when I was twelve years old. And I think I've given back more than I ever took."

I can't trace my own interest and career in the outdoors to any specific thing, but I was fortunate enough to have parents and grandparents who encouraged it. Some adults seem to know exactly how to focus youthful curiosity and introduce kids to the adventure and mystery around them. David Williams's grandfather certainly did.

"My brother, Skip, and I had been trying to catch some bullfrogs in this pond, and our grandfather came up with an incredible scheme," said David. "He told us to get a wide plank and tie a long string to one end of it. A candle was affixed upright in the middle of the plank.

"When it gets dark, he told us, you light the candle and slowly pull the plank along the edge of the pond. The candle will attract all sorts of moths and other insects, and the bullfrogs will leap up on the plank and sit there catching the insects. We thought it was a swell idea, and we set it all up just the way he told us.

"That evening, we lit the candle and skirted the edge of the pond with the string until we got back to the pier, then we waited until we figured enough insects had been attracted. We could hear those old bullfrogs jug-a-rumming around that pond, and we began to pull the plank along the edge. I'll never forget how excited we were. We were absolutely convinced that when that plank rounded the last bunch of cattails, it would be stacked up with bullfrogs.

"You know something? There wasn't a danged frog on that board, but I guess it was a good thing because we had never stopped to figure out how we were going to get all those frogs off the plank and into our sack. It was a heck of an idea, though."

Who knows whether that caper had anything to do with David's career (he's art director for *Wild-life in North Carolina*), but it was surely a significant chapter in his introduction to the great outdoors. It wouldn't surprise me to learn that every naturalist, every outdoorsman, could tell similar tales. And somewhere among their childhood toys may be a box of memories filled with such things as turtle shells and beanshooters. It wouldn't surprise David to learn that in the attic back home is plank, a candle, and some string—a ship of frogs whose real cargo was a lifelong love of nature's mysteries.—*Jim Dean*

American Bullfrog (Jack Dermid)

Core Sound Memoir
A Carolina Profile

JULIAN HAMILTON, JR.
as told to Lawrence S. Earley and Ted Dossett

The stories of Julian Hamilton, Jr., so frequently make him grin that you wonder how he corrals the thick wad of tobacco bulging his cheek while getting off one of his sonic booms of laughter. There's a sort of tug-of-war going on across his face between muscles that want to make room for his smile, and those that want to prevent a domestic catastrophe. The fact that he can maintain a tobacco chewer's decorum while still being true to his humor is no small measure of the man's rough-hewn amiability.

Born in 1925, Hamilton has lived most of his life in Beaufort, save for a few years' stint in the U.S. Navy in the latter stages of World War II. He's worked as a commercial fisherman and more recently as a toolmaker at the Marine Air Base at Cherry Point. He's better known as a decoy maker of some stature, and one of the area's most knowledgeable sportsmen.

Today, Beaufort sports a newly restored waterfront district that makes it a favorite berth for East Coast yachts while attracting thousands of tourists each year. Years ago, Beau-fort was the commercial fishing center of North Carolina, where the menhaden boats set sail for the Gulf Stream to haul in the sea gold.

But for men like Julian Hamilton, Jr., and his father Julian, Sr., Beaufort was also the stepping-off point for fabulous waterfowling. In hunting camps in towns and villages like Atlantic, Lola, Cedar Island, and Portsmouth Island, local sportsmen sought the ducks and geese that flooded the waterway in the winter. Waterfowl got into Hamilton's blood early and stayed there. He's hunted Canada geese just about all his life and has raised them for decades, trying to breed strains of the Canada line that he remembers from his youth. He learned to carve decoys by looking at the birds themselves, but also spent some time at the knee of the legendary carver Mitchell Fulcher.

It was a hot day in August when *Wildlife in North Carolina* visited Julian Hamilton in Beaufort. He had a lot to say about his life in Core Sound.

You know, up until about ten years ago, my feet and hands were always cold. I remember my daddy saying, "Son, there's a black duck in the decoys, you want to shoot him?" And I said, "Yeah." He said, "Well shoot him." I said, "All right." He said, "Are you going to shoot him?" I said, "Yeah." Directly he got up and shot the black duck. I was so cold I couldn't get up! I would never have admitted I was so cold that I had to go back to camp. I was maybe fifteen. I can still see that black duck— the black duck jumped and my daddy put him right down. It's a funny thing how you can see things that far back.

Way back there, we hunted from the time they come 'til they left, unless it got too cold. Cold affected us all. I mean, it was just too bitter to go sometimes. I still think about it when I get up in the mornings and it's bitter outside. I had a many a drop of ice hit me, many a drop of it. And anybody else who's lived around the water knows what I mean.

I've had people with me from the Middle Western states and this dampness goes clean through their bones. I've gone to my blinds in the morning, when I started out, and by the time we got to the blinds the dogs would be covered with ice and I'd be a sheet of ice, too. 'Course I didn't have maybe but a mile to run, no danger as far as I was concerned. I could always go back. The water I hunted in was relatively shallow. There were a lot of sloughs and creeks that you had to cross, but I never did think about anything like that. All I was interested in was getting everything set up.

We had a big freeze, I'd say ten or fifteen years ago. My cousin and I went down to our hunting camp near Portsmouth Island in a big boat pulling a small skiff loaded with decoys. And we stopped to the Mullet Shoal and it was freezing then. And my cousin and I took the skiff and the decoys and went and killed some geese so we'd have something to eat, and that night it froze about a half a mile out in the sound. And we couldn't get out. We had wooden boats.

In about seven or eight days all our grub was giving out and one of the fellers we was with was a diabetic and I think he had one shot left. The day before some of them had started to the big boat. There was ten pounds of flour aboard her. I wouldn't go because I knew there were weak places in the ice, although there were three or four inches or more on the shore, that's how thick it was. They got within three or four hundred yards and they broke through the ice. I reckon the good Lord was looking out for them because the water didn't go in their boots, just to the tops. They managed to roll back onto the ice. I had a laydown box and a piece of aluminum pipe, and that afternoon

one of the fellers shoved that out there to the big boat and got the ten pounds of flour and radioed back that we were all right.

One of the boys said he was walking down the path and there was a Long Tom standing there. We call the great blue heron a "Long Tom" hereabouts. Feller said he walked right up to him and the Long Tom stood right there. And the Long Tom was frozen right in the path. Stone dead. So it happens in the wild.

When I was a boy, my daddy would take me hunting. We'd put the decoys out, throw 'em out there in the deep water where the causeway to Morehead City is now. We had a dog named Ted. We would throw our decoys out there early, daylight, and kill us some ducks and that dog, of course, he'd bring everything in. And he'd bring all our decoys back in, too. My daddy'd take me to school, and then he'd go to work. That happened for years until they got to building the causeway.

When the other boys were playing ball, I was hunting. I was out there fishing or hunting. 'Cause I loved it. And still do. There's nothing in the world like it.

I believe they had the roads built clear to Atlantic by the time I was born. They didn't have the road to Cedar Island until after I was born. Of course my daddy remembered when there wasn't any roads between the communities. They got back and forth by boat. My grandfather ran the mail boat from Atlantic to Beaufort, and the people went on those. He had to pick up a lot of stuff for different people whenever he run the mail from Atlantic to Beaufort.

When I was a young boy my fa-

ther had a camp abreast of Lewis's Creek on Cedar Island. We went there by sailboat. He and I have sailed from here right on down to the camp on Cedar Island. And we always allowed one day to go. Now you've got outboard motors that can get out there in thirty to forty minutes and come back that afternoon. We'd have to have a whole day to get down there. That was a spritsail boat, twenty-one foot. We always went for a week at a time. There were so many geese around when we'd go to sleep at night it would sound like bees. It was a steady roar of geese out there. That is how many there was.

Eventually, the boats got thicker and the people got thicker. Three men owned the camp, and by and by one of those men started bringing hunters in and he built some more camps. Well, it was crowding us and the geese were getting thinner. My father didn't want any of that so we moved down toward Portsmouth Island. That has been about thirty some years ago.

One Sunday, I borrowed my cousin's skiff. She was about twenty foot long. And we went down to the new camp, my father and one of my dogs. The seas were about two foot to the shore side when we decided to leave. The shoal was about fifteen hundred to two thousand yards from the shore and when I dropped off in the deep water and headed to the leeward the seas started breaking in the stern. Well, I couldn't run her no way that they didn't break her in. So I turned her sideways and just did open the throttle, and about halfway to Wainwright Island the steering cable broke. We had put on our foul weather stuff, but we were still wet as seas were breaking right over us and I guess I was trying to

Lawrence S. Earley

Julian Hamilton, Jr., looks over several of the many decoys he has made. Hamilton learned his craft from Mitchell Fulcher, a legendary decoy maker also from Carteret County.

pump her out. Anyway, the steering cable broke. I got that fixed. It didn't seem like no time before we were at Wainwright, come down there sideways, just the wind blowing us.

We changed clothes at Wainwright and I fixed the steering cable a little better. And it was cold. I went on to the leeward of Harbor Island until I got up close to the shore and headed across to Cedar Island Bay. In Cedar Island Bay the seas were deeper but long, about six-foot waves, and so I could keep her headed down. About the middle of the bay, when I come out on the sea, I looked right off her bow about ten foot or less and there was a loon asleep out there in that storm. And I was just about right on top of him when he woke up and dived.

Would a man think that a bird would be out there asleep in a storm? But he was.

But anyway, we went on up to Circle Bay, and I reckon I had to bail out about thirty minutes. And when I got back, I told my father, "Well," I said, "that's the last time I'll ever stick her out there like that." It must have scared me for me to tell him that, but that was the last time I ever stuck her out there when it was that bad. I shouldn't have done it, but I wasn't but twenty-five. I should have known better.

You better not get too confident when you're on the water. You better not ever get too confident.

Talking about loons, the people of Harkers Island were noted for eating them. It's illegal now, but they shot 'em in the spring of the year when they come over the beach. And the people of Salter Path did the same thing. They acquired a taste for 'em, just like some Yankees acquired a taste for collards and corn meal which they don't have up there, I don't guess. I guess they killed a lot of loons because when I was growing up the only thing I ever fished with for bluefish and mackerel was a loon's leg. That's all we had to catch bluefish with. You had to bleach the bone and you put it on a wire leader and if we were going to go sailing we throwed our lines overboard. Would catch a fish or two while we were going.

My father was meat hungry. When he grew up he said everybody on Atlantic was meat hungry. (They called Atlantic "Hunting Quarters" back then.) They took their salt fish and went to Little Washington and traded it for salt pork. You know

what salt fish is, don't you? A while back, they didn't fish year-round like they do now. They always put their fish up in the fall of the year and had salt fish all year long. Then later on they started catching fish the year-round. But they salted their drums, their mullets, spots, and hog fish. I remember one time before they had any ice, my cousin and I caught twenty-two flounders, big flounders, in the daytime. And I asked my daddy, I said, "What are we going to do with all these fish? We can't let them go to waste." We were about twenty miles from Atlantic. And he said, "Well, we'll salt them." And that was the first time I ever salted a flounder. And they kept real good.

But he said they killed anything to get some meat when he was a boy. He said that was how hungry they were. Of course I feel sorry for anybody who can't get all they want to eat nowadays. They are too lazy or just something is wrong with them. People don't do like we did. I was taught to cut the goose's head off right by the eyes so we could eat the brains. There was none of it wasted. And it was good.

During the Depression we ate sea fans and stuff like that. For three months one time all we got to eat came out of the water. We'd take a pointed shell and dig the sea fans up and open 'em up. 'Course it's just a big scallop, you know, but it tastes a little different from a scallop. We'd catch shrimp that big around, an inch and a half around. Shrimp grow real fast anyway. They were probably two-year-old shrimp that survived. And we'd catch the biggest kind—we'd call 'em "corn-cob" shrimp. I hear of people catching some big shrimp once in awhile, but it's just old shrimp that survived.

It used to be that folks in these

parts raised geese for hunting. That's right, they used them as live decoys. And they sold for a big price. The way they raised 'em was like this. The people of Davie Shore used to turn their geese out in the spring of the year into the marshes, to nest and hatch their eggs. In the middle of the summer, when the water got scarce, the geese swam over to Davis's Island where there was an artesian well, the first around. Geese and ducks love to go to ponds to drink fresh water. The people had cows there with slatted wooden fences to keep them in, and the geese would feed in the pasture with their goslings. They'd stay there until the people drove 'em back in the fall. Or they came back on their own.

The people at Cedar Island, they hatched their geese on the mainland and drove them over to Hog Island in boats. The geese scattered all over, naturally, but of course they never left. That fall, the people would go back over there before hunting season and drive their geese back across.

Each person marked his geese so he could recognize them. At Davie Shore, Alonzo Willis cut the outside toe and the inside toe and the petty toe and cut a V out of the web on the right hand side of the foot. He cut the toenail, that is, just enough so it wouldn't grow back. That was his mark. Lenny Davis cut all three toes and the petty toe on the right foot. Over at Cedar Island, Rupert Styron's mark, which he took from his father, was a left hind petty toe. Of course, most didn't have to look at the marks—they recognized their geese as individuals. But there still were fights.

The reason why the geese never left, of course, was that the people had pinioned them. They would cut the bone on the lower side of one wing equivalent to about eight feathers. They'd do that when the geese were goslings, right after they were hatched, although sometimes they didn't do it until the goslings came back in the fall. People told me that when they'd drive the geese back to Davie Shore, the goslings would jump up and fly ahead, and the old goose would swim just as hard as she could to follow them.

These geese didn't all make good decoys. You couldn't hunt some of them. They wouldn't stand still and honk. They'd flap their wings and just wouldn't stand to the strap (live decoys were often tethered to a stake). And that would scare the geese away quicker than anything I know. A long time ago, before I remember good, there come a bad time and the geese got so poor they couldn't fly. And my cousin got him half a dozen geese—all you had to do was show up over there and pick 'em up. And he brought 'em home and was going to have him some live decoys. But the next year, when he went back, he staked them out and they laid down on the water just like shingles. They laid flat. They

was just afraid. It was their wild nature coming back into them. He brought 'em back home and give 'em away. The geese that were good for wild decoys were the ones you raised at home from the original wild stock.

Well, when they outlawed the live decoy, the price dropped and most everybody got rid of their geese, except those who really just loved to look at 'em and raise 'em. I enjoy raising geese. It was more fun for me to go catch a crippled duck or goose through the marshes than it was to kill one. In other words, I wanted to look at them. I had redheads that could eat out of my hand, and the wild geese that had their wing broke I could pick up.

The Canada goose, as far as I'm concerned, has the most sense of all. I've had 'em to go and learn how to open the gate and turn the whole flock out and I've had 'em do most anything.

The first time I went hunting I was so young I didn't have a gun. Later on, anytime my father went on a hunting trip, I was to go with him. He would take me out of school any time. I told my younguns the same thing. I think that all

younguns ought to be taught what it is like out there in the field and how to take care of themselves in a bad time. I know people who wouldn't take their younguns out for nothing in the world. But I think they miss the better part of life if they don't take their children hunting with them. I don't care how young they are. The first time I carried my oldest boy fishing, we laid him on the pilot house. He was six months old. He just went to sleep.

The future of wildlife in these parts is mighty bleak. It's not the gunners that's going to kill 'em. It's civilized man. They're just populating so many places and changing everything so bad that wildlife is just not going to be able to raise. The habitat is going and that's the key to the whole thing.

So it don't look good to me. As long as I can go, just go, just kill one or two and go, I'm satisfied. I'm happy. That don't mean that I'm real crazy about getting up in the morning when it's freezing or something like that. It takes a special kind of idiot to want to do something like that.

Some North Carolina Decoys and Their Makers

J A M E S   S.   L E W I S,   J R.

The time may come when the old duck hunter is content to put his gun away, throw the patched-up waders in the garbage can, and reflect in comfort on occurrences that could be considered pleasant only in retrospect: wind-driven, icy rain that flattened the brown marsh grass and sent a trickle of cold water down the back of your neck; the whistle of overhead wings as you crouched in the darkness before daybreak; the cold day you stepped off into water over your waders but stayed shivering to limit out. But, then, there was that perfect shot when you connected dead center, with a twenty-foot lead on a passing teal speeding downwind at sixty miles per hour. May our accommodating memories exclude the many easy shots we've missed.

However, it may turn out that memories are not an adequate substitute for the excitement and punishment that are a part of waterfowl hunting, so where does the hunter turn? In many cases, he turns to the collecting of decoys. This interest is not limited to hunters, however, for collectors are spread widely across the continent. It is not rare to see a fine collection of waterfowl or shorebird decoys that has been put together by a woman who has never fired a gun, and who may never have seen a wild duck on the wing. The art, which in some degree was whittled into the shaping of every old hand-carved decoy, assures it permanent attractiveness.

Although collectors and dealers have been gathering what they could find along our North Carolina coast for years, it is still possible to uncover in some old fish house, boat shed, or barn a specimen of a type to thrill a collector. Rarely, a whole rig remains in the hands of a descendant of one of the old market hunters, but it is hardly for sale.

Through the years, regional characteristics of decoys have come to be fairly well recognized by collectors. Examples, beginning with the Northeast, are St. Lawrence River decoys, Delaware River decoys, and Upper Chesapeake Bay decoys (Susquehanna Flats), all of which have strong regional markings. In the midcontinent, the Illinois River and the charming little Louisiana decoys

have distinct styles of their own. Besides having features that are peculiar to the areas of their origin, the decoys of some skilled artisans have such distinctly individualistic styles that experienced collectors can positively identify many decoys. These are exemplified by the well-known decoys of "Shang" Wheeler, the Ward Brothers, Ira Hudson, and Charles Perdew, to mention only a very few. In our own state, the Dudleys, John Williams, Ned Burgess, Alvirah Wright, and Mitchell Fulcher had their own recognizable styles.

Presented here is the information I have been able to dig up on some of the early makers of North Carolina working decoys (used for hunting as differentiated from those used for ornamental purposes).

At this point, it may be well to digress sufficiently to explain that market hunters were a tough and hardy group who, before 1918 when the sale of game became illegal, made their living by selling the waterfowl they killed. Along our coast they did most of the shooting from sink boxes which, with several

Ruddy Duck / John Williams, Knotts Island (Currituck Co.) 1890

Redhead / Ivey Stevens, Knott's Island (Currituck Co.) 1915

Coot / Ellie Saunders, Poplar Branch (Currituck Co.) 1925

Pintail / Ellie Saunders, Poplar Branch (Currituck Co.) 1925

Redhead / Solomon Beasley, Wash Woods (Currituck Co.) 1925

Redhead / Wallace O'Neal, Aydlett (Currituck Co.) 1930

Redhead / Bob Morse, Churches Island (Currituck Co.) 1935

Gadwall / Bob Morse, Churches Island (Currituck Co.) 1935

Redhead / Ned Burgess, Churches Island (Currituck Co.) 1935

Black Duck / Ned Burgess, Churches Island (Currituck Co.) 1935

Scaup / Rufus Roberts, Churches Island (Currituck Co.) 1938

Canvasback / Wilton Walker, Tulls Bay (Currituck Co.) 1940s

*Canvasback / Callie O'Neal, Churches Island
(Currituck Co.)*

*Widgeon / Blanton Saunders, Poplar Branch
(Currituck Co.)*

*Redhead / J. A. (Joe) Hayman, Coinjock
(Currituck Co.)*

*Redhead / Robert Pigott, Marshallberg
(Carteret Co.) 1920*

*Bufflehead / Eldon Willis, Stacy (Carteret Co.)
1938*

*Red Head / Eldon Willis and Elmer Salter,
Stacy (Carteret Co.) 1940*

*Red Head / Irving Fulcher, Stacy
(Carteret Co.) 1938*

*Bluebill (Scaup) / Irving Fulcher, Stacy
(Carteret Co.) 1938*

*Red Head (hen) / Alvin Harris, Atlantic
(Carteret Co.) 1939*

Goose / John Lupton, Carteret Co. 1940

*Red Head / Ammie Paul, Sealevel
(Carteret Co.)*

*Black Duck / Henry Murphy, Davis
(Carteret Co.)*

Ruddy Duck / Alvirah Wright, Duck (Dare Co.) 1900

Goose / Marvin Midgette, Dare Co. 1930

Goose / Avery Tillett, Kitty Hawk (Dare Co.) 1935

hundred decoys anchored around them, comprised a "battery rig." One still hears the term "battery decoy" applied to the large, sturdy wooden blocks that were carved to withstand the severe treatment to which they unavoidably were subjected.

Any discussion of North Carolina decoy makers must start with the brothers, Lem and Lee Dudley of Knotts Island (also of Wash Woods and Munden, Virginia. It appears they may rightfully be claimed by both states). Both are buried on Churches Island, North Carolina. The talents of these two carvers have not gone unrecognized, as their outstanding work has been praised in the books of Mackey, Barber, Starr, and other writers on the subject. Many of the decoys they made for their own use may be identified by a distinctive "LD" branded in the bottom. Mackey said that a "B" or "ELM" cut into the bottom was positive identification of decoys they had made for other hunters. When unmarked by initials, the unique style of the Dudleys ordinarily serves as sufficient identification.

Besides the Dudleys, another carver of that same Back Bay-Currituck area, whose work has

been acclaimed as superior by writers and collectors, was John Williams of Cedar Island, Virginia. He operated battery rigs for himself and for others in Currituck Sound and Back Bay, and he made many decoys. His ruddies and swans are especially sought after by collectors today. It is not possible to fully describe the work of John Williams without bringing up the name of Ivey Stevens, who worked for and with him. It seems probable that Stevens learned to make decoys under the tutelage of Williams, and that he made many of the battery decoys that Williams used in his rigs. In attempting to determine the species of these worn and weathered old decoys, which usually have been covered with many coats of paint, it often is not possible to be positive of what species even the last coat was intended to depict.

Just as the Dudleys spread their lives and talents across the lines of both states, so did John Williams and Ivey Stevens operate batteries and scatter their decoys widely throughout the fabulously productive hunting area that included Back Bay, Virginia, and Currituck Sound, North Carolina.

The literature describing the waterfowl decoys that were made in

North Carolina pictures them as generally crude, rough, and indifferently painted. In some respects, the work of Williams and Stevens probably exemplified these terms if compared with the finest products from the hands of the best carvers of our more northerly states. However, instead of crude and rough, they might more fairly have been described as rugged and functional. Without delicate wing and tail projections, which would have been vulnerable to damage from handling when hunting, they were made to withstand the bruising treatment necessarily received by battery decoys.

A decoy carver from Churches Island who seems to have escaped the attention that he deserved among the many carvers in the Currituck area was Ned Burgess (1863–1958) of Water Lily. His ducks, which ran the gamut of the various species of both diving and puddle ducks of the area (including coots), were distinguished by a graceful slenderness that often approached elegance. On all of his decoys I examined, the final shaping was done with a rasp, the marks of which remained to show through a paint job which in its muted simplicity obviously was the work of an artist. Col-

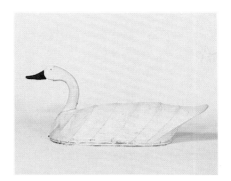

Swan / Mannie Haywood, Kitty Hawk (Dare Co.) 1946

Goose (roothead) / Gary Bragg, Ocracoke (Hyde Co.) 1915

Goose (roothead) / Percy Carawan, Swan Quarter (Hyde Co.) 1935

lectors are fortunate in that, even today, specimens in original paint by this prolific maker still may occasionally be found. Without doubt, Burgess should be ranked with the best of our early decoy makers. He also made a great many canvas-covered geese.

The name Waterfield is still common in the Currituck area, and Malachi (1833–1916), who once lived on Knotts Island, made a great many redhead and blackhead (scaup) decoys for battery rigs. Caleb Geams Waterfield also made battery decoys for other hunters during the latter part of the last century, and it is said that his son George followed in his footsteps in this respect. Reflecting the superstitions of the period, Caleb's wife was accused of being a witch, and this may have led to the tragedy that occurred in the family when George murdered a woman on the island, then later killed himself.

As I traveled southward from Knotts Island, searching for what proved to be extremely elusive information about our early decoy carvers, I was directed to Blanton Saunders of Poplar Branch who told me that he started carving decoys after 1935 when live decoys were outlawed. Until they became illegal,

Blanton kept Canada geese, snow geese, and mallards, which drew the wild flocks to the hunters as no counterfeit waterfowl have ever done since. Blanton's father, Ellie W. Saunders, and his grandfather, Daniel W. Saunders, were not only market hunters themselves but also made decoys and boats to sell to other hunters.

When Blanton started making decoys, decoy makers obtained the juniper (white cedar) by wading into the swamps with cross-cut saws and axes over their shoulders. They felled the trees and sawed the logs into short sections which they then split, with wedges and axes, into blocks of a suitable size for making decoy bodies. The blocks were packed out of the swamp on their backs and seasoned before being chopped and whittled into decoys. Who says those were the good old days? Many sailing vessels were wrecked and pounded to pieces along the Outer Banks, and the masts and spars that washed ashore frequently served as a source of wood for decoys.

Bob Morse and Pat O'Neal were also early decoy makers in the Currituck region. Morse and O'Neal made large battery decoys as well as small boats. Morse lived on

Churches Island. Besides carved wooden battery decoys, Pat O'Neal made canvas-covered slat goose decoys. In addition to decoys and skiffs, this man of wide interests and many skills produced powered cruisers at his boat works and operated a small boat repair business in Coinjock, where he lived.

All of these men were working early in this century. During the same period, Callie O'Neal, a guide who made decoys for his own use only, was operating a battery rig from Churches Island.

Besides the early decoy carvers whose work may be identified by their individual styles, or sometimes by their initials, there were many waterfowl hunters who made decoys for their own use only. The origins of these decoys will never be known. The battery decoys of the Currituck area are characterized chiefly by their large size and simple ruggedness, and it is true that many could be termed crude. Decoy survivors from that era show evidence of much use, and many repaints obviously not splashed on by artists, and they are characteristic of the blocks that still may be turned up in that area by collectors who persevere—and are lucky.

Moving a short distance south

from Currituck, we come to Colington, the home of Mannie Haywood who carved some decoys from solid wood, but is much better known for his canvas-covered wire frames mounted on wood plank bottoms. Some of his decoys may be identified by his initials MH cut into the plank bottom. Besides having a very creditable paint job, his decoys frequently displayed an interesting innovation in the construction of the heads. To overcome the common weakness that caused almost all decoys to crack through the neck, with the grain of the wood, when subjected to the alternate wetting and drying accompanying use, Haywood placed a vertical joint through the head, just behind the eyes. This joint allowed the grain of the wood comprising the neck and rear portion of the head to run vertically, while the grain of the wood in the forepart of the head and the bill ran horizontally, or at right angles to the neck, thus eliminating the planes of weakness in the neck through which cracks occurred. Because of their comparative lightness, canvas-covered duck, goose, and swan decoys were often used in this area.

For most of the information about the early decoy carvers who worked around Back Bay and Currituck Sound, I am indebted to Tilford Wade, a decoy collector and duck hunter of Knotts Island, who spent many hours digging out facts and human-interest stories that could not have been brought to light without his help. Without his aid, this story could not have been written.

Some other decoy carvers who are known to have worked on and in the vicinity of Currituck Sound were J. Adams, Solomon Beasley, Roy Dudley, A. Grady, John Lewark,

H. F. Stone, Wilton Walker, and David Witson. This list could be made much longer.

As we move south of Kill Devil Hills along the Outer Banks we reach territory where waterfowl, and decoys to attract them to the hunter's blinds, have abounded for a long period. But very little information about the decoy carvers is to be had. It is said that Frank Gaskill of Portsmouth Island made roothead brant and geese. Gary Bragg is also said to have made roothead decoys in the vicinity of Ocracoke.

By using rootheads, a device to which some early carvers of Long Island also had resorted, these men overcame the same difficulty that Mannie Haywood and Marvin Midgett of Kitty Hawk had mastered by putting a vertical joint in the heads of their canvas-covered decoys. The choice and shaping of these roots, or knots, required a positive talent which added interest and charm to the decoy. Considering the amount of waterfowl hunting that was done on the Outer Banks, and the great quantities of decoys that were made locally, it is surprising that we are left with so little knowledge of the carvers and so few of their decoys of identifiable origin.

A short distance south of Portsmouth Island, we come to an area (Core Sound) that stretches roughly from Cedar Island to Harkers Island, in which the decoy carvers and their products are better known. In this area, several members of both the Fulcher and the Willis families are well known for the decoys they made during a period beginning well before the turn of the century.

Mitchell Fulcher (1869–1950) of Stacy probably is better known for the artistic merit, as well as the variety and quality, of his work than is

any other carver from this area. He made decoys for both diving ducks and marsh ducks, as well as for geese, and they were known for smooth and graceful lines. The backs of his bluebills were characterized by an interesting dappled effect and his son, Cartey Fulcher of Stacy, says that he obtained this with a snuff brush. For the enlightenment of any reader who may be insufficiently informed about the old, but not extinct, custom of dipping snuff, a snuff brush was made by jerking a small twig from a blackgum tree so as to pull the knot out of the limb with the twig. This exceptionally tough knot was then peeled and chewed (by one of the youngsters, if for grandma's use) until its fibers were crushed to form a small brush. The moistened brush was then used to dig snuff from a can and transfer it for snug deposit between the lower lip and gum. There it might be packed to give pleasure and serve as a stimulus for a period, without showing any (well, hardly any) evidence of its use. Cartey also said that his father, when making heads, used the open end of a .22 cartridge case to stamp circles in which the eyes later would be painted. Besides making decoys for sale to other hunters and clubs, Fulcher served as guide and caretaker at the Green Island Club for many years.

Though this story originally was intended to cover only the state's early makers of working decoys, bridges still exist that span from "early" to "contemporary," and from "working decoys" to "ornamentals." Irving Fulcher of Stacy was, after a lifetime devoted to it, still making working decoys in 1976. Eldon Willis, also of Stacy—with occasional help from his son Roy—was making working decoys into the 1970s. For many years, Eldon Willis and Elmer Salter (1902–64) operated as a partnership which produced hand-carved decoys for hunters and guides. They once received (and filled) a single order for 1,000 goose decoys.

Although there are other active, skilled carvers of ornamental waterfowl, shorebirds, and songbirds in our state, I feel that it would be straying too far from my original purpose to include references to their work here.

Besides handmade decoys, a great many excellent factory decoys (Mason, Evans, Pratt, Dodge, and Wildfowler, to name a few) were used along our coast early in the century, and are still sought by collectors. Since many members of the famous shooting clubs that were located along the Outer Banks were from northern cities, it is not strange that some of them had their own hand-carved decoys sent down.

Known hunter-carvers who worked in the vicinity of Ocracoke, Portsmouth Island, and Core Sound were Wilbur Gaskill, Leckler Lewis (fine silhouettes of ducks and geese) who hunted with Mitchell Fulcher as a youth, John Lupton, Lambert Morris, J. W. Salter, Jodie Styron, Harvey Taylor, Charles Williams, Will Willis, and Bob Willis. Unquestionably, many others could be added.

If any decoys of consequence were made in North Carolina south of Core Sound, I have been unable to obtain any evidence of them.

In winding up this introduction to some of the decoy makers of our coast, it is recognized that much interesting information about the numerous market hunters of the period, many of whom made their own decoys, probably could be unearthed by a diligent researcher, but time is running out. All too soon now, no old-timer will be left to falteringly describe the market hunters and the famous shooting clubs that followed these professionals, and set their own sky-high limits. Few of the early makers signed or marked their decoys, but, as in other areas noted for the artistry of certain carvers, some of our North Carolina makers had such distinct individual styles that their work still may be identified by those who have collected or studied decoys.

The Dudleys, John Williams, Ivey Stevens, Alvirah Wright, Ned Burgess, and Mitchell Fulcher are examples of early carvers whose work speaks for itself. Considering the myriad market hunters, sport hunters, and pot hunters, with their thousands of hand-carved decoys, who gunned from Back Bay to Harkers Island when waterfowl were plentiful and bag limits were high or nonexistent, we have a promising and interesting field which could be explored further.

In the considerable amount of literature that has been devoted to decoys, much has been made of the artistic talent (or lack thereof) possessed by those who created in this form of folk art, and it is true that each region had, among the ranks of its early decoy makers, a small proportion of true artists. However, the great majority made them with only practical considerations in mind: they had to attract waterfowl and to withstand the use and abuse of hunting. If, among the decoy makers who hunted and carved along North Carolina's coast, we agree that a half dozen qualify as artists of some merit, our proportion probably compares favorably with the rest of the country.

Photographs by Ken Taylor.
Decoy collection courtesy of Neal Conoley.

Traditional Boats of North Carolina

MARK TAYLOR

It's a bluebird day as we sail out of Harkers Island in the early morning. Bill Newbold handles the tiller while Hank Murdock—resembling a benevolent, bespectacled Ahab in yellow oilskins—leans against the foredeck and watches for crab pots.

"We'll set a gill net for bluefish off Core Banks, and then go check our crab pots," said Newbold. "It's early, but there might be some blues moving."

We tack across Core Sound and drop 200 yards of gill net perpendicular to Core Banks. In older times the net would have been made of heavy tarred cotton twine, but today a lightweight monofilament net snakes out of a large box mounted on the stern as we run downwind. As the marker buoys pop over the side, Newbold changes course for the eastern tip of Harkers Island and starts a small outboard motor mounted on a side bracket as we drop sail.

"Normally I wouldn't do this, but the wind is dying and we've got forty crab pots to check," he hollered. "We usually do everything but run the crab pots under sail."

Bill Newbold and Hank Murdock, both of Harkers Island, are reviving a classic North Carolina tradition—commercial fishing from a sailing sharpie. Both men are retired, and when Newbold moved to Harkers Island some years ago he decided he wanted to try fishing from a sharpie after learning about the area's maritime heritage.

"I've always wanted to fish from a sailboat, so I had Karl Muller of Harkers Island build me this twenty-six-foot sharpie in 1981. Although I've done a lot of commercial fishing, I had never sailed before. I knew Hank Murdock well, though, and he's an excellent sailor. We decided to try fishing together, and found we made an excellent team. One man handles the net or pots while the other sails the sharpie."

Newbold and Murdock are part of a large renaissance in traditional boats. Until recently, most small working sailing craft were neglected by historians and contemporary boatbuilders. Small fishing boats lack the romance of larger vessels, such as clipper ships, or the elegance and speed of yachts and racing

boats. Interest in traditional boats has revived, however, and most of what we know about the early boats of North Carolina is due to the work of the North Carolina Maritime Museum in Beaufort.

"It's surprising how little we know about the traditional, sail-powered workboats that were used in most areas well into this century," said Michael Alford, Curator of Maritime Research at the museum, who has been studying traditional North Carolina boats for over twenty years. "Most of these boats were fished hard and then discarded, so few original boats remain. Workboats were also generally built by individual fishermen, and the builder usually carried the plans in his head. The men who built and sailed these boats are rapidly disappearing, and when they are gone a fascinating slice of history will die with them."

Alford and the museum staff have developed working plans for several traditional boats through interviews with aging fishermen and boatbuilders, and by measuring and "taking the lines" of the few original boats that remain. Although there were

Traditional sharpie is a fast sailer and excellent work boat. Bryan Blake of Gloucester built this 20-footer in 1974.

Mark Taylor

Mark Taylor

The characteristic round stern is the most difficult part of the construction of a sharpie. This 20-foot sharpie was built by Bill Hettler of Morehead City.

literally dozens of different types of boats used in North Carolina from the 1700s through the early 1900s, three classic sailing craft either evolved in or have strong links to North Carolina coastal waters. These are the sharpie, the shad boat, and the Carolina spritsail skiff.

The sharpie from which Bill Newbold fishes would have been a common sight in North Carolina at the turn of the century. Thousands of these boats were used along our coast, but they were most common in the Beaufort and Morehead City areas. North Carolina fishermen prized the sharpie for its seaworthiness, large cargo capacity, and open work area. And best of all, especially in Core and Bogue sounds, the shallow-drafted vessels seemed almost capable of sailing on a heavy dew!

There has probably never been a boat better adapted to the shoal waters of North Carolina than the sharpie. Ironically, the sharpie was not developed in North Carolina, but was introduced to the state from the North.

"A Rhode Islander named George Ives introduced the sharpie to North Carolina in 1875," said Alford. "Sharpies were widely used for oyster tonging and net fishing in Long Island, and Ives felt that these boats were well suited to North Carolina. He was heavily involved in the seafood and fishing industries in coastal North Carolina, and brought a thirty-four-foot sharpie down to Beaufort. Local fishermen were skeptical of the seaworthiness and sailing characteristics of Ives's sharpie until it beat the fastest fishing boat in Beaufort in a race in heavy weather. Then, they were quick to adopt the boat as their own. Within five years, there were over five hundred sharpies being used in the Beaufort area."

The sharpie is characterized by a plumb or even inverted stem, straight sides, a flat bottom across the beam (there is considerable curve or "rocker" in a sharpie hull fore and aft), and a rounded stern. The boats were usually sailed with a double-masted, leg-of-mutton spritsail rig. This ancient sail plan lacks the low-swinging boom used on most sloops today, but instead features a spar called a "sprit" that extends diagonally across the sail. No standing rigging is needed to support the mast, and the sprit offers plenty of headroom—a feature much appreciated by lone fishermen who hauled nets and handled the boat at the same time.

North Carolina fishermen also found that the sharpie could be built easily and quickly—most fishermen could build one in three to four weeks. Locally available hard pine, oak, cypress, and "juniper" or Atlantic white cedar produced a boat that was inexpensive, solid, and exceptionally durable. Sharpies of all sizes were built in North Carolina, but most ranged from 26 to 36 feet. The smaller ones—from 26 to 28 feet—were usually handled by one man and could carry 75 to 100 bushels of oysters. Larger models were usually worked by two men, and could carry 150 to 175 bushels of oysters.

"Changing times also contributed to the popularity of the sharpie," said Alford. "Improved transportation systems in North Carolina created a large market for shellfish and seafood after the Civil War, and the sharpie was a workhorse of a boat that could help meet this demand. The large, open work area offered plenty of room for handling nets or hauling fish, and the rounded, half-decked stern was convenient to work around while fishing or tonging for oysters. Smaller sharpies were generally used for oystering or fishing for mullet, spot, croaker, trout, flounder, and other species. Larger ones —usually around thirty-five feet— were also used for fishing. Some transferred the catch from smaller sharpies to fish houses on the shore. Many of these larger models were 'buy boats' that roamed the sounds buying fresh fish and shellfish from individual fishermen in smaller boats. Sharpies of all sizes were also used extensively in the menhaden industry, which was developed by several former Rhode Island soldiers who had served in occupied Beaufort during the Civil War."

By the late 1880s Tar Heels had added a few touches of their own to the design. Some innovative fishermen had tried using large sharpies

This Carolina spritsail skiff was built for the North Carolina Wooden Boat Show by Ed Beck (left). Mike Alford, admiring Beck's handiwork, has uncovered much information on the state's early boat designs through his work with the N.C. Maritime Museum.

to dredge or drag for oysters in the sounds, but found that the spritsail lacked the power needed to pull a heavy, iron oyster dredge. They replaced the spritsail with more powerful double-masted, gaff-rigged mains and topsails commonly used on coasting schooners, and the Core Sound schooner-sharpie, commonly called a "Core Sounder," was born. Most of these vessels were from 40 to 45 feet long. The largest Core Sounder was the *Prince*, a 63-footer built in Beaufort in 1899.

"Core Sounders were used much like Chesapeake Bay skipjacks," said Alford. "During the fall and winter, a four- or five-man crew dredged for oysters. In the summer the boats hauled freight. The Core Sounders often ran North Carolina fish to the West Indies and returned with

sugar, molasses, and rum. They also served as buy boats for fishermen, and hauled general cargo in local waters."

Ironically, the man responsible for the introduction of the sharpie to North Carolina was also partially responsible for its demise. George Ives is generally credited with being one of the first to install a small gasoline engine in a sharpie in the early 1900s, and dwindling numbers of sailing sharpies were built after the turn of the century. The huge Core Sounders continued to run into the 1930s, often stripped of their rigging and delivering freight under power in local waters. However, the sharpie lives on in the Harkers Island boats and Core Sound trawlers and shrimpers that make our coast so picturesque today. The round

stern, flat bottom amidships, and straight bow of these boats betray their sharpie lineage.

The shad boat is another North Carolina boat design—as beautiful a vessel as has ever graced our waters. It has its roots in the log dugout canoes used by coastal Indians. Early settlers modified these Indian dugouts by splitting them down the middle, adding a broad plank for a midsection that often included a carved keel, and joining the sections with ribs made of twisted tree roots. These boats were called "kunners," which is probably a corruption of the Indian word for canoe. Small kunners were paddled or rowed, and larger kunners were equipped with a spritsail.

In the early 1870s a boatbuilder named Washington Creef of Roa-

North Carolina Maritime Museum

North Carolina Maritime Museum

This flat-bottomed spritsail skiff skippered by an Audubon game warden was photographed in 1905 (top). The largest of the Core Sounders was the Prince (bottom), a 63-footer built in Beaufort in 1899.

noke Island went the kunner one better. Local shad fishermen needed boats to work their pound nets, which were large weirs made of wooden stakes that ran perpendicular to the shore. Large schools of migrating shad were intercepted by these nets, and were diverted into holding pens called "pounds." The ideal boat for working a pound net was under 27 feet so it could enter the pound and remove the fish. It also had to be shallow-drafted, seaworthy, and capable of hauling a heavy load. In addition, it should carry a large spread of sail so that it could work in the light breezes of summer.

Creef began by making a half-hull model of a small round-bottomed boat with a sharply pointed bow, shallow keel, and square stern. The keel and garboards (planks adjacent to the keel) of the boat were carved from a single log—as in a kunner—but the hull was finished with carefully joined planking. He rigged the boat with a spritsail, but added a single innovation—a small "flying topsail" was attached to the top of the mast and operated independently of the other sails. This topsail enabled the boat to catch the slightest puff of wind coming in over the treetops when it was working a pound net close to shore.

"Shad boats were prized by fishermen because of their seaworthiness, comfort, speed, and graceful lines," said Alford. "Unlike sharpies, shad boats were difficult to build, and a large group of boatbuilders who specialized in shad boats soon developed around Roanoke Island."

To build a shad boat the boatmakers first felled a huge white cedar tree, and hauled both the main log and stump back to the building site. The main log was carved into an elongated Y that formed the keel and garboards of the boat. The stump was split into sections and taken to a sawmill in Elizabeth City where it was cut into two-inch slices on a huge bandsaw. These slices were to form the ribs and stem of the boat. Referring to his half-model, the builder selected a stem and ribs that matched the contours of the model. These were fastened to the log keel and garboards. Then, the boat was carefully planked so that the planking met the log keel and garboards in a graceful curve. Finally, the boats were painted white or gray and a colorful stripe was added along the gunwales. This was unusual because most North Carolina workboats were devoid of ornamentation.

The construction of shad boats changed around the turn of the century. Builders switched to using dead-rise planking (planks met the smaller keel at an angle instead of faring the planking into the single log that formed the keel and garboards) because large trees had grown scarce, and plank ribs replaced the natural crooked ribs and stem cut from stumps. Many of these shad boats were built for waterfowl hunting clubs on the Outer Banks, and the last shad boats made in North Carolina were built around 1930 by the Dough family of Roanoke Island for the Church Island Gun Club on Currituck Banks.

Fishermen who owned original shad boats prized them for their speed, and the boats were often used for smuggling liquor during Prohibition.

Fortunately, about a dozen original shad boats remain, and these boats are still being used under power by commercial fishermen in the Manteo area. "All of the remaining shad boats are of the original design with the one-piece, log keel and garboards," said Alford. "Some of these boats are probably a century old. The boats that were built later with dead-rise planking didn't hold up as well, and have all disappeared."

The Carolina spritsail skiff is another classic design that evolved in our waters. This boat was often called the "mule of the coastal fisherman." Most skiffs ranged from 16 to 22 feet and were used for clamming, oystering, crabbing, fishing, and general transportation.

The dead-rise hull of the spritsail skiff had one unique feature—it lacked a keel. The center planks of the shallow, V-bottomed hulls met in a single seam which swelled to form a watertight joint. This reduced the draft of the hull considerably—a twenty-footer drew only four to six inches of water with the centerboard up.

"The dead-rise Carolina spritsail skiff was an excellent workboat and a very fast sailer," said Alford. "These boats carried a large spread of sail, and fishermen often raced their boats for pleasure on Sunday afternoons and holidays. However, there were differences in the design of these boats throughout the state. In the rough open waters of Albemarle Sound, for example, freeboard was increased and side decks were added to dead-rise skiffs to make them better sea boats. Some Carolina spritsail skiffs were also built along sharpie lines. These boats had the flat bottom, straight sides, and plumb bow of the sharpie but lacked a round stern. They had a shallower draft than a dead-rise skiff, but weren't as fast or as seaworthy."

These boats were not used only for casual fishing and pleasure sail-

ing, however. A twenty-foot spritsail skiff routinely hauled several fishermen, a large net, and up to a thousand pounds of fish or shellfish. In fact, Hank Murdock lives next to an elderly man on Harkers Island who raised a family net fishing, oystering, crabbing, and clamming from a small spritsail skiff.

Until recently, traditional North Carolina boats were found only in aging photographs and fading memories. The original sharpies and spritsail skiffs are gone, although a few rotting hulks probably lie undiscovered in remote marshes and creeks. Only a handful of shad boats remain to remind us of a time when tough men sailing small boats wrested a living from the water.

Happily, a new day is at hand. The work of the North Carolina Maritime Museum has prompted a surge of interest in traditional boats, and gleaming white sharpies and spritsail skiffs built for recreational sailing are now docked amidst sleek fiberglass yachts on the Beaufort waterfront. Many people are also watching Bill Newbold's fishing with keen interest. He was recently featured in *National Fisherman*, a trade journal for the commercial fishing industry, and some knowledgeable observers feel that Newbold is proving that traditional sail-powered workboats such as the sharpie and spritsail skiff have a place in the future of commercial fishing. When I accompanied him, we returned to the dock with two boxes of crabs and a large tub of bluefish. On the run back to Harkers Island he quietly told me about his fishing as we watched Core Banks turn golden in the late afternoon sun.

"I began fishing with the sharpie for the joy of fishing from a classic

boat, but I've found it to be a very practical boat for inshore fishing today. Like most fishermen, I go after whatever is in season. Much of my work is clamming, and I just beach the boat on a bar and get out. Since this boat draws only eight inches of water with the centerboard up, she is ideal for oystering and crabbing in shallow waters. She'll also haul a load—I once brought in three tons of fish, although that was kind of risky. She's also a good sea boat. We fish in winds up to thirty-five knots, and in the spring and fall we go five to fifteen miles offshore and set gill nets for spot, croaker, and Spanish mackerel.

"Of course, there are some limitations to fishing under sail. We can't go as far as a powerboat, and have to allow extra time in case the wind doesn't cooperate. However, fuel costs are minimal and this boat is very simple—there's nothing on it that I can't fix myself. A few years ago when fuel prices jumped, Hank and I were making money when most fishermen weren't. We're either revisiting the past or welcoming the future—depending on what happens to the price of fuel."

Death of a Turtle

Waves of heat rose from the white gravel that covered the railroad bed, and hot tar oozed from the ties. Ahead, the rails curved and disappeared around a bend. Just down the embankment to the right lay the river, an artery of 58-degree water that ran parallel to the tracks baking in the late summer sun.

Something caught my eye. A large box turtle moved feebly on the gravel, trying to climb over the smooth, hot steel. How long had it been trapped between those rails, and how had it gotten there? I carried it into the thick undergrowth, and left it in a moist, shaded spot. Maybe it would live.

Back on the tracks, I followed the curve for another 200 yards looking for the path to the river where I planned to fish. In that short distance, I found four other box turtles, all trapped between the rails. All dead.

After taking a closer look, it was easy to see how the turtles had become trapped. Here and there were small openings under the rails where the turtles, seeking the warmth of the gravel and ties, had crawled through. Once between the rails, they could not find the openings again, and eventually perished in the heat. A more effective death trap could hardly be devised. If that many turtles could die in that short stretch, how many more had been claimed in the fifteen miles of rails along that river? How many are similarly trapped in the countless miles of rails that crisscross the nation? Here is a creature with few, if any, natural enemies and a lifespan of up to 138 years. Yet, seeking only warmth, it finds death.

As I stood hip-deep in the river and cast tiny flies to an occasional rising trout, I felt unsettled by what I had seen. Yet, it was not the plight of the box turtles that bothered me most. I knew I had no answers for them, nor would I seek any. That is precisely the problem. Virtually every-

where we look, we are confronted with environmental problems both large and small for which there seem to be no easy solutions. Perhaps no solution at all. Indeed, many of the problems are so knotted and confused that it seems hopeless to even seek an answer.

Those box turtles were trapped by more than just rails; they were caught in the kind of deadly tradeoff that is becoming more and more common. Sure, a railroad bed might be designed to prevent their entrapment, but it would never be done. It would be too expensive, there are too many miles of track, and box turtles are understandably a low priority for the rail industry. Furthermore, no studies have been made to learn the extent of the problem. Which means that a certain unknown number of box turtles had been, and would continue to be, expendable—sacrificed to the greater benefits we all share from railroads. And if there is blame to be placed, is it not therefore shared by us all?

More wildlife is crushed on our highways each year than is killed by all other means combined. The automobile is our biggest predator, yet, except for a few deer and chipmunk crossing signs, what has ever been done? What can be done? For every environmental battle we fight and win, we lose countless others, and, in many cases, we don't even choose to fight. Instead, we simply accept the loss as a necessary and unavoidable price for progress. And ironically, some of our energy is wasted in bitter contests that should never even occur. For example, many well-meaning people seek to ban hunting, yet properly regulated hunting has no adverse effect on wildlife; in fact, the money spent on management and habitat improvement from licenses and taxes on sporting gear protects and enhances wildlife populations. Without it, many species—and not just those sought by sportsmen—

would be far less numerous than they are today. Yet, while we squabble, our heritage of wildlife and natural resources is slipping away.

A few box turtles trapped on a railroad may indeed be expendable, but we face other sacrifices that are far more critical. Thousands of pesticides are being pumped into the environment, virtually without regard to their impact on wildlife. Again, far too little is known about their effects, not just on wildlife, but on human life as well. The long-term impact could be as disastrous to the earth's life as all-out nuclear war, yet most of us seem no more concerned about it than we are about a few sunbaked box turtles. Solutions may exist, but we don't seek them effectively. Can't be helped, we say. Agriculture is essential, and some loss is inevitable. But at what point does the loss balance the gain? Will we even recognize that point, and can we afford to wait that long?

The same is true of our rapidly disappearing woodlands, wetlands, and other undeveloped wild areas. Taken individually, the loss of this habitat to a shopping center, a cloverleaf, or a housing development may not seem drastic, but the overall trend is frightening. Someday, if we last that long, we may be in the Supreme Court fighting to save the last half-acre vacant lot in the middle of a megapolis extending from Key West to Nova Scotia.

When I left the river that day, I walked along the tracks to the car. A box turtle (the one I had saved?) was at the edge of the gravel, climbing toward the rails. I carried it to the car and put it in a small cardboard box. One turtle, heading to Raleigh, a shell within a shell moving at 55 miles per hour, its future beyond its control. I felt an intense kinship.—*Jim Dean*

Jane Rohling

Johannes Plott's Famous Hunting Dogs

CURTIS WOOTEN

"The Plott hound can run like a fox-hound, fight like a terrier, tree like a coonhound, and has the nose of a bloodhound," Von Plott once said. One of six hunting hound breeds recognized by the United Kennel Club (UKC), the Plott is different from the other hounds in common use in North America today. Many claim it's more aggressive and faster, with a willing-to-mix-it-up attitude and catlike agility in a fight. These traits endear it to the rugged mountaineers of North Carolina who chase bear, boar, and raccoon. The Plott hound takes its name from the family that developed the breed. In a manner of speaking, the dog has been two hundred years in the making, and much of that has taken place here in the mountains of our state.

The story of the Plott hound began in 1750 when two brothers who had worked as gamekeepers for wealthy landowners in Germany left that strife-torn country in search of a better life in the New World. Their provisions for life in America were meager but among them were three brindle- and two buckskin-colored hunting dogs—part of the stock their wealthy landowner employers had used to hunt wild boar and stag. The brothers thought they might be helpful in hunting the bear, buffalo, and deer they had heard about in the colonies.

One of the brothers never made it to America. He died en route and was buried at sea. The other, Johannes, then sixteen, arrived at Philadelphia in September 1750, took coastal boats and walked to New Bern, and traveled inland to what is now Cabarrus County where other German immigrants had preceded him. Just west of the Uwharrie mountains, he established a farm, married, and fathered several sons.

The dogs he brought with him proved useful in hunting for food as well as tracking the bear, mountain lions, and wolves that preyed on his livestock.

The Plott dogs were different from other hounds found in the Carolinas at the time. Most other hunting dogs were descendants, in some fashion or another, of the English foxhounds that were popular in the colonies. The Plott dogs were not so "houndy." They were more like mastiffs with short ears, bench legs, barrel chests, somewhat pointed noses, and a slightly flagged tail. Their voices were not so melodious as other hounds and they were hot-nosed—that is, they were not particularly good at following a cold track. But that was no disadvantage at the time. Bear were plentiful and dogs with expert tracking ability were not always in demand. What was needed were hounds that could take a suitably warm track, jump the game, bring the animal to bay, and then hold it until hunters arrived. The Plott dogs filled that bill.

It may not be proper to refer to the early Plotts as hounds. According to Taylor Crockett, a current-day Plott owner and breeder who lives near Franklin, Mont Plott, the great-great grandson of Johannes, "would bristle right up if you called his dogs hounds. He said they were a 'cur dog,'" a cur being a breed of hunting dog recognized by old-time mountaineers.

At any rate the Plott dogs were fierce, iron-willed dogs that could track, chase, and fight black bear,

Photograph courtesy of Plott family

John Plott holds a group of Plott hounds on the Plott family farm west of Waynesville. John and his two brothers, Sam and Vaughn ("Von"), were instrumental in getting the Plott hound recognized by the United Kennel Club in 1946.

mountain lions, and wolves with un-equaled ability. They had an intensity for the hunt and they soon had a reputation for tracking big game and holding it at tree or bay until the hunters arrived. When marauding bears or wolves raided the livestock in the area, it was the Plott dogs that were brought in to hunt them down.

There is no way of knowing the exact stock of these German dogs, and the subject has given rise to a great deal of speculation. They were catch dogs used on wild boar, some say, related to the boxers and great danes. Lawrence Plott, a six-generation descendant of Johannes, who now lives in Waynesville, spent nearly fifteen years in Germany after his arrival there during World War II. That allowed him to do a considerable amount of research into the ancestry of the Plott dogs. He says that probably the closest relative to the current-day Plott is the Hanoverian Sweisshund. The breed is old enough to have spawned the

Plott dogs and was developed—and is still found—in the same part of Germany from which Johannes immigrated. Both breeds are similar in appearance, coloring, and physical makeup, and they display the same hunting traits and characteristics.

Having worked with dogs in Germany, Johannes knew the importance of breeding and worked to maintain and improve the qualities of his pack. Only the best were bred and the best of their offspring kept. Those too aggressive or clumsy were

Photographs courtesy of Plott family

Vaughn Plott stands with Plott's Happy, Plott's Balsam, and Plott's Link in 1954 (above, left). Photo from Plott family album (above, right) shows all three brothers at a bear hunt in 1932. Vaughn is at left with golf cap, John holds rifle in the middle, and Sam is at right, bending over.

killed by the quarry they brought to bay, and those that showed a lack of desire or cowardice were dispatched on the spot by the hunters. These selective practices produced a breed of dogs that were clever in fighting cooperatively with other pack members when dangerous game was cornered. They produced a breed not only with the drive and guts to hold dangerous game like bear and wild boar, but also with the sagacity during the showdown to survive to run and fight another day. It's a characteristic that sets the Plott apart from other hounds.

In 1780 the Plott dogs passed into the hands of Johannes's son, John. In 1800 John traveled west looking for a new home, and is said to have been shown by Chief Junaluska a valley on the eastern slopes of the Balsam Mountain range in what is now Haywood County. John made claim to 1,700 acres there and settled in what is now called Plott Valley, located just west of Waynes-

ville. He and his sons soon established a reputation as renowned bear hunters and the breeders of the best "bar" dogs around.

Over the next two hundred years the Plott packs passed through the hands of George, Henry, John, and, in the late 1800s, Montreville (Mont) Plott. All were premiere bear hunters and sticklers for maintaining the breed.

The Plott dogs stayed, more or less, in the Plott family over those years. The Plotts never sold a dog, although they did give them to neighbors and hunting companions. Vaughn (Von) Plott, son of Mont and a fifth-generation Plott breeder, is quoted as having said: "People would ride in here on mule with a tow sack and go home with a pup. They'd come from miles away to get one of those brindle dogs. People had to have them to keep their farms safe from wild animals." Many of those dogs were bred to other hounds, with performance on the hunt the only criterion considered. But the bloodlines of the Plott family dogs are said to have been kept intact. They were a family pack and the pride of ownership, the pride of training, and the love of hunting kept the line going. Although their popularity grew locally, they were little known outside the Carolina mountains.

By the late 1800s the Plott hounds' reputation had spread across the state line into the mountains of northern Georgia, reaching the ears of one Elijah Crow of Rabun Gap. A bear hunter of considerable reputation himself, Crow had a pack of bear dogs he considered second to none. They were known as leopard-spotted bear dogs, or leopard-spotted curs, a breed recognized by hunters in the southern Appalachians at the time, but which has since disappeared.

Crow was so intrigued by the stories of the Plott hounds that he packed up his own dogs and gear and traveled to Plott Valley to meet the Plott family and see for himself what the Plott dogs could do. Mont Plott welcomed Crow and the two became immediate friends. For several weeks they hunted their dogs— as separate packs and together, noting their performance. Each man was impressed with the other's dogs.

When Crow returned to northern Georgia, he took with him one of Plott's old stud dogs, to which he mated one of his best bitches. The following year he returned to Plott Valley bearing with him a pup, the result of the crossing of the Plott and leopard-spotted cur hounds. That dog, named Old Thunderer, became an excellent bear dog and was subsequently used as a stud dog by Mont Plott. That outcross was

the first admitted introduction of new blood to the Plott dogs since Johannes settled in Carolina in 1750. Another outcross to a dog having leopard-spotted cur blood is said to have been made by Mont's son John and grandson "Little George" in 1928.

Mont Plott had five sons, three of whom (John, Sam, and Vaughn) carried the traditions of hunting bears and breeding Plott dogs into the twentieth century. John and Vaughn kept separate packs, which became known for their individual traits. John and his son Little George maintained a short-eared strain of Plotts, said to be much like their ancestors. Known for their speed, feist, and willingness to mix-it-up with bear and boar, they were generally more efficient and evasive fighters and for that reason were preferred by many bear and boar hunters. Vaughn, or "Von" as he was universally known, bred a longer-eared strain that had a colder nose and a better voice. Gola Ferguson, a friend and hunting companion of the Plott brothers, had a first-class pack of Plott hounds of moderate earage, which he developed by breeding his Plotts to a Blevins hound.

The Blevins hound was a brindle-colored dog with a black saddle that took its name from a Yancey County family. All evidence indicates that the base stock of the Blevins hound was Plott. In the late 1800s a patriarch of the Blevins family obtained some hunting stock from Mont Plott and during the next two decades returned to Plott Valley for additional stock. Outcrosses the Blevins's made to hound stock— probably black and tan but possibly other breeds, no one knows for sure—produced a top-notch bear

dog that was known for its keen nose and melodious voice. From these hounds the Blevins family assembled one of the finest packs of bear dogs in existence and they became known as the Blevins hound.

The cross of Gola Ferguson's Plott hounds with a Blevins in the 1920s produced a blend that was deadly on bear and wild boar. Two of Ferguson's dogs named Boss and Tige—the result of the Blevins cross —became noted throughout the Smokies for their outstanding qualities. Both were extremely good trackers, had excellent mouths, were fast trailers, and "ran to catch a bear"—the ultimate compliment a bear hunter bestows upon a dog. They were long-staying fighters and both were excellent tree dogs. Students of Plott hounds breeding say that the Plott-Blevins cross made by Gola Ferguson is partially responsible for the sensational dog that exists today. Of the eighty-one dogs initially registered by the UKC, seventy-nine can be traced to one or both of these famous Plott hounds.

Between 1908 and 1912 a group of northeastern and European businessmen attempted to establish a European-type shooting preserve on Hooper's Bald in the remote mountains of Graham County along the North Carolina-Tennessee line. They enclosed several thousand acres with rail and wire fences and stocked elk, buffalo, Russian brown bear, ring-necked pheasant, and European wild boar and other exotic game animals. Long before the enterprise was abandoned, the wild boar had escaped and were well on their way toward establishing themselves in the surrounding mountains. Equipped with three- to four-inch tusks and the quickness of a deer, the boar was a formidable adversary for hunters and hounds. The bear-fighting Plott hounds were found to be adept at trailing and holding wild boar as well.

By the 1920s and 1930s the Plott hounds were becoming better known outside the area. In addition to the Plott families and Gola Ferguson, the Cable family of Swain County had a first-rate pack, as did the Phillipses of Graham and Clay counties. In the 1930s *Life* magazine ran an article on the Plott hounds, which sparked interest in the breed. About the same time bear-boar hunts began being staged in western North Carolina and eastern Tennessee, which gave a large number of hunters from around the country first-hand knowledge of the dogs.

During the 1930s efforts were begun to have the Plott hounds recognized as a separate breed, and in 1946 the United Kennel Club granted this recognition and established standards for the breed.

The originators of the breed never dreamed that their hounds would attain the fame they now have among hound men, nor did they envision that the Plott would become a popular raccoon hound. "Fact was, back when I was hunting with Gola Ferguson and them, if a Plott cropped that would run a coon when a bear track was available, they'd get rid of him right quick," said Taylor Crockett.

It is sheer numbers that have brought about the shift. Big game hunting—for bear, boar, and mountain lion—is a rather specialized sport for which the Plott is recognized as the premiere hound in most quarters, but by comparison there is a rather limited number of areas across the country where that type of hunting is done. The ranks of raccoon hunters, on the other hand, are legion and they create quite a demand for good raccoon dogs. Just as the Plott filled the bill when a big game hound was needed, the breed is meeting the challenge for first-rate raccoon hounds.

The modern Plott is generally a darker-colored dog than the original stock of Johannes Plott. Two of his dogs were buckskins, a color not allowed by present-day registration standards. They have a better nose, a more melodious voice, and a more houndlike appearance than the original Plotts. Most houndsmen consider these changes improvements that make the dogs more versatile, more applicable to most of today's hunting situations. And, the change in emphasis from a dog that will fight a bear to one that trees raccoons may also have altered the temperament of many Plotts, possibly for the better. Though by nature gentle and easygoing with people and other dogs, the Plott will fight to the death when turned upon, which has given it a bad reputation with some dog owners. "Some people's objection to the Plott is that they're a little bit hard to handle," says Crockett, "and they are if you don't know how to handle them.

You have to keep them apart or they'll fight amongst themselves. I've lost more dogs, had them kill each other, than I have lost to game."

The Plott hound is the oldest American-bred hunting dog breed. Although the black and tan and redbone breeds were registered earlier, they don't go back nearly as far as Plotts. And, as has been mentioned earlier, the Plott hound ancestry is different. Though other breeds have been crossed fairly recently with the Plott dogs to produce the Plott hound we know today, that crossbreeding was made on an already established strain or breed that bore little resemblance to the foxhound that gave us our other hounds. That ancestry has produced a hunting dog with a difference.

What is that difference? Taylor Crockett says, "It's generally his aggressive nature. A Plott that pans out like he's supposed to is fast on the track, he's gritty, he's got lots of what I call go-power—enthusiasm; lots of desire and heart."

Add to that a word that keeps cropping up whenever a conversation turns to Plotts—courage. A Plott will not quit a fight. Even though maimed by the crushing slap of a big bear or torn by raking claws or gnashing teeth, the Plott will attack again—and again until he is either hauled off by the hunters or finished by the bear. It is that "grit" that endears the breed to a growing number of houndsmen.

I'm a Bear Hunter
A Carolina Profile

CLYDE HUNTSINGER
as told to Lawrence S. Earley

At a certain point, the road to Hot Springs plunges sharply and commences to twist and turn like a writhing snake. The forest swallows you up here and you know you are truly in Madison County. On one side gnarled slopes rise steeply and fall away just as abruptly on the other. Here are the protected hollows and coves and ridges and trails where live a hardy breed of people who like their isolation straight up, like shot whiskey.

It was this Appalachian landscape and its people that Clyde Huntsinger knew well, and he talked about them in the summer of 1980 from his mobile home in Hot Springs. Except for a few years in the U.S. Army, Huntsinger lived his life in Madison County, working first as a barber and then later as a wildlife refuge manager in the Rich Laurel Area under the North Carolina Wildlife Resources Commission. In 1971, a bad heart forced him into retirement.

Like the people he lived among, Huntsinger spoke plainly and spoke his mind. Poaching was a common problem among the independent mountain folk, and he pursued poachers with an uncommon zeal. "The way I feel about game," he said, "it belongs to everybody. When the poacher goes in there and kills that deer illegally, as far as I'm concerned he's a rustler, just the same as if he went out there and rustled some rancher's cattle."

He was a hunter, first and foremost, and his talk that summer day was full of past hunts, of bear chases and "wonderful quail hunting" back in the days before clean farming. There were plenty of wild turkey in Madison County at one time, he said, but local story had it that two Tennessee hunters with repeating rifles exterminated them one season long ago. He had spent so much time in the woods, he said, there wasn't a ridge or a trail in the surrounding six or seven counties he hadn't been on.

"When I die," he said that afternoon, "I want to be buried in a casket made of oak and hickory—not a pine in it—because I want to be surrounded by something that the deer and the bear got some good out of." In July 1982, a year after this interview, Clyde Huntsinger died at the age of fifty-nine.

I'm a bear hunter. I love a bear hunter. I love a bear hunter to death. I'd still bear hunt if I was able, but I'm just not able. I go up on the side of the road sometimes in my pickup or car and set and listen to a race, and if nobody's never been on a good bear hunt or been in a position where they could hear this he's missed it all!

There's nothing to me like a good bear fight and a good chase. I'm not particularly interested in killing the bear. I've killed four bear in my life. I could have killed a lot more but I didn't do it. I like to hear them dogs catch that bear. Dogs as a general rule are not going to hurt that bear, but he's going to hurt some dogs if they press him.

A bear hunter, he's got to be pure in heart. And if he's going to follow them dogs, he's got to go temporarily insane because when you're bear hunting here in these mountains you're going through laurel slicks and thickets and briers and everything else. A fellow I know, he

Black Bear (Leonard Lee Rue, III)

likes to bear hunt. We were hunting on Shelton Laurel and he actually tore his clothes off of him trying to catch up to them dogs. The dogs would stop the bear, they'd fight awhile and they'd go again. Just about the time he'd get up with 'em they'd break and go again. They actually had to go get him some clothes to get out of the woods. Now that's the pure in heart. That's what I'm talking about.

A bear hunter, he's going to raise a gang of pups. And he don't want them dogs to run a thing in the world but a bear. He don't want 'em to run a deer. When that dog barks he wants to know that it's a bear. He wants 'em to be straight bear dogs. And he invests a lot of money —it's nothing to see a bear hunter pull out a thousand or fifteen hundred dollars for one dog. That's not unusual at all here in the mountains.

A good bear dog is bred into him just like a beagle. A beagle that's worth his salt will run the first rabbit he ever smells. It's bred in him. Bear dogs are just like beagles. Some beagles are exceptionally good rabbit dogs, and some are not. And some dogs are exceptionally good bear dogs and some are mediocre. It's a tough deal. You got to start a pup out with old dogs that know what they're doing. And preferably them pups are from dogs that are experienced bear dogs. You don't go out on the side of a road and pick up a dog and it run a bear; in fact most dogs are scared of a bear, scared to death of 'em. A good bear dog is hard to come by.

In all of my years I have seen four dogs that you could turn loose and sit down and when they barked it was a bear. Now there was just as good a dog that could run a bear and put him up a tree or fight that

bear. But you had to find a track and turn the dog on that bear, or he'd get out and run anything. I've seen four dogs that you could bet your life that when that dog barked it was a bear. When that dog barked, you could turn the other dogs loose, have a good bear chase, probably kill a bear.

Mr. John Plott of Haywood County, a very dear friend of mine, who I hunted many years with, and also his father—their ancestors are the originators of the Plott hound. Now that was a dog that was bred up from various other dogs. Had a little bulldog in it, had the old-timey cur in it. I've owned Plott dogs; owned one called a Leopard Plott, just as spotted as a leopard, beautiful dog. They're awful gritty dogs and for fighting a bear I don't think you could hardly beat 'em. But if you could get a black and tan or a redbone or anything, I think they're a better trail dog.

Now there'll be a lot of arguments on that, but I've hunted with all of them even down to a feist. The first bear I ever killed was from two little dogs about the size of a lap dog. And one year on management hunts when I was on Davidson River, a group of bear hunters checked in. They used ten dogs at a time, you know. One feller come in with his bear dog and it was a feist dog. Some of them laughed at him. I said, "Now, boys, let's give the dog justice. I know what a feist will do." Well the next day we turned the dogs loose, that feist was the one that treed the bear first. It made some of them Plott dogs look might punylike. This little feller running through the woods, and he had the bear up a tree. Taken all the way around, I prefer the Plott—but don't count out other dogs, too.

The mountaineers, the boys here, are the old true bear hunters. They used to leave this country and go down to the coast to go bear hunting. Down in Hyde County and all in through there. We didn't have no bear up here to hunt. We'd load up and go to the coast. Now that's back in the days when men wasn't getting but ten cents an hour. We'd pool our money in together. Have a dog trailer. Go all the way down there. Camp out in the woods. Find us a place where we could get water, and bear hunt. All I was interested in was a good bear chase and a good fight. If someone killed one it was all right. If he didn't it was all right. Many a trip we didn't kill a bear but had maybe fifteen races. It'd get in them swamps and get away from us.

But when we first started hunting down there them people didn't know nothing about bear hunting. We was a curiosity. People would come to camp to look at them mountain boys and them vicious dogs they had. Yeah, we was a curiosity to them people. They'd come to camp just to eyeball you and look you over. They thought we was a terrible bunch.

When I was a boy back in the 1930s and early 1940s here in Madison County, we had wonderful quail hunting. It wasn't unusual at all to go out and get up from six to ten covey of quail on that small farm. Every farmer grew his own wheat for bread. Most of them also grew either barley, rye, or oats and rather large corn crops. There was no farm tractors to speak of at all at that time. Work on the farm was either done by mules or horses and they had to raise a lot of grain for feeding livestock, cows, chickens, horses, and mules. And threshing machines would go from farm to

Black Bear (Ken Taylor)

farm throughout the county to thresh grain for the farmers.

After I returned from military service in World War II I got home on New Year's Day in 1946 and a big change had taken place. For some reason or another the farmers had quit growing that particular wheat and small grain, had cut down on the size of the corn, and just about had eliminated the quail population. We did have some rabbit, squirrel, very few raccoons—you'd find a track once in a while and people guarded it with their life 'til somebody caught it. There was always a few bear in the Upper Spring Creek area, but mighty few; there was not a huntable population of deer in the county, although there has always been some deer hunting as long as I can remember in the Rich Mountain section.

Right now in Madison County the bear hunting is the best it's been in its history. There's a lot of deer now. The coon population has picked up, and the Wildlife Commission deserves the credit for the hunting and fishing we have today.

I went to work for the Commission March 17, 1952. At that time nobody that I know'd of worked for the Commission for the money there was in it because I drew less than a hundred and fifty dollars a month, clear pay after everything was took out. Me and my wife moved into the old John Rock station in Pisgah Forest—it was an old log house built during the Vanderbilt reign when they owned all that property before they turned it over to the government. We didn't have any electric lights. My wife chased snakes and spiders and everything else all over that old log house—she didn't appreciate that too high.

When I first went to work as a

game lands manager for the Wildlife Commission it was fist and skull. You wasn't Mister; you was "Blankety-Blank." I've had guns pulled on me, I've had a shotgun pulled on me and it cocked and loaded up with buckshot. Man said he's going to kill me. And if you wasn't able to stand up to it, that was just it.

Poaching has a different meaning to me than to the average person. The way I feel about game, it belongs to everybody. It's on my land today, it's on your land tomorrow, and it's on Tom, Dick, and Harry's place the next day. When that man goes in there and kills that deer illegally, as far as I'm concerned he's rustling, just the same as if he went out there and rustled one of them rancher's cattle.

A poacher—he picks his time to go, and you've got to think like him. If it's a-pouring rain, you'd say, well, for the poacher out there now would be a good time to go. That man would be laying up, that's the time for you to get on his back. Now he won't hunt too much in the snow, because he knows you can track him. But now that rainy, dark night, you say, well, he's going to lay up. You got to think like the poacher thinks.

The hardest poacher you had to catch was the man who had patience. Now if he was a man just going in the woods and coming out today, he wasn't all that much trouble. It's the old down-to-earth poacher that was going in there and staying a week at a time or two weeks at a time, that was a tough nut. He took his rations with him, and he had him a camp right in the middle of the biggest thicket he could find, and he didn't stir much, he didn't go far away from that. He made a beeline to where he was going and he stayed there. And if you walked up on a camp unexpectedly, nine times out of ten if he was in camp you never found a gun. He had them guns hid. You'd have to get out and hunt 'em up. You know'd they was there.

Uncle Perry Davis, an old warden who went to work during the Vanderbilt days, he used to help me some on Davidson River. He had a saying: If you wanted to catch a man, you get a real good poplar board clear of knots and a good sharp knife and a whet rock. You know'd reasonably well where that man would come to hunt. He said, just take your board and your good sharp knife and your whet rock and go up there and sit down, and take your food with you. And he said, start whittling, real slow, when your knife got dull, whet it up. He said, before you get that sixteen-foot board whittled up you'll catch that man. That's pretty well right.

A poacher'll hide his tracks a lot better than a deer does or bear does. Animals, as a general rule, are a lot easier to track than a man is. If a down-to-earth good poacher knows what he's doing, you'll never find him, you'll never find where he's

been. He's that particular and he's that careful, because he don't go through the woods a-stirring up the leaves and doing this and that. What he does is just so minute that the average person would never see it.

I can track a man across a bare rock. I learned it as a boy, growing up. Watching for animal tracks. If someone tells you you can't track a man across a bare rock, he's one kind of fool. You can, because you'll see grit on there that's been disturbed. Now where a man steps on that bare rock there's grit laying there and when he puts his foot there he moves that grit and there'll be a small, minute scratch. He could be a-walking on a bed of moss, and to me it's just as plain as walking in the snow.

There's hardly a ridge, trail or a hollow in Madison County, Buncombe County, Henderson County, Haywood County, Graham County, and part of Yancey County and part of Mitchell County that I haven't been on. I've got out on the Blue Ridge Parkway, come on down through the Wilson boundary and out at Cane River Gap and through that country there. I've walked in it and camped in it and hunted in it

from the time I was just a boy. It wasn't nothing for us to load up and go twenty or thirty miles away, stay a week and hunt. Most of these boys in the mountains here, they grow up with a gun in their hand; they know how to shoot it.

Peace of mind, that's what you get in the woods. You're hunting legally not a-bothering nobody, nobody to bother you. And the satisfaction that you get out of outwitting a deer, or outwitting a turkey or outwitting a trout fish in a hole somewhere, that's wonderful! You can't learn that in a book. It's experience. I wouldn't give you two cents to kill the biggest deer in the woods, and the average hunter wouldn't give you two cents. It's the satisfaction of going up there and killing that deer and lying a little— killing it about thirty or forty yards out there and swearing it was two hundred and running like hell, that's what there is in it. And bringing it out legally, and tying it on your jeep or your pickup and showing that deer off. That's the fun, the satisfaction in it. That's the thrill of hunting.

PART TWO
Flora and Fauna

"Late Afternoon," courtesy of artist, Larry Barton

Stalking the Old-Time Apples

DOUG ELLIOTT

It's early March as I write this—long past apple time—but on my desk are several Winter John apples. Through their greenish-yellow base color show crimson flecks, and there is a little blush of lavender here and there. Their skin is wrinkled, but the white flesh is predictably firm and delightfully tart. Their tangy flavor has mellowed considerably during the four months since that brisk, breezy day last fall when I picked them.

Just about anyone who's been raised in the mountains or who's looked at apples in the western part of our state has come across Winter Johns or some of the other old and almost-forgotten varieties of apples. Until recently, an apple was just an apple for me. That was before I started ranging the hills and hollows with Theron Edwards, a sharp-eyed mountain man from Yancey County raised in the mountain tradition of self-sufficiency and still in touch with much of the old-time wisdom and ways. After a couple of seasons of seeing apples through Theron's eyes, I felt like someone who had been shown a rainbow in full color after seeing only black and white.

Doug Elliott

There were once more than eight hundred varieties of apples; many that have not disappeared can be found only in old orchards.

The fact is, there's an incredible variety of apples in the mountains of North Carolina. And by biting into a few of these old-time apples we can tap the richness of a rapidly disappearing culture and life-style.

When I asked Theron how many types of apples he knew, he rattled off a list of more than twenty varieties. Just the names of these almost-forgotten breeds left my head reeling with delight. Some were named for what they resembled, like the elongated, lopsided Sheep's Nose apple, the oval Crow's Egg, and the yellow Bellflower. Others took people's names, presumably the ones who developed the variety or who first brought it into the area. So there's Stark apples, Betsy Deatons, Black Hoovers, Striped Ben Davis's, and Ducketts. Still others, like the Winesap, Sweet Russet, Stripey, and Spice apple, are named for their distinctive tastes, color patterns, or both. The Spitzbergen and the Virginia Beauty refer to their place of origin; the Horse apple is so big and sour that it is considered fit only as feed for horses; the Limbertwig was named for the distinctive shape and flexible limbs of the parent tree. And who knows how the Leatherman, the Milam, the Democrat, and the Knotley Pea got their names. Many of the apple varieties I mention here are found only in a particular area, perhaps as small as a portion of the county. And some names might be a local name for a widespread variety. For example, Theron showed me what he called a "Northern Spice Apple" that looked suspiciously like a common New England breed called "Northern Spy."

One of the great proponents of preserving the many varieties of apples was L. H. Bailey whose 1922 book, *The Apple Tree*, lamented that, of the more than eight hundred varieties listed in nurserymen's catalogues in 1892, not more than a hundred were available at the time of the book's publication.

"Why do we need so many kinds of apples?" Bailey asks. "Because there are so many folks," he says. "A person has a right to gratify his legitimate tastes. If he wants thirty or forty kinds of apples for his personal use, running from Early Harvest to Roxbury Russett, he should be accorded the privilege. There is merit in variety itself. It provides more contact with life, and leads away from uniformity and monotony."

Today, according to the North Carolina Agricultural Extension Service, 90 percent of the state's commercial apple crop is made up of only three varieties: Red Delicious, Golden Delicious, and Rome Beauty.

In the North Carolina mountains, people have developed an appreciation for a variety of apples because apples were used in so many ways. In the old days, apples were not an occasional treat. They were a staple food. From the planning of the home orchard to the drying of the apple slices, every way possible was used to extend the apple season and preserve the fruit. In the absence of modern refrigeration, various kinds of apples came to be known not only for their taste but also for their rate of ripening and their capacity for preservation. Each apple had its specific season and purpose. Some apples are early apples and some are better late in the season. Some are for drying, some are best suited for sauce while others are best for can-

ning. There are juicy ones for cider and hard ones for storing, and, of course, there are plain old eating apples.

During the season, some of the best old-time eating apples are Crow's Eggs, Bellflowers, Black Hoovers, Virginia Beauties, and Spice apples. The small yellow Spice apples actually have a distinctive wintergreen-mint flavor. Some eating apples will keep for months, while others might be right for eating during only a few weeks of the season. Theron showed me a little apple called a Stripey. Early in the season the apple has a crisp, tangy, white flesh; but if it gets too ripe or you let it sit around the house too long, sometimes for even a few days, its crisp texture turns mealy. "It'll almost choke you," says Theron of its sawdustlike texture. As good as this delicious morsel is fresh from the tree, you'll never find it in the supermarket.

Sauce apples and canning apples each have different properties; they aren't just labeled as cooking apples. Good canning apples are firm-fruited and won't turn brown while a whole panful is peeled and sliced. The slices hold their shape as they are exposed to the rigors of home canning. Some good canning apples are Winter Johns, Pippins, Milams, Sweet Russets, Knotley Peas, and Spitzbergens. Although it is possible to make sauce out of almost any apple, the best have a soft texture that will break down into sauce with little cooking. Bellflowers and Stripeys are ideal for sauce making. Juicy apples like Winesaps and Sheep's Nose lend themselves well to cider making. Pippins and Crow's Eggs are favorite pie apples. The large Striped Ben Davis is a favorite baking apple.

Good canning apples are usually

good drying apples because of their firm flesh. Apple drying was an important home industry in many parts of North Carolina. Itinerant merchants traveled the back country buying or trading dried apples. Theron tells of peeling and slicing basket after basket of apples that were dried on racks over the cookstove. In some areas, the apples were cored and sliced into rings which were dried by stringing the slices on a pole. Drying is one of the simplest and, if you have a wood stove, one of the most efficient ways to preserve apples. Just slice the apples thinly and spread them on window screens (preferably nylon screens) suspended a few feet above your wood stove or other heat source. The drying usually takes three days to a week. During warm, dry weather (a rarity in the Appalachians) apples can be sundried, but they must be taken inside every night to protect them from the dew. Traditionally, people who were preparing apples for the market peeled them to make a more refined product. However, this is not necessary, especially if the apples have not been sprayed.

The art of preserving fresh eating apples nowadays has been relegated to the realm of horticultural science and refrigeration engineering. Modern storage houses are vapor-sealed and have massive refrigeration systems that maintain a constant temperature of 31 degrees Fahrenheit and a relative humidity of at least 85 percent. However, the old-time methods of storing apples are still worth knowing, not only because they may be of use to those who might like to store a few bushels of apples for home use, but also because they demonstrate a creative relationship with the environment and

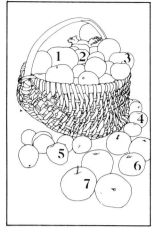

Fall's colorful crop overflows this basket handcrafted by Lula Street of Yancey County. Among the favorites are: Black Hoovers (1), Winter Johns (2), Ben Davis' (3), Stripeys (4), Crow's Eggs (5), Virginia Beauties (6), and the Golden Delicious (7). Black Hoovers, Virginia Beauties, and Crow's Eggs are especially good eating apples. The Stripey is crisp and tangy early in the season, but quickly turns mealy if it gets too ripe. No doubt that is one reason why some of the old apple varieties are not sold commercially. The Golden Delicious, along with the Red Delicious and Rome Beauty, comprise 90 percent of North Carolina's crop.

Doug Elliott

Photographs by Doug Elliott

a sensitivity to nature that is disappearing from our modern world.

For the person versed in the art of apple storing, the first thing to consider is the phase of the moon. As Theron tells it, "keeping" apples are best picked on the "down side" of the moon (when it is waning). During this phase, any bruises that occur will most likely dry up and not ruin the apple. However, if you make hard cider or home brew, you'd best make it during the "comin' up" of the moon, since things "work" or ferment better as the moon is waxing.

Next you must choose a good keeping-apple variety. Winter Johns and Hardenings are the favorites in our area. The apples are picked carefully, each apple lifted upward to snap off the stem. If it is pulled so that the stem rips out of the apple, decay can soon ruin it. In colonial days two men, a picker and a packer, harvested each tree with gloved hands. The picker handed two apples at a time down to the packer who carefully laid the apples in straw on a sled. (A sled jiggled and bumped less than a wagon or a wheelbarrow.) When loaded, the sled was skidded over hay to the packing cellar.

The apples were then stored in cellars. In Vermont and Connecticut where there was ready access to quarries, some apple cellars actually had marble shelves to keep the fruit

From blossom to fruit, spring to fall, the apple is closely associated with the Appalachians. Although apples seem distinctly American, they actually originated in Persia and were brought here from Europe. The apple gatherer (opposite page) climbs high among heavily laden boughs to gather Winter John apples from a tree found at an abandoned mountain cabin.

cold and dry. Sometimes they even had windmills that operated fans inside them to keep the air moving. Noah Webster recommended packing apples in heat-dried sand. Others used grain or dry straw. Sometimes really special apples were hung "by their tails" (stems) from the cellar's rafters. One favorite down-home Appalachian apple storehouse is a hollow chestnut stump. It is cleaned out, lined with dry leaves, filled with apples, and covered with more dry leaves and some slabs of bark to shed the rain. Theron has also piled apples on the ground and then covered them with a thick layer of "loose blade fodder"—dried corn leaves—tied in bundles. This insulates the apples from severe cold, yet allows plenty of air circulation. "They'll keep all winter," Theron says.

The apple tree, like most of us who call ourselves American, is not native to the Americas. Some crab apples are an exception, but the apple tree actually originated in Persia although it had been cultivated in Europe for at least two thousand years before it was brought to the New World. Despite its foreign origins, no tree has contributed more to America than the apple tree. Besides the vinegars and tonics, it's given us apple jack, apple brandy, apple wine, and apple cider. There's apple jelly, apple sauce, apple butter, apple cake and pie; and don't forget

apple leather (broiled and dried apples), candied apples, baked apples, scalloped apples, apple grunter, and apple crisp. There are apple toys such as apple-faced dolls and apple games such as bobbing for apples. Apple wood is prized wherever a hard, fine-grained wood is called for. In colonial days, it was used for machinery, particularly cogs, wheels, and shuttles. Even the apple tree bark can be used as a vegetable dye to give vivid golds and yellows.

Jonathan Chapman, better known as Johnny Appleseed, said, "Nothing gives more yet asks less in return than a tree, particularly the apple."

Whenever you roam the hills and the hollows of the Appalachians and come upon an apple tree, stop and look around. You will probably see others as well and perhaps some ancient rose bushes, lilacs, or other cultivated plants. Nearby, you may see the ruins of an old cabin, perhaps no more than the fallen chimney and a depression in the ground that marks the cellar where many an apple was stored. Living in the space age, it is difficult for most of us to understand the richness as well as the hardships of that kind of life. Other than reading a little history and listening to the music and the stories of the old-timers, there aren't many ways for us to get a flavor of the old times—unless it's through the flavor of old-time apples.

Cutting the Tree

Someone once told me that there are three ways you can tell when you are getting old. One, he said, is that you begin to lose your memory. He couldn't recall right offhand what the other two were.

I could probably help him out. My son recently said to me, "Dad, you're over the hill and picking up speed all the time." I accepted that with grace befitting my growing maturity, but the truth is that I have noticed a developing trait that is an even surer sign of middle age. I find myself comparing today's customs and traditions with those of a few years ago—unfavorably, I might add.

Take the business of Christmas trees. If you want a Christmas tree this year, you'll probably go to one of many lots where commercially grown trees are staked out and tagged. You'll pick one out, pay for it, cram it in the trunk or tie it on the roof, and take it home. Actually, it's a nice little family tradition, and kids of all ages enjoy looking over the various trees until they find the one they want. The lots offer a wider choice of both sizes and kinds of trees than ever, and the tree you pick is likely to be far handsomer than any you could buy or find a decade ago.

This is a fairly recent development in North Carolina. It hasn't been so many years ago that, if you wanted a tree, you had only a few choices. In the relatively small eastern North Carolina town where I grew up, you could run down to the neighborhood grocery and check out the red cedars leaning against the side of the building. A big tree might set you back $4.00, but you could get a pretty good one for $1.25. If you were interested in exotics, there might be a few scraggly blue spruce that consisted of a trunk and about four limbs, some of which still had a few needles clinging stubbornly to the tips. Spruces were usu-ally more expensive than cedars, but I never understood why.

The other alternative—one that most people chose—was to take the family on an afternoon drive in the country and find your own tree. Even if you didn't know a farmer who would let you look for a tree, there was plenty of unposted woodland around where no one cared if you cut a cedar. I don't need to tell you that's not the case anymore, and fewer families still prowl the fields and woodlands to find a wild tree.

Nostalgia may be the rust of memory, but, even if my recollections of the annual family tree-cutting trip are flawed, it was still an exciting event for a kid. I can recall running through the woods and the overgrown fields hoping to be the first of three brothers to find the perfect tree. There was more than a little competition between us, and we quickly learned that the best cedars—full-bodied and bright green—usually grew in the edges of fields, and especially along hedgerows or fences. I didn't know it then, but the seeds are eaten by birds and are "planted" with the droppings that accumulate when the birds light on the fences, power lines, or hedgerows. That's why the trees often grow in straight lines as though a farmer had planted them.

Seldom did we find a truly perfect tree. Some were too tall, others too brown, and many had only one good side. But sooner or later, a decision would be made. Dad would saw it down, and we'd help drag it back to the car while the heady scent of cedar would be fueling our already rampant Christmas spirit. (Mine was usually so rampant that by the time Christmas Eve arrived, I was running a fever, but you couldn't have gotten me to sleep with a half gallon of paregoric.)

Now, I know that Christmas is a very personal

thing, and everyone has his or her own little traditions. Furthermore, I know that a Frazer fir is probably the most classic of all trees, and we've decorated some lovely ones. And yet, for me, the only real Christmas tree is a cedar. Nothing smells better than a cedar. I don't care if you have to wear gloves to put it up. I don't care if it drops every needle two days after it's up. So what if the tip is too light to properly support a star. Cedars are Christmas trees.

And while I'm warming to the subject, I might as well admit another lapse in taste. All these little white lights look beautiful, but every house in every neighborhood looks just exactly alike. Shucks, you can ride for blocks without seeing a tree with colored lights—big, old-fashioned colored lights like a proper eastern North Carolina red cedar ought to have.

I may never cut another wild cedar, but something in my blood still stirs when I see a really good one while I'm driving down a two-lane blacktop. And my soul is at peace when I can look across a bleak December field and see a distant farmhouse with a string of colored lights draped out front on a bush, and a peaked row of blue lights in each window.

I think these are the colors of hope, but I could be wrong. And I really don't hold it against you if you've got a fir and white lights. There's no such thing as bad taste at Christmas.—*Jim Dean*

Debbie Conger

Willie and Me and the Two-Moon "Turkles"

PAUL KOEPKE

"You want to hold or chop?"

"I chop 'im."

I passed the ax to Willie and turned to the garbage can that served as a temporary holding pen for the snapper. The turtle was a big one, a twenty-five-pounder, that Willie had hooked while fishing in my pond and managed to play until I came galumphing up with the dip net and heaved· it ashore. I had hoped that he would have taken it off in the topless carton I offered but he assured me, with wide-eyed solemnity, that he was not taking *that* to his bosom. Since there was nothing else to carry it in alive, it was obvious that the beheading would have to take place on the premises and that I was to be master of ceremonies.

The turtle was on its hind legs, leaning against the side of the can and glaring at me with baleful yellow eyes. Displeased with what it saw, it opened its powerful, toothless jaws and hissed. Clearly, it had the same Sam Smallish, I-hate-you-one-and-all-damn-your-eyes disposition as the rest of its species. I eased the can over on its side, slid the tur-

tle to the ground, and grasped it firmly by the tail. As I lifted it, the head snaked out, hoping for a whack at my brisket, but as soon as the front of the plastron touched the surface of the chopping block it was quickly withdrawn and the waiting began. I maintained a firm grip on the tail, keeping the turtle's rear slightly elevated, until its head emerged again to take stock of the situation, extending further and further. Then the ax blade flashed with one clear, clean stroke from Willie and the deed was done.

Willie went on his way rejoicing with visions of sweet, tender turtle fried in egg and cornmeal dancing in his head, but I did not envy him the hot, messy afternoon that lay ahead. He will need a cauldron of scalding water, a short, sharp knife with plenty of backbone, and a lot of elbow grease before this behemoth winds up in the pan.

A brief immersion in the hot water, using the tail as a handle, will suffice to soften the skin and claws so that they may be readily removed, but then the real work begins. The turtle will be placed on its

back and steadied with blocks or wedges firmly affixed to the table surface to eliminate any rocking or sliding caused by the rounded carapace. The plastron will then be loosened by severing with the tip of the knife blade the cartilaginous material that binds the plastron to the carapace. With the plastron retained as a movable but still useful pressure point, the knife will then be inserted along the interior surface of the carapace to loosen the meat from the shell, particularly at the points where the heavy leg muscles are attached. With this accomplished, the plastron will then be removed, the viscera extracted, and the edible remainder cut into sizes suitable for frying. Also, since Willie's turtle is a big one, it will be necessary to make fillets of the neck and leg meat which will otherwise be too thick to fry properly.

Good luck to Willie and his turtle dressing. Meanwhile I have the severed head to deal with. There are many old wives' tales that have long since been discredited, but, when these worthy crones advised not to pick up a newly severed snapper head, they were not just mumbling in their gruel. The things can bite. Hard. I found a stout twig and rapped the snout. Nothing. Another rap. No response. The third rap did it. The jaws had the twig in a death grip and I tossed them both into a briar patch for the ultimate delectation of whatever was interested. I never cease to marvel and, as often as I've done it, this recurring ritual never fails to bring to mind the time in my high school biology lab when a snapping turtle's heart lay beating hour after hour in a saline solution while, in an adjacent bubbling beaker, the same turtle's flesh was being loosened from its skeleton. Such is the tenacious grip these creatures have on life.

Turtles are plentiful in and around Two-Moon Pond: mud turtles, box turtles, cooters, pond sliders, the smelly little stinkpots, and the spotted turtles that my Ocracoke friends call "highland hicketies." But by far the most prominent are those tough, formidable holdovers from the Pleistocene like the one Willie and I had just dispatched.

Chelydra serpentina is a pretty fancy name for a grim old U-boat of a beast that spends its winters in some muddy burrow and the warmer seasons lying in wait on the pond bottom or cruising below the surface seeking anything those merciless jaws can crunch. But having little Latin and less Greek, it remains unperturbed by polysyllabic niceties and continues its ceaseless predatory rounds.

This year, after a particularly severe winter, I saw a snapper's conning tower rise for the first time on a blustery first of March. It apparently liked what it saw and, with plenty of food available, it appeared more and more frequently as the

weather warmed, and it was soon joined by others.

The snapper's tastes are catholic, to say the least. Newts, fish, crayfish, snakes, muskrats, smaller members of its own species, anything, in short, that lives and moves in the pond of a size worth the trouble is considered fair game. Fishermen must look sharp to their stringers, particularly if any fish they catch are bleeding, and waterfowl are in great danger of being seized from below, never to rise again. This spring, for example, a female red-breasted merganser disappeared below the surface with flaps of protest before our eyes. When we reached the spot, a subaqueous old meat-grinder of a snapping turtle was already tearing it to shreds. But despite their fabled voracity, their depredations have had only a minor impact on our pond life. We keep no domestic waterfowl and I feel certain that they are no more of a threat to the fish population than the kingfishers, herons, and ospreys who are regular visitors. And since they are a definite asset where muskrat control is concerned, I bid them Godspeed, and, unless inadvertently hooked by Willie, allow them to cruise unvexed.

With the coming of April and the warming of the water, the snappers are moved to participate in what passes with them for the process of reproduction. The encounter usually takes place in the northeast quadrant of the pond and always on the surface. A thrashing tumult in the water is the signal that an amatory engagement is underway and year after year I play the voyeur, fascinated by what seems to be one of the most brutal copulative procedures in nature.

It is clear at the outset that neither of the pair can stand the sight

of the other. The male is the aggressor who will not be denied, while the female is equally determined that she will see him sliced to ribbons before she will submit. And so they face off like two Civil War rams, maneuvering slowly for an advantage, edging into striking position so that their sharp, hooked beaks can be brought into play. After forty-five minutes or an hour of this cut-and-slash, the raw, pink flesh of their gashed heads and necks is plainly visible and it is only then that the male finds the opportunity he seeks. A flattish plastron fits poorly on a rounded carapace, however, and soon they are plastron to plastron, locked in a love-hate embrace which sets them slowly barrel-rolling until their union is consummated. The rolling procedure is quite necessary, as it turns out, since, due to the overhang of the carapace and the leeway afforded by the plastron, only the bottom turtle, upside down, can get its head out of the water to breathe.

When at last they part, the impregnated female swims slowly off to the shallow, muddy end of the pond while the male, his stint in the lists of love complete, lies puffing and wheezing on the surface until he gets his wind back and can resume his interminable search for something else to snap at.

A Hindu mystic was once asked about his concept of the earth, and he replied that the earth was an island floating on water in a huge bowl resting on the back of an enormous elephant which was supported by a colossal turtle. When asked what held the turtle up, he indicated that it rested on yet another even greater turtle. When pressed further he finally replied, "Let's face it; there's always another turtle." And so it is at Two-Moon Pond. Catch them as we will, there is a seemingly endless supply of snappers, for there are ten ponds of an acre or more within a half mile of ours and, when the wanderlust is on them, they may well leave the old homestead and move off to more congenial waters. On a number of occasions, by day or night, I have come upon them, lumbering across the lawn like miniature Sherman tanks and headed for my pond. One moonlit night, in fact, I went to investigate a hitherto unnoticed hump in the lawn near the water's edge and found myself standing in the immediate rear of a large snapper. As I bent over for a closer look it suddenly wheeled 180 degrees with remarkable agility for a creature so cumbersome and made for the protection of the water. I was in the way, of course, but not for long. I bounded into the air like a springbok and, when I landed, the turtle had vanished into the dark

pond. From that time forth, I did my nighttime hummock checking from a respectful distance with a flashlight.

Perhaps the greatest problem in playing host to these big, surly brutes is that occasionally one will swim too close to the vertical runoff pipe during overflow and find itself firmly pasted in place by suction. The protective shield around the mouth of the pipe has long since turned to ferrous oxide, and only a stub of the cedar post which once supported it remains above water. As a result, whenever a snapper gets hung up it must be removed, either manually from a boat or by trying to snag a flange of its shell with a large Hopkins lure and a surf rod from the shore. Manual removal from a boat is not bad if the turtle is in head first and half strangled, but, if it has made contact plastron down, it is usually in a towering rage and firmly stuck. To get it free without

benefit of a stable platform and adequate leverage is dangerous and almost impossible. I therefore prefer to cast twenty feet with the treble-hooked lure until a purchase is secured and heave. The turtle usually comes loose with a mighty slurp and the overflow continues. As for the Hopkins lure, that always winds up somewhere in the big winged elm immediately behind me. I lose a lot of Hopkins lures that way.

And so the wheeling seasons come and go, and in and around our little watery world the snappers lurk in some secluded hideaways or slip effortlessly like gray-green shadows through the dark water, pausing now and then to up snorkel without a ripple and as quietly disappear. But inevitably the day will come when there will be a cry of "Big turkle!" from Willie and it's the dip net detail once again for me.

Those Incredible Hummingbirds

JANE ROHLING

If you saw a bird the size of a bug, with wings that vibrated so fast that they disappeared, feathers that flashed in the sun like polished metal, and a bill like a darning needle, would you be surprised? And, if this bird could fly backwards, forwards, upside down, and sideways—would you believe your eyes?

That's the way it is with hummingbirds: they seem to belong more to the magical realm of fairies and unicorns than to our ordinary world. That's undoubtedly why some of them have been given such names as "purple-crowned fairy" and "fork-tailed woodnymph."

These extraordinary little birds are found only in the Western Hemisphere where over 320 species have been discovered. Evidently, their ancestors found the ocean barriers too vast to cross, but in the New World they have expanded their range from Saskatchewan to Tierra del Fuego, adapting to widely varying climates. The ruby-throated hummingbird (*Archilochus colubris*) is the only species of hummingbird that calls North Carolina home—in fact, it is the only species normally found east of the Mississippi River and one of only four species found as far north as Canada.

Hummingbirds have practically redefined the meaning of the word "flight" with their abilities in the air. Scientists have long been impressed with their aerial feats and have recently used high-speed photography and stroboscopic lighting to unravel many of the mysteries behind hummingbirds' flight. Stroboscopic lighting uses a tube capable of firing many bright flashes in an incredibly short amount of time. It is extremely useful in examining movement, because it stops action many times each second and allows the viewer to see each step.

At his house in Chapel Hill, Carl Buchheister, president emeritus of the National Audubon Society, told me about some of these experiments. He has been a hummingbird watcher for many years.

"Flight speeds of hummingbirds are very interesting," Buchheister said. "Their wingbeat has been calculated using stroboscopic photography. When they're hovering getting food from a plant their wings beat fifty-five times per second. Can you imagine that speed? It only takes one second to say 'Lucky Strike.' And that's fifty-five complete beats up and down. . . . And when they're backing away from a plant it's about sixty-one beats per second, and when they're on their way, just starting out they're at about seventy-five beats per second." In quick maneuvers like courtship flights, their wings move up to two hundred times per second.

Another scientist, Crawford Greenewalt, experimented with hummingbirds in a wind tunnel to measure the speed of the hummingbird's flight, and found that a female rubythroat could achieve a speed of 29 miles per hour while struggling against the adjustable air stream. In plunging flight they have been clocked at over 60 miles per hour!

These feats are possible only because hummingbirds have a different structure from other birds. Whereas all other birds except the swifts articulate their wings freely at the shoulder, elbow, and wrist, the hummingbird's wing rotates mainly at the shoulder. The long paddlelike

wing is virtually all-hand. Actually, the hummingbird model is a unique design somewhere between the insects and the birds. But if the hummingbird model were extended to the size and weight of a swan, its wings would have to be 32 feet long.

It takes some pretty strong wing muscles to power any type of flight and in most strong flying birds the pectoral muscles account for 15 to 25 percent of the body weight. The hummingbird's flight muscles comprise 25 to 30 percent of its weight.

There are other advanced aeronautical features in this tiny muscular package. Most birds get power only on the downstroke, but not the hummingbird. With each lift of its wings, the hummingbird tips the front edges backwards so that power is maintained on the upstroke and the downstroke even when the bird is upside down. The result of this double action is an explosive acceleration and a speed that is astonishing for so small a bird.

Greenewalt compares a hummingbird to a helicopter: "If a helicopter hovers, the rotor is in a plane parallel to the earth's surface—so are the wings of a hummingbird. As the helicopter moves forward or backward, the rotor tilts in the appropriate direction—so do the wings of a hummingbird. The helicopter can rise directly from a given spot without a runway—so can a hummingbird."

There are a few other birds that can fly backwards or hover, but none can do so with the ease of a hummingbird. And no other birds, not even "whirly birds," can fly sideways. How the hummingbirds do that remains a mystery.

Hummingbirds must expend an enormous amount of energy to power their muscular body. Indeed,

Jane Rohling

A three-inch blur, the ruby-throat at the trumpet vine (left) *is North Carolina's only hummingbird species. Flame azalea* (above) *is another hummingbird favorite.*

they have the highest energy output per unit of body weight of any warm-blooded animal, and they burn up fuel at a fantastic rate. While hovering, a hummingbird expends ten times more energy than a man running about nine miles an hour.

Even at rest, the metabolic rate of a hummingbird is more than 50 times as fast as a human's. Its heart is the largest of all warm-blooded animals (relative to its size), and it beats 500 to 1,200 times per minute, depending on the bird's activity.

A small bird with such a high metabolism faces some significant problems. For one thing, it has to obtain enough food to fuel its energy output. While humans can get along on a charge of fuel three times a day, hummingbirds have to refuel almost continuously. Like athletes, they have chosen sugar as their high-energy fuel source because it enters the blood speedily and delivers fresh fuel to the muscles in the shortest possible time. Every day a hummingbird visits from 1,000 to 2,000 flowers, taking in more than half its weight in nectar. A man's daily output of energy is about

3,500 calories. The daily output of a hummingbird, if calculated for a 170-pound man, is equivalent to about 155,000 calories. A man would have to consume 285 pounds of hamburger, 380 pounds of boiled potatoes, or 140 pounds of bread a day to meet these demands!

Another problem faced by the hummingbird because of its high metabolism and frantic activity is conserving its fuel supply and maintaining its body heat. The hummingbird's body temperature is normally a little higher than ours, about 104 degrees Fahrenheit, and its small body loses heat very rapidly. Very small warm-blooded animals in a cold climate have to eat a great deal at short intervals to provide the fuel that maintains their body heat, or come up with another solution to the problem.

One solution hummingbirds have found to the problem is to go into an unconscious, comalike state called torpor. In torpor the bird's body temperature drops, its breathing and heartbeat are reduced, and the bird is incapable of movement. Its body uses about one-twentieth the amount of energy it would during normal sleep in this condition. When the temperature rises, the bird slowly wakes up.

"A friend of mine actually went out in the garden one day and found flat out on top of a flower a hummingbird that looked as if it were dead," recalled Buchheister. "She picked it up and took it into the warmth of her house. In a few minutes it awakened from its condition of torpor and began to fly around the room."

If food has been scarce and a hummingbird is forced to go to sleep without sufficient nourishment, it will go into torpor to

Hummingbird nestlings are tended only by the mother, who plunges her bill deep into their throats to regurgitate nectar and insects. Two nestlings are the average brood, and they stay in the nest anywhere from 10 to 30 days depending on the food supply.

stretch its energy reserves—even if it's not cold outside!

The hummingbird's second solution to maintaining its warmth is more conventional—it simply heads south for the winter. The rubythroat migrates 2,000 miles from its breeding range in the eastern United States and Canada to spend its winter vacation on the Yucatan Peninsula. It usually heads south with the first frosts of fall—early October in North Carolina—and returns around mid-April. During the week before departing on this incredible journey, the rubythroat adds 50 percent to its normal body weight, all of it fat. This reserve fuel supply is crucial to the bird's survival, for it must cross the Gulf of Mexico on a 500-mile nonstop flight.

The rubythroat's northern migration is timed to keep pace with the opening of its favorite flowers. This is risky business, since even in the southern states it faces the danger of late-killing frosts. The birds show an astonishing toughness in weathering storms, cold, and rain, but the death of the flowers they need for food is sometimes more than they can stand.

Soon after they get settled into their summer homes, it's time for the courtship rituals to begin. The courtship flight of a male ruby-throated hummingbird is an impressive sight to behold—even for the female hummingbird, who certainly knows something about flight. The male rises high in the air, then swoops past the female within inches, rising again on the other side. He is careful to orient himself so the sun best shows off his flashy colors as he swings back and forth like a tiny iridescent pendulum, until the female is finally overcome by his charms.

Jane Rohling

Kay Frazier

Immediately after mating, the male flies off into the sunset, leaving the female to build the nest on her own. The rubythroat's nest is about the size of a walnut—so tiny that a soft-drink bottle cap will cover it. The female chooses her materials with the greatest of care, using fine down from plants like the milkweeds or dandelions or the wooly scales from fern stems to line the inner cup. Coarser materials—bud scales, moss, bits of stems, leaves, and bark—are used for the bulk of the nest. The exterior is decorated with small pieces of lichen that camouflage and beautify the finished product. All of this is woven together with spiders' webs, which are also used to tie the nest securely to its twig support.

Hummingbird nests are very hard to find because they look so much like a knot on a limb that you don't even notice them. They are often located on fairly low, downward-sloping branches, often near or over water. Occasionally the location of a nest pleases the owner so much that she is reluctant to abandon the site and will build a new nest on top of the old one.

In North Carolina, the ruby-throated hummingbirds lay their first clutches of one-half-inch eggs in May or June. Carl Buchheister says, "The eggs are always two in number and pure white, and the birds usually raise two broods a year. That's a pretty good rate of increase. If all of them lived, we'd be knee-deep in hummingbirds." But all of them don't live. Only one-sixth to one-third of them are reared successfully, yet large numbers of these attractive creatures survive.

After an incubation period of about two weeks, the young hummingbirds peck their way into the world—black, blind, and no bigger than bumblebees. The length of time they will stay in the nest varies from as little as ten to as many as thirty days, apparently depending on how frequently they are fed. And the feeding of baby hummingbirds is a fearsome spectacle to behold. The mother feeds them almost entirely on insects that have been partially digested in her crop. In what resembles a sword-swallowing act, she inserts her bill so deeply into the young birds that you'd expect it to come through the other side. She

Hummingbirds, like bees, pollinate many flowers and are attracted to flower shapes and certain colors, especially red. Columbine (above, left) is a favorite, as is the Atamasco lily (above, right). The hummingbird's metabolic rate is incredibly high: if it weighed as much as a 170-pound human, it would burn about 155,000 calories a day. The average adult male human burns only about 3,500 calories a day.

then pumps nourishment into them by regurgitating the food she has brought.

Although the young are fed mainly insects, the adults feed primarily on flower nectar, and like bees and other nectar-eating insects the hummingbirds provide a pollination service to flowers. Many of the flowers they frequent have evolved pollination mechanisms, such as special flower shapes or colors, specifically to attract hummingbirds. Extremely long floral tubes with nectaries at the end cannot be reached by most insects, limiting access to hummingbirds' long bills and tongues.

Studies show that a common flower color such as red is advantageous to both hummingbirds and flowers. It is an advertisement that attracts hummingbirds to sources of food as soon as they arrive in a new area. The result: the flowers get pollinated and the birds get fed.

Birds that have learned to associate red with food often investigate any red object they see. Buchheister related an incident at an Audubon summer camp in Maine: "We were on a field trip one day and we came across a shallow stream bordered by a very large area of cardinal flowers. There were at least forty hummingbirds going in and out, hovering at plants. It was an unbelievable sight. One of our staff members went in among the flowers wearing red shorts and soon had hummingbirds swarming all around her."

In spite of their love of sweets, hummingbirds cannot live on nectar alone. They have to supplement this

Jane Rohling

Nectar from such flowers as Jewelweed is a favorite food; however, hummingbirds must supplement this carbohydrate diet with proteins, fats, and vitamins obtained by eating tiny insects.

carbohydrate diet with proteins, fats, and vitamins, which they get from the minute insects and spiders they eat. In fact, some ornithologists believe that hummingbirds first visited flowers for their insects inside them, and developed their sweet tooth later on. Flies, gnats, aphids, tiny beetles, and spiders are all fair game for hummingbirds.

One might assume that tiny creatures that are adorned like jewels and frequent flower gardens would be peaceable by nature, but there is nothing peaceable about hummingbirds. The rubythroat is a nervous, irritable little bird which resents any intruders into its territory. From the time the young leave the nest, they are about as likely to do battle with their mothers as with young from a neighboring nest. At feeders they are so determined to keep others away that it seems they'd rather fight than eat. And they'll attack anything—from bumblebees to hawks—regardless of size.

As with many wild animals, man

has posed the biggest threat to the survival of hummingbirds. In the nineteenth century hundreds of thousands of them were killed and shipped to Europe for use in ladies' accessories. In one week during 1888, over 400,000 hummingbirds' skins were sold at a London auction. Many species of hummingbirds were originally recorded by naturalists not in the tropical forests of South America, but in the shops of taxidermists and milliners, and some species probably became extinct before they were even identified.

Fortunately the fashions have changed, and this country and many others prohibit the capture and export of hummingbirds. Now the greatest threat to hummingbirds is loss of habitat. Tropical forests, where many hummingbirds spend all or part of the year, are being destroyed everywhere they exist. Yet, even in the face of this threat, hummingbirds have a better prospect for survival than many birds because of their supreme adaptability. Some species have benefited from the spread of agriculture and the multiplication of human homes surrounded by flower gardens.

These pint-sized birds that Audubon called "glittering fragments of the rainbow" are certainly as fascinating to study as they are beautiful to watch. So plant a few flowers, hang out a feeder, and invite hummingbirds to lunch. In return they'll entertain you with their antics and add a little color to your life. I'd say that's a pretty good return for a small investment.

Magnificent Monarchs

HARRY ELLIS

Since ancient times, man has observed with awe and fascination the seasonal movements of the big orange and black monarch butterflies, the only ones that annually migrate both north and south like birds. He has watched the flocks move southward in autumn, wondering how such delicate, wind-tossed creatures were able to find their way over long distances and, after the howling gales of winter had passed, return again northward to the flower-filled fields of spring.

The monarch (*Danaus plexippus*) is known and recognized by more people than any other American butterfly. Hundreds of bright-eyed school children know it by sight and are able to call it by name. It flits in summer over fields, gardens, and meadows throughout the United States—with the exception of the Rocky Mountains and the far western deserts—and well into Canada.

The most widespread of all our butterflies, it is also one of the most numerous. At a time when some thirty species of our American butterflies have rapidly declined during the past decade, and some of them may soon be listed as endangered species, it is heartening to know that the monarch is as abundant as ever.

With the passing of winter, the monarch follows the spring northward. Descending to young, tender milkweed plants, the female lays her eggs singly, here and there, until she has laid a total of four hundred or more. Each pale-green, bullet-shaped egg, intricately ribbed and so small that the naked eye can hardly see it, is glued to the underside of a milkweed leaf. Not many days afterward, both male and female monarchs, exhausted from their efforts, fall to the ground and fly no more. But the northward migration has not ended. There is only a pause, as a new generation matures and prepares to resume the journey.

In a week or ten days, a tiny, black-headed greenish caterpillar hatches from the egg, with an intensive craving for milkweed leaves—its only aim in life to eat and grow. Shedding its skin from time to time, its size increases with each successive moult, until in two weeks' time it is a large, boldly marked caterpillar with stripes of yellow, green, and black, nothing about it remotely resembling a butterfly. Now a full-grown caterpillar, it soon stops eating, grows restless, and leaves the milkweed plant searching for a proper place to enter the pupal or chrysalis stage of its life. Finding a suitable twig, it attaches itself, hanging head downward. Within hours, a kind of convulsion seizes it and the body begins to contract and expand, causing the skin to split between the eyes. The split progresses upward along the median line of the back, and finally the green chrysalis bulges forth.

Where a moment ago there was only a caterpillar, we now see a brilliant, jade-green cask, bejeweled with a row of shining gold dots half encircling the chrysalis, and hanging by a thin black stem. One of the most beautiful objects in nature, it has been called "the green house with the golden nails." But in ten days or so, the green and gold vanishes and the walls become transparent, revealing the developing orange

Harry Ellis

The incredible journey of the adult monarch butterfly from Canada to Mexico is interrupted as the colorful insect sips nectar from a goldenrod plant in the Blue Ridge Mountains.

and black wings of the monarch butterfly. The miracle of transformation to a winged beauty is now near at hand.

Suddenly, without warning, the chrysalis is rent at the bottom and the butterfly bursts out and hangs to its fractured walls. The flame-colored wings, crumpled at first, gradually expand and become straight, and the swollen abdomen becomes more slender. Then, unexpectedly, with a contraction of the body like the first breath of an infant, the monarchs sail away—into blue skies and green fields.

Such a radical change from a crawling caterpillar to a brilliant butterfly recalls to mind the old fairy tales where an enchanter waves a wand and a man becomes a beast or a beast becomes a man. In the case of monarch metamorphosis, however, nothing could be further from the truth, for we know that such change comes only through a series of unerring steps, following the specifications of "nature's blueprint."

The spring migration is now resumed, the new generation driven northward by an inborn instinct. They, too, after traveling hundreds of miles, mate, lay eggs, and, with tattered wings beating feebly, also soon die. The eggs hatch and the larvae mature into adult butterflies that continue the journey, each successive brood penetrating farther north until they cross the border into Canada, reaching as far as Hudson Bay before the summer ends. These monarchs also mate and produce the year's final generation of monarch butterflies.

But now in this northern latitude summer is coming to an end. There is a biting chill in the air at night as the year's energies begin to wane. Nectar-producing flowers are becoming less numerous. In these late-maturing butterflies, there is a reversal of the migratory urge. It is no longer northward, but southward. The monarch hordes are now gathering for one of the most astounding migrations in the animal kingdom. They will be traveling to a land that they have never seen, guided by an unfathomable instinct.

Much information about the monarch's comings and goings has been acquired by Canadian zoologist Dr. Fred A. Urquhart and others under his supervision, through tagging many thousands of their wings with thin, paper adhesive labels bearing a number and an address. One monarch, tagged and released north of Lake Ontario on September 18, was recaptured in Mexico on January 25, some 1,870 miles away. Another, after being tagged, flew 80 miles in one day.

Soon the southbound migrants can be seen flying against a vast expanse of blue sky, some in large flocks resembling sunset-colored clouds, others not traveling in flocks at all, but journeying singly as lone individual voyagers. They wing their way over forests and mountains, lakes and rivers, cities and deserts, others of their kind joining them along the way.

Down across the Appalachians they come, pouring through North Carolina's Blue Ridge Mountain gaps like chips passing on a swift stream. Traveling the same migration routes that their forebears have used for centuries, it is as if, in some mysterious way, each monarch, though it has never made the flight before, somehow "remembers" that its ancestors went down a certain Blue Ridge valley or flew over a particular chain of mountains on the way south.

Always migrating during the daytime hours, they rest at night in trees, chilled and sluggish, but when the morning sun has warmed them they are off again. Occasionally they pause briefly in meadows along their flyways to sip nectar from goldenrods, asters, and other late-blooming wildflowers.

Violent windstorms and heavy rains take a toll of migrating monarchs. Otherwise they have few enemies. Both the caterpillars and adult butterflies are distasteful, and probably poisonous to birds and most animals. As a result, they are rarely attacked by predators, which recognize them by their "warning coloration." Birds have learned so well to shun them that another butterfly, the viceroy (*Limentitis archippus*), with wings that mimic the color and pattern of the monarch, but lacking the bad taste and toxic characteristics, flies through the air safe from attack.

As the autumn chill advances and a whisper of approaching winter is in the air, the flights become more hurried. Their flight path is from northeast to southwest across the United States, most of the flocks passing through Texas and on across the Mexican border.

There are two distinct monarch populations in the United States— one in the eastern and midwestern states and the other in the western states. The western monarchs winter along the central and southern coast of California in groups of cypress, pine, and eucalyptus trees in congregations numbering many millions of butterflies.

After crossing Texas and the

The life of a monarch begins with a pearllike egg (above), which is laid on the underside of a milkweed leaf in spring. When the egg hatches, a tiny, greenish caterpillar with a shiny black head crawls out (near right). After two weeks of molting, it is a boldly striped caterpillar about to change once again (far right).

After attaching itself to a twig, the caterpillar splits its skin between the eyes and the green chrysalis bulges forth (above, left). When the old caterpillar skin drops off, the new chrysalis changes into a jade-green case half-encircled with golden dots (above, middle). In ten days, a developing butterfly is visible within the thin walls of the chrysalis (above, right).

Photographs by Harry Ellis

most marvelous compass of all, they have reached their winter home at last. At this high elevation, the winter temperature stays around freezing, keeping them in a semitorpid state in which they use up little of the reserve energy and body fat that will be needed for the return migration.

As the months pass, eventually winter begins to loosen its grip and the daylight hours grow longer. One by one, the hills and meadows to the north are touched by the green fingers of spring.

Here, high in the Sierra Madre, the monarchs stir a little, flash their wings, and engage in short flights away from their wintering trees and then back again. But soon, in the increasing warmth of a certain spring day, hundreds of them are off, winging northward, with the rest of their tribe soon to follow. On the spring flight, they travel as individuals, with no inclination to gather in flocks. Over forests, farmlands, and meadows they fly, until in the fields below are clusters of fresh, green milkweed plants. Here eggs will be placed and another generation will begin anew.

The life cycle of the monarch butterfly has come full circle.

Mexican border, the eastern monarchs, which we have been following, wing their way deeper into Mexico. Here, at an elevation of 9,000 feet, they descend like swirling autumn leaves and blanket the fir trees on a 20-acre area in masses so dense that twigs and branches

bow and sometimes break under their weight, though each butterfly weighs but a hundredth of an ounce.

On fragile wings they have come, from half a continent away, to this distant pinpoint on the map of Mexico. Guided by instinct, that

When the transparent case bursts, a fully developed butterfly emerges, hanging from its old case for a while before flying off to continue its migration northward.

Everything but the Squeal

Anybody old enough to remember life before television, and fortunate enough to have spent that part of it in rural North Carolina, will undoubtedly associate late November with three happenings. Traditionally, that's the time when the major hunting seasons open and harvest is celebrated by Thanksgiving. It is also time to begin to look for hog-killing weather.

One hopes—but with shaky conviction—that it is not necessary to explain that this does not mean a spell of weather cold enough to freeze hogs. Instead, it means the arrival of weather that is cold enough to keep the meat from spoiling during the slaughtering and butchering process. That may not sound like a gala event to you, but on countless small farms across North Carolina, hog killing has always been a bit special. The work is too hard to call it a holiday, but the gregarious pleasures are too pervasive to call it drudgery.

Not many farm families kill hogs anymore. Regulations now control the sale of homemade pork products, and farmers no longer smoke hams to sell for extra cash. Some families still kill a few hogs for their own use, but even this practice is dwindling. Also, there aren't as many small family farms, and farmers on those that remain often find it simpler to buy pork products at the grocery.

There are two—perhaps three—good reasons to lament this decline. First, there's the loss of a colorful tradition. Those who, as children, romped along the fringes of a hog killing have treasured memories. Thick clouds of steam rose from the huge cauldrons as the carcasses were scalded to remove the hair, then hoisted on poles and gutted. Every member of the family had some task in the butchering process. Hams were trimmed, bacon was cut, sausage was ground and seasoned, intestines were cleaned, and tenderloins were carefully wrapped. Virtually every part of the pig was used, and it usually took two days from dawn to dark to finish. There was always much laughter from the men working or standing around the fire, and from the long butchering tables spread with paper where the women cut, chopped, ground, and packaged everything but the recently departed spirits of the hogs.

Then, there was the seemingly inexhaustible array of homemade goodies—many of which have never been tasted by today's generations. Fried pork fat was crumbled to make cracklings which were added to biscuits or cornbread, and, if anything tastes better than a clabber (sour milk) crackling biscuit, I've never had it. There were also scrapple, liver pudding or mush, souse meat, spicy sausage, chitterlings, and many other concoctions. Fresh ham was a special treat, and, though it was once as common in the fall as smoked ham, it is rarely seen today. The odor of hams slowly curing in the smokehouse permeated the neighborhood, and the only aroma that smells any better than that is the inside of a tobacco barn.

The demise of hog killing has changed the eating habits of many farm families (arguably for the better if you consider the reduction in cholesterol). Still, there is something mighty appealing about a breakfast of fried scrapple, crackling bread, homemade sausage or barbecue, navy beans, fried eggs, molasses, and black coffee, and such a combination was not unlikely.

The loss of tradition and the dwindling of many homemade pork products are two evident changes, but something else seems to have passed into history, something more subtle. The purchase of a wrapped package of pork chops in a huge supermarket is an impersonal act, far removed from the gore and reality of a hog killing. Indeed, many people today might never eat another slice of bacon if they had to attend a hog killing and see the hog dispatched with a .22, scalded, gutted, and butchered. By and large, those are likely to be the same people who cannot abide anyone who would shoot a deer and eat the venison.

That unrealistic view is part of the price we've paid in the transition from frontier to farm, and from farm to metropolis. I suspect that we could use a little more of the kind of gore associated with hog killing, and a little less of the impersonal kind we see today on television. For certain, few farm-grown kids ever doubted the source of a ham biscuit or a mess of fried squirrels. An image of my Northampton County grandmother comes to mind, her arms elbow deep in a huge tub of sausage. The last thing on her mind was, "Poor pig."—*Jim Dean*

North Carolina Division of Archives and History

Our Wild Orchids

DOUG ELLIOTT

We think of them as rare and exotic blossoms embellishing the limbs of lush jungle trees, hanging in horticulturists' hothouses, or brightening the bosoms of society. However, these are not the only places orchids are found. We can see countless native species not a stone's throw from many of our homes.

The orchid family is one of the largest and most widespread plant families. There are about 170 species in North America and one-fourth of these can be found within North Carolina's borders. In fact, orchidologist Donovan Correll writes of having observed 14 species growing in and around less than an acre of sphagnum bog in Henderson County.

Though they aren't as large and showy as some hothouse hybrids, wild orchids are every bit as beautiful and many have unusual life cycles, uses, and associated lore that make them even more interesting.

A few of our native orchids are valued for more than the beauty of their flowers. The roots of several have been used as remedies. Both the pink and the yellow lady's slip-per roots have found their way into the crude drug trade under the name "nerve root." For many years, nerve root was listed as an official drug and used as a sedative and a nerve tonic. It is still sold in some herb shops and health food stores.

The tiny coral root orchid has a peculiar jointed, coral-shaped rhizome—or underground stem—and tiny nondescript flowers. One of its common names is "fever root" and, traditionally, it has been used as a medicine to reduce fevers by promoting perspiration.

Adam and Eve root is another orchid whose paired corms (tuberlike rootstocks) are more distinctive than its flowers. The plant was so named because the two corms are quite nearly linked together. Even today, these roots can be bought in shops specializing in magic and the occult. In occult lore, Adam and Eve root has the reputation for helping maintain the bond between lovers—in a solemn ceremony, the two lovers each receive one of the roots. The woman takes the "male" or "Adam" root and the man takes the "female" or "Eve" root. The "sex" of the roots is determined by placing them in water. Adam will float and, alas, poor Eve (according to this disgracefully chauvinistic legend) will sink. This part of the legend really works! Tradition also says that, as long as the pair retains possession of their respective roots, their bond will remain strong and true. There are no guarantees on this, of course. Still, in these times of tumultuous interpersonal relationships, can we afford to snicker at a potential herbal remedy?

The ancient Greek botanist, Theophrastus, was probably the first to take botanical notice of orchids. When he unearthed a terrestrial European orchid similar to our Adam and Eve root, he noticed the characteristic pair of rounded corms. He didn't associate them with Adam and Eve, but rather went behind the fig leaf and named the plant "orchis" from the paired tubers' resemblance to a portion of the male anatomy.

Orchids are among the most highly evolved and highly specialized of plants. It is said that their ancestry is in the lily family. Lilies are characterized by the fact that they have three petals and three sepals. (Usually lilies look as though they have six petals because their petals and sepals are almost identical.) As with lilies, nearly all orchids have six petallike parts, but the lower petal is usually enlarged and is called the lip. (Sometimes, as in the snowy orchid and the grass pink, the lip is the uppermost petal; more on that later.)

The reproductive parts of the orchid—that is, the male stamens and anthers and the female pistil and stigma—are united into a single organ called a column. Nearly all orchids are pollinated by insects and some have evolved to such a degree that they can be pollinated only by a single species of insect.

The stratagems that these orchids use for getting insects to cross-pollinate them are so sophisticated that they almost seem devious. The most extreme example of this is provided by the Mediterranean ophrys orchid which not only looks like, but even smells like a certain species of female wasp. It is pollinated when the male wasp mounts and tries to mate with it. As he fumbles about, he picks up the pollen which eventually rubs off when his misdirected lust carries him on to the next fraudulent flower. Mimicry, compelling fragrances, and sweet nectars are their lures. One-way funnels, hair triggers, spring traps, adhesive plasters, and collapsible flaps are their means. Pollination is their end.

The pink lady's slipper or moccasin flower is pollinated by a small bee which, in search of nectar, pushes its way through the elastic folds of the cleft in front of the inflated lip. There in the lush banquet chamber it feasts on the nectar secreted on hairs. When ready to depart, however, the inviting inward-funneling entrance will not serve as

Doug Elliott

The shoelike shape of the lip gives the yellow lady's slipper its name. This handsome flower is one of more than three dozen wild orchids that grow in North Carolina.

an exit. And the frantic buzzing testifies to this until finally two little gleams of light guide the bee up the narrow neck. As the well-fed captive pushes its way up and out into freedom, the column is placed so that it must first strike the stigma and deposit any pollen that it may be carrying at the time. Then upon leaving, the beleaguered little beast is dispatched with a new load of pollen from one of the two anthers to be delivered to the next flower on its itinerary.

The Habenarias are our largest orchid genus. There are about fifteen species in North Carolina. They are often called the "rein orchids" in reference to the long straplike spur the flowers have. The name "Habenaria" is Latin and means "strap" or "rein." This long spur serves as a nectary and contains the sweet syrup that attracts insect pollinators. Because the spur is so long and narrow, the only insects that pollinate it are those with long-sipping mouthparts, such as butterflies and moths. When the insect inserts its hairlike "tongue" into the nectary, the pollen clings to the mouthparts in such a way as to contact the stigma of the next blossom visited.

The showy orchid and the kidney-leaf twayblade use a sticky, fast-setting cement to attach the pollen to insects. When the bumblebee (or smaller insect in the case of the twayblade) alights and pushes its head into the opening of the flower, it ruptures a little membrane which exposes the cement. Attached to it are the pollen masses that adhere to the bee's head, looking like an extra pair of antennae. These are then carried in the proper position to be delivered to the next flower.

The calapogon or grass pink produces no nectar and little or no fragrance. To one used to looking at orchids, it appears to have its flower on upside down, because its lip is the uppermost part of the blossom. One wonders how this topsy-turvy little posy with apparently so little to offer would ever manage to get itself pollinated. Let me assure you, this designing little nosegay has it all

Lefty Kreh

Curtis Wooten

Doug Elliott

Curtis Wooten

The purple fringed orchid (top, left) and the showy orchid (top, right) are two of the most handsome wild orchids found in the state, and are far more common than the rare whorled pogonia (bottom, right). The yellow fringed orchid (bottom, left) blooms *in late summer in bogs, meadows, and grassy hillsides in the Coastal Plain and mountains. Wild orchids are found in every county in the state in a wide variety of habitats.*

Doug Elliott

Doug Elliott

Grass pinks (top, left) seem to wear their beard and lip upside down. They are found in wet pinelands and seepage slopes primarily in the Coastal Plain, but also in uplands. The pink lady's slipper (near left) is far more common than the yellow lady's slipper, and sometimes grows in large groups along mountain streams.

Curtis Wooten

Doug Elliott

The round-leaved orchid (bottom, left) is a delicate denizen of our woodlands, while the rare snowy orchid (bottom, right) decorates bogs and wet meadows in the Coastal Plain and mountains.

Split-second pollination occurs when the nectarless and odorless grass pink attracts a bee with its gaily colored fringe (1). The fragile lip gives way beneath the bee (2), causing pollen carried by the bee to be deposited on the orchid's stigma. Simultaneously, the bee picks up new pollen from the orchid's column.

worked out! The brightly colored lip, swaying in a spring zephyr, hails a passing bee, its multicolored fringes promising a solid foothold and the hope of luscious nectars within. However, when the bee lands, the lip collapses with startling suddenness. The bee strikes the column with his back when he falls. Cradled by the two upturned petals on either side, he is prevented from sliding off. While in this position, any pollen the bee may be carrying is deposited on the stigma. Simultaneously, new pollen is attached to the insect to be carried to the next flower. This whole process takes hardly more than a second.

Orchid fruits are most frequently dry, rounded capsules. The most notable exception to this is the elongated beanlike fruit of the vanilla orchid, which gives us vanilla flavoring. Many of our native orchids produce capsules containing thousands of seeds, and other species are even more prolific. There are well over three million seeds in a capsule of a large tropical cynoches orchid.

"If orchids produce so dern many seeds," one is tempted to ask, "why aren't they more common?" Nobody seems to know the whole answer to this. It may be that, in spite of all the fancy gimmicks these highly evolved creations have developed to encourage insect pollination, they don't always work. Out of even a large population of orchids, relatively few produce seed pods. Also, during the relatively long time between pollination and the ripening of the seed capsule—sometimes several weeks—the orchid may lose its flower through injury or by the hand of an indiscriminate wildflower picker.

Even when the seeds do manage to ripen and disperse, their problems are far from over. The seeds are so small that they contain no stored food (endosperm) to sustain them while they germinate and become established. They are completely dependent on a fungus. This fungus actually infects the seed and aids the transfer of nutrients from the soil to the embryo and eventually to the roots of the young plant. This is called a "mycorrhizal association." ("Mycorrhiza" means "fungus-root.") Some of the larger orchids with green chlorophyll-containing leaves and well-developed roots may not maintain this relationship with the fungus. However, other orchids like the coral root, which has almost no chlorophyll to manufacture its own food, must maintain mycorrhizal associations all their lives. With all these obstacles in the way, it is fortunate that the few fruits that do mature contain the huge number of seeds that they do.

Orchids are found in every county in the state and they can be seen in practically every habitat, from the edges of salt marshes on the coast to the slopes of the highest mountains. North Carolina even has an orchid that lives in trees. This is not un-

Seed capsules of crane fly orchid (below) contain thousands of microscopic seeds. In winter (right), the stalk of this orchid stands erect with seed capsules attached.

Photographs by Doug Elliott

seed
capsules

previous
summer's
flower
stalk

withered corm
from previous
season

winter leaf
forming new
corm which will
produce flowers
next spring

In winter, Adam and Eve orchid's corm and stalk wither with seed capsules attached, while its winter leaf forms a new corm from which next spring's flower will burst.

usual for tropical orchids, but in temperate climates this is highly exceptional. Though it is fairly common in Georgia and Florida, the green fly orchid reaches the northern edge of its range on the coastal plain of North Carolina. In fact, the area around Lake Waccamaw is considered to be the northernmost location of an epiphytic (tree-living) orchid in the entire Western Hemisphere. The green fly orchid grows in clusters on the limbs of trees near water. Epiphytic orchids are not parasites. They take no nutrients from the trees they grow on. Their roots do anchor the plant but they actually function more like leaves.

Orchids can be seen in every season of the year. In fact, we have two that are most conspicuous in winter when they are not blooming. These are the crane fly orchid and the Adam and Eve root. These orchids grow in rich woods and closely resemble each other in their appearance and style of growth. Late in the fall, after the trees have lost their leaves, these orchids' seed capsules ripen and begin shedding their seeds.

Meanwhile, up from the ground an inch or so from the seed stalk emerges an oval-pointed leaf that is green on top and purple on the underside. The leaf remains there all winter collecting the sun's energy and storing it in the growing corm at its base. In late spring, the leaf dies as the new flower stalk arises from the same corm.

These low-key plants never manage to have a leaf and a flower at the same time. As the summer flower passes, the fall leaf emerges. At the base of each new leaf, a new corm is forming and the corm from two seasons ago withers away, so there is usually just a neatly linked pair. Because a new one is produced each growing season, the plant actually moves a few inches from year to year.

If you wanted to go on an orchid-watching excursion and see as many different kinds as possible, you might do best to head for the mountains in late May or the Coastal Plain in early September. These are often considered peak times and places. In the mountains, there is a great deal of seasonal variability because of the varying altitudes. On the same day with a little travel, you can see early spring flowers on the mountain tops and early summer flowers at the lower elevations. Be sure to look in as many different habitats as possible: rich coves, dry woods, and acid bogs. On the Coastal Plain, look in soggy pinelands, hardwood forests, and open savannahs. Above all, don't overlook those ditches along the roads. Sometimes they contain the richest flora.

Habitat destruction, such as the draining of marshes and bogs, the indiscriminate clearing of land, and the general spreading of pavement over the landscape, is the worst threat to our orchid flora. Picking or attempting to transplant wild orchids is also strongly discouraged and in many instances it is illegal. Most orchids have such specific requirements (sunlight, soil moisture, temperature, and pH) that they do poorly or will not survive at all when transplanted to gardens.

Many people equate orchids with diamonds. As the diamond is considered king of the gem world, orchids reign supreme over the world of flowers. One never finds a perfect diamond in nature; they are always in the rough. However, perfect orchids are common. Each facet, cut, angle, and curve, every glint of light, and every sparkle of color seems the work of a master.

Discovering the World of Spiders

HARRY ELLIS

Not many steps from my back door in the Blue Ridge Mountains of North Carolina is a vacant lot, overgrown with a dense tangle of grasses, weeds, and low-growing vegetation. Soon after I acquired it some years ago, I noticed that this little tract was the habitat of a great variety of spiders in many forms, colors, and sizes. Here on an area only a few hundred feet in extent was an amazing diversity of spider life.

For years I had been fascinated by these eight-legged creatures—that immense zoological order, the Araneida, with 35,000 known species worldwide. There are over 2,000 species in the United States, with approximately half of this number represented in the state of North Carolina.

A few years ago, I set out to make an investigation of the spiders within the confines of this small fraction of an acre, and through several seasons was deeply engrossed in a project of observing and photographing them. As time passed, my growing interest in spiders led me farther and farther afield. Loaded down with photographic equipment, I have climbed our highest mountains and tramped through miles of lowlands and swamps, amid swarms of pesky mosquitoes, in search of rare spiders.

Spiders differ from insects by having eight legs instead of six, only two body sections—the cephalothorax and the abdomen, and usually eight eyes. While many insects feed on vegetation and the sap-bloods of plants, spiders must have fresh-killed animal prey. This they procure by two different methods, according to the species, and they can be divided into two major groups: the hunters and the trappers.

The hunters devise no webs as traps to ensnare their prey, but either stalk it and chase it down or wait for it quietly in ambush. Crab spiders (family: *Thomisidae*) remain hidden in flowers awaiting insect visitors, their coloration in many cases matching the flowers on which they rest. The wolf spiders (*Lycosidae*) are keen-eyed hunters of large size and great strength that prowl about among the grass roots chasing insects and leaping on them like predatory wolves. One day I watched a large wolf spider (*Lycosa aspersa*) stalking a green tiger beetle. Finally, it pounced on it and the battle was quickly over. When young wolf spiders hatch from the egg sac, they climb on the mother's back and for a week or more are carried with her wherever she goes. With amazing acrobatic ability, the jumping spiders (family: *Salticidae*) spring upon their unlucky prey like leaping tigers. Sometimes, anchored with a silken dragline, they leap from buildings and other objects, capturing their prey in midair.

One of the hunting group, at least on certain occasions, becomes a fisherman. Fishing spiders (*Dolomedes*) sometimes dive under water to capture small fishes. One day in midsummer, as I stood on the edge of a small, slow-moving stream that wound its way through a Carolina meadow, I became engrossed in watching a cloud of midge flies dance and whirl across the glassy surface. Then suddenly my eye caught a flash of silver at the water's edge near a clump of rushes. Looking closer, I saw a large fishing spi-

Harry Ellis

One of the most common spiders is the black and yellow garden spider, which weaves a large orb web. These spiders are often called writing spiders because of the design on the web that looks like script.

der (*Dolomedes vittatus*) dragging a tiny wriggling fish from the water. Soon its struggles ceased, as poison fangs sank into the fish's flesh and powerful digestive enzymes began dissolving body tissues. While insects make up the bulk of this spider's diet, I am convinced that the incident I had witnessed is not a rare occurrence. I had watched and photographed a piscatorial gladiator of the spider world in action.

The female fishing spider carries her huge, round egg sac in her jaws until ready to hatch. She then weaves green leaves together into a silken nursery and hangs the sac inside. Just outside, she stands guard over the hatching young with a fierce maternal instinct that is perhaps unequaled among nature's smaller creatures.

To me, the ingenious trappers of the spider world that hang silken nets and snares of many forms for trapping their prey are the most amazing of all. The silk for web weaving is released from glands in the abdomen through fingerlike appendages known as spinnerets, the strong elastic threads being pulled from them by the back legs. Here, a high degree of specialization exists, each group of spiders weaving its own particular style of web. There are orb webs, funnel webs, sheet webs, and bowl and doily webs, to name only a few. Web spinning is generally done by the female of the species. Sometimes immature males construct very imperfect webs, but these activities are abandoned on reaching maturity.

Funnel webs of the grass spider (*Agelenopsis naevia*) are found in almost incalculable numbers in eastern fields and meadows. The front of the web is a flat hammock with a funnel-shaped tube leading downward among a tangle of grasses. Here in the dark funnel sits the spider, inviting all "guests" that land on the silken platform to "walk into my parlor."

Of all our many species of spiders, only a few are dangerous to man. Chief among these is the notorious black widow (*Latrodectus mactans*), common throughout most of the eastern United States. The female is a shiny, black spider with a red hourglass marking on the underside of her abdomen. The much smaller male, not known to bite humans, is often eaten by the female after mating. Black widows are so abundant around my home in western North Carolina that within an hour I have collected more than two dozen specimens around old trash heaps and in the dark corners of cellars and basements. Here, the coarse, irregular webs are hung with a funnel-shaped retreat near the center. The venom of the female is more virulent, drop for drop, than that of a rattlesnake and may be more toxic per unit measurement than that of any other living creature. In spite of this, the bite, though extremely dangerous, is seldom fatal to humans. This is due to the small amount of venom injected. The eggs are laid in a silken sac that, when cut open, exposes two hundred or more tiny gleaming "pearls" with an iridescent sheen. Out of this number of eggs, perhaps only a half a dozen spiders will escape their natural enemies and survive.

From man's earliest beginnings, he has been closely associated with spiders, certain species following his footsteps, sharing his caves, wigwams, and dwellings. And today, there are few homes where the house spider (*Theridion tepidariorum*) cannot be found, as this small,

Photographs by Harry Ellis

The bowl and doily spider constructs a shallow web in the grass (top, inset), *and early morning dew often turns a meadow into a sparkling fairyland. Camouflage is a specialty of the crab spider* (lower three photos), *and this species can change color to match the red, yellow, or white flower background while waiting for a passing meal.*

The fishing spider is a large and aggressive hunter capable of capturing and eating tiny fish.

yellowish-brown spider is the most common cobweb weaver in houses and attics.

Some spiders are found only in remote wilderness areas far from human habitations. The Appalachian cliff spider (*Hypochilus thorelli*) is restricted to isolated regions of the southern Appalachians, especially the southern Blue Ridge and the Great Smoky Mountains where it is often quite abundant. It is a large, long-legged spider of brownish-mottled coloration. The circular web, shaped like a lampshade, is hung under a dark, overhanging cliff. Here, inside the net the spider sits, waiting for insects to become ensnarled in the mesh, its coloration and pattern against the rock a perfect example of protective camouflage.

The orb-weaving spiders comprise a large family, represented by several hundred species. Their finished webs, arranged like wheels with spokes and spirals, represent the supreme pinnacle of engineering achievement among all spiders that hang silken traps and snares for capturing insects. The symmetrical orb web is the most intricate and complex structure made by any living thing, a masterpiece produced by a master craftsman endowed with an almost incredible complexity of instincts acquired through evolution. It is yet a riddle beyond our explanation that a lowly creature, having no more than a glimmer of what we would define as intelligence, comes from the egg fully and ideally equipped with all the needed reflexes and instincts for the construction of such an amazing device.

I often arise at dawn on misty autumn mornings and walk down country lanes and over fields and meadows to witness the beauty of many hundreds of orb webs, each radiantly bejeweled with dewdrops, every silken filament transformed into a shimmering necklace of pearls. But, the orb web is fair only to human eyes. To the spider, it is a means of survival; to the insect, it is a cruel death trap. Overall, it represents a link in nature's greater ecological web of checks and balances that stretches so far back into time.

From the center of their great orb wheels, the black and yellow garden spider (*Argiope aurantia*) and the banded garden spider (*Argiope trifasciata*) hang head downward where, at any vibration of insect claw or flutter of moth wing, they rush forth to wrap their victims like mummies in coils of lethal silk. Other orb weavers, like the shamrock spider (*Aranea trifolium*) and the marbled spider (*Araneus marmoreus*), build retreats of leaves woven together with silk above their webs. Inside her retreat, each spider waits with claw on a signal line, feeling every vibration of her woven universe. Should an insect become entangled in the sticky spirals of the web, the spider is ready to swing down the nonviscid radial lines like a graceful artist of the trapeze.

Not only are we captivated by the ethereal beauty of their webs, but also a number of spiders themselves command attention by their striking patterns and bright colors. Many of the orb weavers belong to this group. Some species of jumping spiders are covered with rows of iridescent scales that, when viewed at a certain angle of light, display a flashing brilliance of changing coloration. Certain wandering spiders (family: *Ctenidae*) are patterned in rich shades of orange and reddish-brown and are among our most handsome arachnids.

Recognized by the red hourglass mark on the abdomen of the female (left), the black widow is perhaps best known for its poisonous bite.

Photographs by Harry Ellis

Female black widows (above) guard egg sacs which contain tiny pearllike eggs (top, right). Black widows are commonly found around old trash heaps, and the venom of the female is more virulent, drop for drop, than that of a rattlesnake, although the bite is seldom fatal to humans.

Photographs by Harry Ellis

A fishing spider (above, left) stands guard as her young hatch from the egg sac. The wolf spider (above, right) carries her newly hatched young on her back.

On the other hand, some of our spiders are strange and grotesque in form and appearance. The spiny-bodied spider (*Micrathena gracilis*) and the arrow-shaped Micrathena (*Micrathena sagitta*) have bodies adorned with several rows of sharp, needlelike spines and tubercles which, no doubt, offer some degree of protection against birds and other enemies. In the long-jawed orb weaver (*Tetragnatha*), the front jaws are so greatly elongated that they appear completely out of proportion to the rest of the body, giving it a gruesome, unnatural appearance.

My investigations into the realm of the spiders have added a whole new dimension to my interest in na-

ture. I have learned that no one need go far afield or to faraway jungles or distant shores in search of natural wonders. There are marvels just as intriguing, almost in our own backyards—material aplenty for a lifetime of investigation. In my surveillance of spider life, I have made no discoveries new to science, but have found lasting pleasure and a sense of awe and wonder at their marvelous instincts and amazing skills. Spiders are complex and interesting creatures; and, in spite of the prejudice and fear that often surround them, almost entirely harmless and worthy of our understanding.

The Ultimate Survivor

DOUG ELLIOTT

"The possum is to be met with no where but in America . . . and is the wonder of all Land Animals," wrote John Brickell in 1737. Brickell was a physician who lived in Edenton in the early 1730s before North Carolina was even a colony. In his book, *The Natural History of North Carolina*, he described the opossum and offered a number of eighteenth-century interpretations of opossum behavior and lore.

As a naturalist, I have always had at least a passing interest in opossums, not only because the possum is the only marsupial on the continent, but also because of the great amount of attention given these creatures in American folklore. However, a certain occurrence one bright May morning turned my passing interest into a full-time passion.

As I was walking down a wooded road listening to bird calls, I heard a raspy clinking sound I couldn't identify. It had a distressed, urgent quality to it, but, as much as I scanned the trees, I couldn't locate it. Then my eye caught some movement. On the ground in front of me was a very distraught baby opossum. It was about four inches long with sooty gray fur, "shoe button" eyes, and tiny pink hands and feet. Its delicate ears and naked tail were black on the parts close to the body and pink on the extremities. As I watched, it backed away on wobbly legs, giving me the characteristic toothy grimace known as the "possum grin."

Apparently, the little opossum, which I later determined was a female, had fallen off its mother's back the night before. I gingerly picked her up, and, not knowing what else to do, popped her onto my head. She immediately grabbed hold with miniature clenched fists, and there she stayed for most of the next month.

I named her Blossom. As she got bigger, she usurped an overalls pocket for her daytime sleeping quarters. Then she moved into a shoulder bag, and eventually adopted a padded corner in the house or car. She was very unemotional and docile, and slept all day and for a good portion of the night if all her food needs were met. She was fairly well box-trained. There was a beautiful existential purity to her being, an acceptance and lack of attachment in her primitive simplicity.

In this age of environmental consciousness, it might behoove us to have an evolutionary look at opossums like Blossom. They are the oldest living native mammals on the continent. Toward the end of the reign of the dinosaurs some eighty million years ago, the first mammals that appeared were little opossum-like marsupials (pouched animals). In North America, these marsupials evolved into many forms (eleven genera at least); but, as higher mammals came onto the scene and competition got stiffer, these early marsupials gradually disappeared. The sole exception is one genus, *Didelphis*, that survives as today's opossum.

In spite of the millions of years that have elapsed, the "modern" opossum has retained essentially the same generalized form, habits, and intelligence as its first Cretaceous ancestors. In North America, this very generality seems to have been

Opossum With Young (Jack Dermid)

the opossum's key to success. (To get an idea of the specialized directions in which marsupials can evolve, have a look at Australia's marsupials. There is an incredible diversity of forms, from marsupial wolves to moles and kangaroos.) Had the opossum become specialized for a particular type of habitat, food, or behavior, it probably would have had to compete with other more intelligent placental mammals and lost out. While in other parts of the world the more highly evolved marsupials are rapidly succumbing to pressures of human populations, here in America Br'er Possum seems to be rubbing elbows with humanity and actually thriving. Opossums are able to live everywhere from vast wilderness areas to urban business districts. In precolonial times, the opossum was found only in the South, but today it can be found all the way up into Canada and west to California. Much of this range expansion has taken place during this century, probably aided by the advent of the garbage can.

Even though the opossum has now moved north, it is still a southerner at heart (or bodily at least), and it has not quite adapted in its new territory. Most northern opossums (and even some that live in the higher altitudes in the North Carolina mountains) lose the tips of their naked tails and ears to frostbite.

The opossum's behavior in the face of danger is another manifestation of its primitiveness. John Brickell was probably not the first and was certainly not the last person to refer to opossum as slow-witted. "They are a very stupid Creature, being altogether negligent of their own Safety, and never strive to flee from their Enemies as it is natural for all other wild Beasts to do."

Opossums have no specialized escape mechanisms. They can climb trees, but they can be easily shaken out. They are not fast runners. I have caught many of them after only a short chase.

The most famous protective opossum behavior is, of course, "playing possum." Brickell noted the phenomenon and described it this way: "They are hard to kill, for I have known their skulls smashed and broken in pieces, so that they seemed to be quite dead, yet in a few Hours they will recover and creep about again." Studies have shown that playing possum is not really a "feint" but a true "faint." Apparently when the threat becomes more than its simple psyche can bear, some sort of mental overload switch is flipped and the opossum conks out into the oblivion of a catatonic state. In this condition, its heartbeat and breathing are barely perceptible. It will revive when the situation calms down. Brickell reported, "it is a common saying in Carolina, that if a Cat has nine Lives, a Possum has nineteen."

Another factor in the opossum's survival as a species is its high reproductive rate. A female usually raises two litters a year. The sex life and reproduction of the opossum is the source of some of the most bizarre fact, fiction, and folklore in the animal kingdom. Alas, much of it is too bizarre for a family magazine—especially some of the myths. The truth is strange enough.

Take, for example, the gestation period of an opossum. For comparison, an elephant's is twenty-three months, a human's is nine months, and a cat's is two months. An opossum's is an incredible thirteen days.

Thirteen days (plus or minus six hours) after conception, four to

twenty-four baby opossums are born. They are blind and hairless with undeveloped hind feet and tail, and at this stage are literally embryos. Each is about half an inch long and weighs about the same as a paper match. A human baby born in the same proportion to the size of its mother would be about the size of a nickel. Even so, these infants are endowed with developed front limbs (complete with tiny deciduous claws that drop off once they are in the safety of the pouch), and they have strong, muscular mouthparts.

The newborn opossum makes the journey to the pouch on its own, completely unaided by the mother. If the infant falls off or misses the pouch, it is lost. There is no providing in the mother's primeval brain for the rescue of fallen babes, and observers of opossum births report that as many as 40 percent of the young may never reach the pouch. Once in the pouch, the ordeal is not yet complete. The tiny opossum must locate one of the thirteen pinhead-sized nipples; if all the active nipples are already occupied, it will perish. If the infants do find a nipple, however, their problems are over until they are about two months old when they leave the pouch and ride on their mother's back. (They do not hang with their tails wrapped around hers.) "The young ones . . . remain sporting in and out of this false Belly till they are able to fend for themselves," Brickell reports. They are completely weaned and on their own by the third month.

Opossum legends and myths are common among many native American groups, including the Cherokees and Catawbas of the Carolinas and the Aztecs and Mayans of Mexico and Central

America. In most of these legends, opossums are viewed with little esteem by North American Indians. According to one Cherokee friend of mine, before the white man introduced his complex obscenities, the worst thing one Cherokee could call another was "possum manure" and the Catawbas referred to the opossum with a word that translates as, "He who slobbers much fluid."

However, south of the border, according to the hieroglyphic codices left by the Aztec and Mayan civilizations, the opossum played an important role. In the Dresden Codex, the Mayans depict opossums as bearer deities called *mams*. (No doubt this was derived from the opossum's habit of carrying its young on its back.) These *mams* appeared during the last five days of each year and they carried on their backs the prognostication of the new year. The Florentine Codex tells us that the Aztecs considered the opossum to be good eating and its tail was used to make tea or salve.

Of course from ancient times to present, the opossum has been much more utilized as a source of food than of medicine. Brickell tells us that "their Flesh is generally fat, white and well tasted, several Persons eat of them [and] prefer them before Pork, but their ugly tails are enough to put one out of Conceit with them."

Many of us have seen "Eat More Possum" bumper stickers, but few know that the origin of this catchy slogan is directly traceable to the Possum Growers and Breeders Association of America, Inc. The association, which boasts a membership of over 40,000, has its headquarters in Clanton, Alabama, where Frank Basil Clark presides as the international president. Clark says he was born and raised in Hanging Dog, a small community out in the far western tip of North Carolina, but he has lived in Alabama since well before the inception of the possum association. Recently I met him in City Hall in the mayor's office where I learned that, along with his duties as president of the Possum Growers and proprietor of the town's only drive-in theater, he is also mayor of this bustling central Alabama town of 6,000.

"Yes, it seems my work is never done," he confided. "I'm mayor from nine to five, I run the theater from five to midnight, and slop my possums from midnight till dawn." Mayor Clark sports a sleek handlebar mustache and snakeskin cowboy boots. He is a blend of southern "good ole boy," deadpan comedian, and shrewd politician. Even so, his interest in possums is genuine, and he envisions a time when possum ranching—like catfish farming—may prove profitable. "We think possums might be the answer to the world's food problems, but right now it is more profitable to raise them for research," he said as he made a phone call to a buddy, Curtis Smith, and arranged a tour of Smith's possum ranch. As we drove over, he told me that Smith had just sold most of his possums and he only had a dozen or so left (his breeding stock). At least I could get an idea of the layout.

Smith greeted us as we pulled into the driveway of his modern house and escorted us to a wooded grove where the possum cages were arranged in and around a barn. While he went from cage to cage, feeding and watering the animals, he explained that raising possums for research showed increasing promise.

"We can't even afford to eat them anymore," Clark lamented. "Medical research labs are buying them up as fast as we can produce 'em."

Apparently, because of its unusual life cycle and its embryonic young, the opossum has become an important experimental animal for medical researchers who are studying ways to combat birth defects and other diseases in humans. The scientists want only possums that are raised in captivity because they are healthy, easy to handle, and have pleasant dispositions. "There's nothing sweeter than a peach-fed possum," says Clark, still not willing to give up the gustatory delights afforded by a platter of possum and sweet potatoes.

Like Clark, Smith has also been successful in the political arena. He is a newly elected Alabama state representative, and, of course, he attributes his political victory to his involvement with the Possum Growers and Breeders. Both he and Clark sum it up this way: "If you put your possum first, everything else will fall into place."

PART THREE
Special Places

"Backwater at Pamlico," courtesy of artist, Robert Herr

A Quest for Wilderness

GEORGE ELLISON

Horace Kephart led a life that many people might envy. He was a scholar and one of the most influential university librarians in the nation, yet he chucked it all to live in a wilderness—a wilderness that he helped shape into what is now the Great Smoky Mountains National Park.

Kephart came to western North Carolina in the summer of 1904 while much of the area was lightly settled and still considered the wildest remaining chunk of real estate in the East. Why he came was largely a mystery then; and, to some extent, the mystery remains. It is clear, however, that he wanted to combine writing with a wilderness-frontier experience "so that I might realize the past in the present." He was also seeking a "Back of Beyond" in which he could find a "place to begin again."

That he was at least partly successful is beyond question. During the some twenty-seven years that he lived in and around the Smokies, he hunted and fished, and wrote countless national magazine articles and books, two of which were important and influential. The first, *Camping*

and Woodcraft, proved to be a storehouse of practical advice, lore, anecdotes, and adventure, and it became the standard work in its field. It became a virtual handbook for the Boy Scouts.

Kephart's most significant book, however, was *Our Southern Highlanders*, a classic study of our southern mountains and the people who lived there. This book, along with his later role as a publicist for the movement to form a national park, secured Kephart's fame as an important and colorful figure in the history of the nation, and especially in the Southern Appalachians.

Kephart's life is a study in contrasts. He was born in East Salem, Pennsylvania, in 1862, his ancestors having been among the first settlers of the mountain wilderness west of the Susquehanna. His father, Isaiah L. Kephart, was a teacher, editor, and clergyman. In 1867 the family moved to Iowa where Kephart attended Western College for a year. In 1876 they returned to Pennsylvania and he entered Lebanon Valley College, graduating A.B. in the spring of 1879. That fall he enrolled

in the College of Liberal Arts at Boston University. In addition to studying under Alphaeus Hyatt— the distinguished zoologist—he enjoyed "the blessed privilege of studying whatever I pleased in the Boston Public Library." Thus evolved the career he was to follow for the next twenty years.

In 1880 he went to Cornell in Ithaca, New York, where he assumed supervision of cataloging the library's holdings, while also taking courses in history and political science. At the library he worked for Cornell's first librarian, Willard Fiske, who became a friend and benefactor. In 1885, Fiske brought Kephart to Italy to assist in cataloging the world's finest collections of Dante and Petrarch, Icelandic history and literature, and the Rhaoto-Romanic language.

In 1886, Kephart returned to the United States and accepted a position as assistant librarian at Yale College in New Haven, Connecticut. The following year, he married Laura Mack of Ithaca. While in New Haven, Kephart began his career as a writer. Most of his early writings are related to professional library matters, but he was also developing an interest in American frontier history. Largely as a result of this interest, he accepted in 1890 the directorship of the St. Louis Mercantile Library Association, "the oldest library west of the Mississippi." Here Kephart built one of the finest collections of Western Americana then in existence. He became an authority in the field, consulted by such writers as Hiram Chittenden and Emerson Hough.

As an exceptionally competent librarian, Kephart resided with his wife and children in St. Louis for over a decade. After the turn of the century, however, his outlook on life underwent fundamental changes. His interests and writings shifted from librarianship to outdoor life, firearms, and frontier history. He became disenchanted with the basic context of his homelife. A serious drinking problem arose. As time passed his main pleasure came from solitary excursions into the Ozark mountains and the Arkansas swamps. "I love the wilderness because there are no shams in it," he wrote in his notebook at this time. The extended wilderness trips alienated the library's directors; and late in 1903, he was forced to resign from the Mercantile Library. In April 1904 he suffered a nervous collapse and was taken to his parents' home in Dayton, Ohio. His wife returned with the children to Ithaca.

While Kephart was in Dayton, he became increasingly preoccupied with the desire to combine a literary career with a wilderness existence. He wrote that he was "looking for a big, primitive forest where I could build up my strength anew and indulge in my lifelong fondness for

hunting, fishing and exploring new ground." He used U.S. Geodetic Survey maps to pick out the wildest mountain area, which turned out to be the Smokies.

Traveling by train with all his gear, he arrived in western North Carolina during the summer of 1904, and initially set up a camp on Dick's Creek several miles west of Dillsboro in Jackson County. In October, he obtained permission to use an abandoned two-room cabin on the Little Fork of the Sugar Fork of Hazel Creek in the Smokies, and lived there until 1907. Deep in the virgin woods, Kephart studied the flora and fauna of the area. He was fascinated by the mountain people and their culture, and eventually he gained their friendship and confidence.

"They were like figures taken from the old frontier histories and legends that I had been so fond of . . . they interested me more than the ultra-civilized folk of the cities," he later related. Kephart not only studied the people, he also became enchanted with the simple and direct challenge of living efficiently in this environment. By 1906, he had compiled enough material and practical lore to publish *Camping and Woodcraft*.

Kephart left the Hazel Creek watershed in 1907 and traveled in other parts of the Southern Appalachians. In 1910 he returned to Swain County, where he lived in a boardinghouse in Bryson City most of the year. But during the summers he camped, mostly by himself, at various sites in the Smokies. Bryson Place, about ten miles up Deep Creek from town, was the spot he liked best. Here he would set up camp for the entire summer, hauling in by wagon or on horseback the

supplies and equipment he required, which included a small folding desk and writing materials.

Two books on subjects on which he was an authority, *Camp Cooking* and *Sporting Firearms*, appeared in 1910 and 1912. The first edition of his major work, *Our Southern Highlanders*, was published in 1913 (revised and expanded in 1922). Drawing on materials he collected firsthand—primarily on Hazel Creek and in the Bryson City area—or that he carefully researched, Kephart produced a literary work that is historical, sociological, and autobiographical. No book devoted to the southern mountains has been more widely known, read, and respected.

After 1913, Kephart published *Camping* (1916) and *The Camper's Manual* (1923), edited a series of eleven volumes of adventure and exploration (*Outing* Adventure Library, 1915–17), and labored on a novel entitled *Smoky Mountain Magic* that never got out of typescript. He was active in the establishment of the Appalachian Trail, particularly in plotting the route the trail was to follow through the Smokies and on into north Georgia.

But his most important writing and the major portion of his energies during the 1920s and early 1930s were devoted to the movement that culminated in the establishment of the Great Smoky Mountains National Park. Kephart's role in the movement was considerable. He wrote articles for periodicals and newspapers advocating the establishment of a park in the Smokies, carefully explaining time and again why the area should be preserved. Many of his pieces were accompanied by the excellent photographs of his Japanese friend, George Masa, who spent as much time in the Smokies

When Horace Kephart arrived in the Smokies, he was determined not only to live in the wilderness but also to write about and document the area and its people. He kept voluminous notes and journals which subsequently became the foundation for his best-known book, Our Southern Highlanders.

with Kephart as he did in his Asheville studio. Together they caught the spirit of the high mountains and watersheds in words and pictures.

Kephart did not live to see the park become an actuality because he was killed in an automobile accident near Bryson City in 1931. Still, he died knowing that the park was assured. In the November following his death in the spring, when representatives of North Carolina and Tennessee went to Washington to present the deed for the lands to be included in the park, Secretary of the Interior Ray Wilbur recognized Kephart's part in the park movement: "I wish that I could name every one of the men and women who have worked devotedly to see this new national park come into being, but I am sure you will join me in appreciation of the persistent and idealistic interest of Mr. Kephart, who not only knew these mountains and loved the people, but saw in them a great national treasure."

Two months before his death, the

U.S. Geographic Board designated that a peak on the high divide of the Smokies, about eight miles northeast of Clingman's Dome, be named Mount Kephart. He was the first living American honored by such a decision.

Kephart's motivation for wanting the region preserved as a park was concise. "I owe my life to these mountains, and I want them preserved that others may profit by them as I have," he said. Still, there is reason to suspect Kephart might have wished that the whole area could remain exactly as he found it—preserving not only the majestic mountains, forests, and wildlife, but also the unique way of life he found there among the scattered human inhabitants.

But Kephart knew that change was coming. Indeed, it was already under way in the form of massive timber operations. Given the alternatives, he settled on the best compromise despite some lingering personal regrets. On September 12, 1928, he wrote in a letter to his son George:

"The long and difficult task of surveying, examining titles, estimating values, etc., of the Smoky Mountains National Park lands is finished. The purchase money is all in hand. Legal difficulties have been overcome. And now, at last, the actual purchase or condemnation of the whole area will proceed to a finish. It was a big undertaking, and beset with discouragements of all sorts; but we've won! And now congratulations are coming in from all over the U.S. Within two years, we will have good roads into the Smokies. And then—well, then, I'll get out."

Life in the Southern Highlands

These black and white photographs taken by George Masa and Horace Kephart are from the archives at Western Carolina University. They depict a way of life that has largely disappeared. The accompanying quotes are from Kephart's Our Southern Highlanders.

She knows no other lot

"Many of the women are pretty in youth; but hard toil in house and field, early marriage, frequent child-bearing with shockingly poor attention, and ignorance or defiance of the plainest necessities of hygiene soon warp and age them. At thirty or thirty-five a mountain woman is apt to have a worn and faded look, with form prematurely bent—and what wonder?"

Horace Kephart's cabin at Hazel Creek

"When I went south into the mountains I was seeking a Back of Beyond. This for more reasons than one. With an inborn taste for the wild and romantic, I yearned for a strange land and a people that had the charm of originality. Again, I had a passion for early American history; and, in Far Appalachia, it seemed that I might realize the past in the present, seeing with my own eyes what life must have been to my pioneer ancestors of a century or two ago."

The Turpins befriended Kephart in 1904

". . . the great mass of mountain people are very like persons of similar station elsewhere, just human, with human frailties, only a little more honest, I think, in owning them. The worst of them still have good traits, strong characters, something responsive to decent treatment. They are kind-hearted, loyal to their friends, quick to help anyone in distress."

Bob's father gritting corn

"Now, yan's my field o' corn. I gather the corn, and shuck hit and grind hit my own self, and the woman she bakes us a pone o' bread to eat—and I don't pay no tax, do I? Then why can't I make some o' my corn into pure whiskey to drink, without payin' tax? I tell you, 'tain't fair, this way the Government does!"

Mountaineers moving to town

"The mountaineer, born and bred to
Spartan self-denial, has a scorn of
luxury. . . . And any assumption of
superiority he will resent with blow
or sarcasm. A ragged hobbledehoy
stood on the Vanderbilt grounds at
Biltmore, mouth open but silent,
watching a gardener at work. The
latter, annoyed by the boy's vacuous
stare, spoke up sharply: 'What do
you want?' Like a flash the lad re-
torted: 'Oh, dad sent me down hyur
to look at the place—said if I liked
it, he mought buy it for me.'"

Be it ever so humble

"There is something very attractive and picturesque about the little old log cabin. In its setting and ancient forests and mighty hills it fits, it harmonizes, where the prim and precise product of modern carpentry would shock an artistic eye. And it is home. When the wind whistles through the cracks and snow sifts into the corners of the room, one draws his stumpy little split-bottomed chair close to the wide hearth and really knows the comfort of fire leaping and sap singing from big birch logs."

Kephart (*at right*) directing the removal of a North Carolina bear's hide

"The mountaineers have an odd way of sharing the spoils of the chase. They call it 'stoking the meat. . . .' The hide is sold, and the proceeds divided equally among the hunters, but the meat is cut up into as many pieces as there are partners in the chase; then one man goes indoors or behind a tree, and somebody at the carcass, laying his hand on a portion, calls out: 'Whose piece is this?' 'Bill Cope's.' And so on down the line. Everybody gets what chance determines for him, and there can be no charge of unfairness."

Splitting clapboards

"I went down into the valley, wunst, and I declar I nigh sultered! 'Pears like there ain't breath enough to go round, with all them people. And the water don't do a body no good; an' you cain't eat hearty, nor sleep good o' nights. Course they pay big money down thar' but I'd a heap-sight ruther ketch me a big old 'coon fer his hide."

Quill Rose making music

"The mountaineers have a native fondness for music and dancing, which, with the shouting spells of their revivals, are the only outlets for those powerful emotions which otherwise they studiously conceal. Most of their music is in the weird, plaintive minor key that seems spontaneous with primitive people throughout the world. But where banjo and fiddle enter, the vapors vanish. Up strike The Fox Chase, Shady Grove, Gamblin' Man, Sourwood Mountain, and knees are limbered, and merry voices rise."

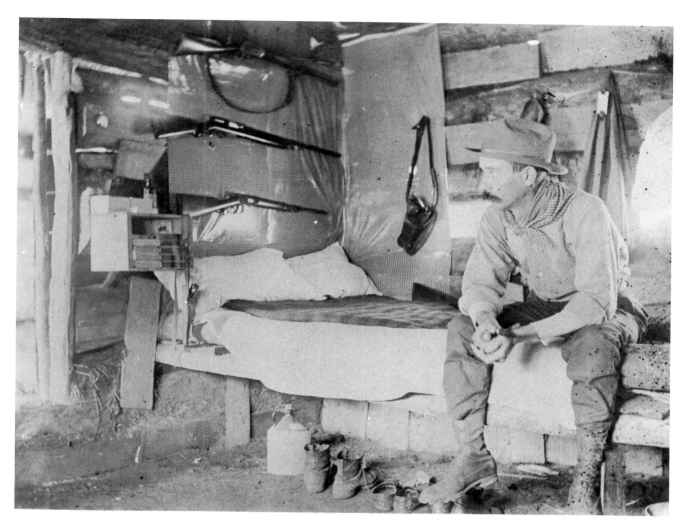

Interior of Kephart's cabin at Hazel Creek

"So, too, in the rudest communities of Appalachia, among the most trifling and unmoral natives of this region, among the illiterate and hidebound, there still is much to excite admiration and good hope. I have not shrunk from telling the truth about these people, even when it was far from pleasant; but I would have preserved strict silence had I not seen in the most backward of them certain sterling qualities of manliness that our nation can ill afford to waste. It is a truth as old as the human race that savageries may co-exist with admirable qualities of head and heart."

Where the Wind Comes From

A few years back, two boys about eight years old wrapped a double handful of cookies in tinfoil, cut two walking sticks out of a ligustrum hedge, and walked up the street to a culvert where a small creek flowed. They followed the creek upstream through backyards and a city park. In the pools, the water was murky, but, where it ran over pebbles, it seemed clear. After walking perhaps half a mile, the boys entered a wooded area and lost sight of the houses. Tall reeds and dense brush shrouded the creek, filtering out the sound of traffic, barking dogs, and mothers calling children home to supper.

At a spot where the creek tumbled over a series of bedrock ledges, they sat down and looked around. This was it, they figured. We're in the wilderness. They ate their oatmeal cookies, and drank out of the most polluted creek in Raleigh.

After I realized that my son and his friend were not going to die of typhoid or something worse, I began to appreciate what they had done. I remembered a boy about their same age who—thirty years earlier—had decided not to go straight home from the swimming pool one summer afternoon. Instead, he had followed a ditch for about a mile and wound up on the moon.

At least that's what I thought it looked like. Actually, it was a huge expanse of waste pine bark that covered many acres of lowland near the Roanoke River below a pulp mill. There were deeply cut trails through the chips, and in one place I found a cave in a shelf of pine bark. I walked that maze half believing that no one had ever been there before. And on the way home, I drank some of the oily water from the ditch (I had a better sense of ritual than plain good sense).

Sooner or later all kids get that first taste of exploration, and it usually taps a lifelong wellspring; an insistent need to go beyond what is known. That current flowed again recently while I was reading A. B. Guthrie's *The Way West*, a fictionalized, but technically accurate, account of the first wagon trains to travel from Independence, Missouri, to Oregon.

At one point a trapper, who had first traveled west in the 1830s, described his feelings upon seeing the same country again as a wagon train pilot in 1845. Even that early, he was beginning to feel boxed in. The trapper "sat his horse and watched thinking how things had changed. This country was young, like himself, without the thought of age. There wasn't a post on it then, nor any tame squaw begging calico, but only buffalo and beaver and the long grass waving in the Laramie bottoms. The wind had blown lonesome, the sound of emptiness in it, the breath of far-off places where no white foot had stepped. A man snuggling in his robe had felt alone and strong and good, telling himself he would see where the wind came from."

Kids drinking from the polluted creeks over a century later were "seeing where the wind came from," although it is a sad comparison. Yet it is a comparison that can only become sadder. In just the past few decades, those of us who care about such things have suffered a steady and relentless loss. Many of the swamps and brackish backwaters I loved as a kid down east are gone, the rivers choked with algae. In the mountains, we exult in stolen moments of solitude, knowing full well that just beyond the ridge the bulldozers are at work. Those places not already accorded wilderness status or something similar are being mopped up, and there is pressure to unlock some of the meager wild country we've set aside.

There will be no more Oregon Trails on this planet, although there will certainly be some to other galaxies. It's our nature to seek them—and, alas, often to leave a trail of destruction.

Maybe that's the best reason of all to lock up what remains of our scattered wilderness on earth. Few of us will explore the vast cosmos, but we can visit the remaining fragments of frontier here and preserve at least the spirit of exploration. And we can do it without the stigma of destruction that accompanied the actual exploration undertaken by our forefathers. It is a substitute at best, but one many of us truly need.

Thoreau long ago wrote, "In wilderness is the preservation of the world." He was speaking not only of the resource, but also of the spirit of mankind.—*Jim Dean*

North Carolina Division of Archives and History

Following the French Broad

JAY DAVIES

The air is thick with dampness as fog creeps up the valley floor toward my balsam-shrouded perch atop Devil's Courthouse. Except for the wind, all is quiet while I trespass in this primeval environment. This rock outcrop is rough and cold. As my hand moves across its crystalline surface, I drift back in time, back nearly a billion years, when the rocks of the French Broad were just beginning to take form from the slowly cooling, molten magma covering the earth's surface.

Over the coming millennia life will make its debut, struggling first as a single cell and later as plants, invertebrates, fish, and more advanced forms. A titanic collision between Europe and North America will cause a tremendous buckling of the earth's crust along the Eastern Seaboard of the United States. The Precambrian rocks will be fractured and tilted, their jagged shards thrust skyward to form the Appalachian Mountains. Over time erosion will continue to modify the topography, but already the course of the French Broad River will have been predestined.

The headwaters of the French Broad begin as springs on the North Fork northwest of Brevard.

I met the French Broad as a stranger. The North Fork and the Davidson, Stackhouse, and Shelton Laurel were only names to me, but that was before I traced the river's route from its origins near Rosman to the Tennessee line, watching as it rushed onward into Tennessee toward its marriage with the Holston River at Knoxville, 217 miles from its beginnings. I followed the river through Transylvania, Henderson, Buncombe, and Madison counties, places rich in history and mountain lore. I talked to the people who lived on its banks and listened to what they had to say about the river. I read the histories and the scientific accounts.

From all these sources I learned what lavish provision the French Broad has made for man. Man has long been a part of the French Broad, hunting game in her forests, building homes from her timber, farming her rich valleys, eating her fish, and drinking her water. The river offered a highway from the heartland of the nation through the almost impassable Appalachians to the market places of the Deep South. She gave clean and abundant water to new industry.

In exchange for all that, men too often sullied the gift, turning her

Jay Davies

clear water muddy with siltation and clogging it with wastes.

Early explorers called wide rivers "broads," and, because this one flowed toward the French Territories, she was called the French Broad. Of course, in the highlands of the North Fork in Transylvania County the river is hardly more than a rivulet. Sentinels of Fraser fir and spruce stand guard. The journey of these trees south from Canada with Ice Age glaciers occurred in the wink of an eye compared to the age of the river. This island refuge high atop the Pisgah Mountains provided a hiding place where the trees could live when the climate warmed and the ice melted.

The West and North Forks have a geologically youthful appearance. Their waters cascading across boulders and rubble bespeak their raven-ous appetite to erode their beds in a frenzied attempt to lessen their grade and achieve a more mature, meandering state. These streams are clear and cold; their gravel bottoms are free of choking silt and rich in aquatic insect life. Brook or "speckled" trout, as they are called locally, persist in the headwaters, while the secretive brown and flashy rainbow dominate the main stream.

Downstream from Rosman, the river follows a lazy, meandering course through a broadening agri-cultural valley. Stark white and gray sycamores line the earthen banks. I floated this section of river and as my canoe glided over the sandy bot-tom I wondered what the stream was like two hundred years ago. Historical records of similar streams in North Carolina tell of water so clear their gravel bottoms in pools

A historical link between towns like Marshall, the French Broad was a vital trade route for lumber and other goods. Marshall is also the county seat of Madison County.

Jim Dean

Curtis Wooten

Trout are found in the headwaters of the French Broad, and the downstream stretches afford good fishing for smallmouth bass and catfish. This angler (top) is hoping for a strike from a muskellunge that may be a yard long. Many fine homes are located along the river. At Hot Springs, Sunnybank (lower photo), which dates from 1875, is one of the survivors of the town's heyday as a resort.

several feet deep appeared only a few inches under the surface. I have found no reason why the French Broad should not have been the same.

As I gazed upon the river's bottom, I realized I was observing the legacy of a century of reckless development and careless exploitation of the land. Today siltation is considered the single most destructive pollutant in North Carolina. Expensive filtration systems are needed to remove suspended sediment before the water may be used, and erosion of topsoil increases the cost of agriculture.

The French Broad is still cold enough downstream of Brevard to provide a respectable trout fishery. Surprisingly, large brown trout are caught each year in small tributaries like Boylston Creek, located near the border of Transylvania and Henderson counties. Some biologists theorize the large trout are nomads that

move into these cold tributaries to escape the warm summer temperatures of the river.

The river downstream from Brevard was not always so clean, however. Bill Allen of Swannanoa recalled a large fish kill that occurred in the mid–1950s. "I'd say every species imaginable was killed: largemouth and smallmouth bass, sunfish, catfish up to forty pounds, carp as large as small hogs, and giant black crappie. Crayfish climbed out on the banks and every tributary, no matter how small, was packed with fish trying to get away from whatever was killing them."

In fact, the French Broad was severely polluted by domestic sewage and industrial wastewater through the 1950s and 1960s. According to Heath Dobson, an environmental engineer with the North Carolina Division of Environmental Management located in Asheville, the pollution completely depleted the oxygen

content of the river in some sections and rendered it unsuitable for fish and wildlife propagation. Once regarded as a valuable resource, the river was viewed with scorn. "Just throw it in the river, it's a dump anyway," became common advice for disposing of garbage and trash.

To some extent this attitude persists today. I talked with the manager of a gravel mining company located on a tributary of the French Broad. He could see the importance of cleaning up the nation's streams, but felt some had to remain as dumps to accommodate industry. His attitude depressed me for he saw only limitations in environmental protection regulations, while I saw them as opportunities for improving our quality of life.

Near the Henderson-Transylvania county line is where the steamboat *Mountain Lily* met her Waterloo. She was an ambitious venture by the French Broad Steamboat Company to provide river transportation between Asheville and Brevard in the late nineteenth century. These "men of vision" exploded tons of dynamite to remove stubborn rock shoals, and constructed massive jetties to deepen the river. Scarcely had she started her maiden voyage, however, when a flash flood swept the *Mountain Lily* from her moorings and she sank. Mud and debris packed the jetties and the *Mountain Lily* rotted into history.

Henderson and southern Buncombe counties are broad agricultural floodplains and the river is nearly seventy-five yards wide in places. Here, less shaded by the trees lining its banks, the river is partially weaned from its dependency on organic matter washed into it and begins to support itself with solar energy trapped by microscopic phyto-

plankton and other algae growing within it. The riverbed is lined with sand, but, as it nears Asheville, rock shoals become numerous.

Old newspapers often show pictures of anglers holding yard-long muskellunge caught from this section. Pollution was thought to have exterminated the species by the late 1950s, but thanks to the recent cleanup of the river and stocking efforts by the North Carolina Wildlife Resources Commission the crafty, elusive, and savage nature of the musky are sovereign qualities able to be appreciated by a growing number of Tar Heel anglers. "The musky provides a challenge that's not matched by other species," says Bill Allen of Swannanoa. "Once he sets his mind to hit, he'll just fascinate you." Bill has seen them hit a boat attempting to grab a plug, and yet other times he has watched them make a run and just as quickly stop without hitting. "It's uncanny," says Bill, "but when they do that, some of them will roll their eyes at you as if they are saying, 'Fooled you didn't I.'"

The Swannanoa River enters the French Broad at Asheville. Her once pastoral valley provided a pathway for pioneer families moving west from Old Fort, North Carolina, and in later years became a trade route. Manufacturing concerns moved to the Swannanoa's banks and along with them came pollution. By the middle of the twentieth century, chemical pollutants were being regularly poured into the river and trash was everywhere.

Bob Watts of Black Mountain canoed the river in the early 1970s. "I was appalled at the amount of man-made junk in the river; plastic milk jugs and garbage bags, rusting automobiles, tires, and garbage were

A fisherman tries his luck from a dam on the French Broad north of Asheville. Years ago, sauger migrated upstream each spring to spawn, and fishermen gathered to catch them until dams like this one blocked the migration and greatly reduced the sauger population.

everywhere. People had a hopeless attitude toward the river, everyone dumped stuff in it, and no one thought anything could be done about it."

A member of the Black Mountain-Swannanoa Jaycees, Bob talked to the membership about cleaning up the river and a following Saturday he and ten other members were standing on the river's bank. "That first day," said Bob, "we were only able to pick up the small stuff in a short section of the river, but it was enough." Word of the project spread throughout the entire community. One company donated a large crane to remove the automobiles and heavier trash. Local governments, institutions, and private business donated other equipment and manpower. Landowners cleaned up the river bordering their property. Numerous citizens volunteered, and even passive onlookers caught the fever and went home to get chain saws and rakes. Gradually the river improved until today it is classified trout water and stocked by the North Carolina Wildlife Resources Commission.

A mile below Asheville the river assumes a different personality. What had been an almost gentle, meandering matron becomes a cascading, impetuous vixen. "Agiqua" was the name given the French Broad by the Cherokee Indians, but the whitewater cascades below Asheville were called "Untakiyastiyi"— "where they raced." Whether or not the Cherokees raced their canoes here is unknown, but the name vividly depicts the excitement that must have been generated in their hearts by this tumbling stretch.

The Newfound Mountains line the western horizon of Buncombe and Madison counties and streams like Turkey, Sandy Mush, and Spring Creek drain their rocky slopes. Agriculture is prevalent and the rolling hills are green in pasture.

This tranquil atmosphere, however, was ripped asunder in November 1977 by a one-hundred-year flood which plowed its way through the French Broad Valley. Damage was extensive as swollen creeks washed across unprotected floodplains and gouged new channels through valuable cropland. Federal disaster relief funds poured into the area, and I was assigned to a team of specialists who helped recommend how the money should be spent.

Jay Davies

Fickle by nature, the French Broad changes its personality throughout its length. From its tumbling origins, it widens and slows in Henderson and Buncombe counties as though gathering energy for the massive rapids further downstream.

That winter I visited farms within the stricken area, helping determine the best way to rebuild the damaged land without causing further stress on the heavily damaged streams. It was puzzling at first how some fields had been extensively eroded by the raging waters, while neighboring land was left relatively untouched. Gradually the evidence built until the cause of the disparity became clear. Farmers who had plowed right up to the stream's bank were usually the worst hurt, while those who had left a buffer strip of native vegetation consisting of trees and shrubs experienced little damage. The narrow buffer strips, often only ten to fifteen feet wide, had stabilized the stream banks and prevented the channel from wandering through the adjacent fields. The vegetation had also reduced the velocity of the overflowing creek and thereby lessened its ability to erode the topsoil as it flowed across the land. Unfortunately, many landowners have continued to farm right up to the creek despite continued efforts by the U.S. Soil Conservation Service

and others to promote good soil conservation practices.

After the flood, many landowners chose to channelize the streams on their property in an attempt to reduce further flooding. This shortsighted practice not only devastated the aquatic habitat for fish and other aquatic life, but also greatly increased the likelihood the stream will flood sooner on neighboring landowners downstream.

As I pass into Madison County the river is 1,000 feet wide in some places, tumbling over a streambed strewn with rock ledges, boulders, and gravel shoals. Small islands are common, and the water is usually muddy and warmer as very little of the river is shaded from the sun's rays.

The sporty smallmouth bass are plentiful in these shoals. Carl Murray of Marshall tells of catching twenty of the scrappy fish in a day, mostly in the one- to two-pound range, but every once in a while a four-pounder. Taking me aside he whispers about a special place on Ivy Creek, located on the southern edge of Madison County, where I am guaranteed to catch a smallmouth on the first cast.

The deep holes in this section of the French Broad often produce trophy musky and large stringers of channel and flathead catfish or "yellow cats." A fifty-pound flathead was caught near Hot Springs a few years ago, and twenty-pound fish are frequent. Fishing for these monsters is the "sit and wait" type with chicken livers the preferred bait. But don't be lulled into thinking this is a lazy man's sport, because once these giants are hooked they make strong surges along the bottom and never seem to tire.

Alexander, a small community located ten miles north of Asheville on the east bank of the French Broad, consists of only a few stores, a gas station, and some homes, but 150 years ago it was the busiest watering hole on the Buncombe Turnpike. Completed in 1828 and considered one of the finest toll roads of the time, the Buncombe Pike ran along the east side of the river from Asheville to Hot Springs and linked the markets of South Carolina with the agricultural heartlands of Tennessee, Kentucky, and Ohio. Through the middle and late 1800s, droves of hogs, cattle, mules, and turkeys were a familiar sight on the pike as they were herded to sale. To accommodate the weary drovers and their animals, "stock stands" were built. Alexander's was king, consisting of a general store, blacksmith shop, sawmill, gristmill, and even a hotel. Here and at others like it, the animals were fed, watered, and sheltered for the night, while the drovers were provided solid, hot meals and a bed.

The lusty way of life along the Buncombe Pike faded into the past by the mid-1880s, when the Western North Carolina Railroad Company completed the last section of track linking Morristown, Tennessee, with Old Fort, North Carolina. The railroad brought prosperity to isolated Madison County. The ring of axes and crosscut saws echoed through the valleys as its vast stands of virgin oak, chestnut, poplar, and hickory were harvested. Marshall, the county seat tightly sandwiched between the river on the west and the mountains on the east, emerged

as a major trading center. Marshall's fortunes have not been without cost as its Scotch-Irish residents have been repeatedly flooded. Invariably when the water receded, however, they shoveled out the mud from their kitchens and stores and began anew.

A few miles downstream from Marshall, according to Cherokee legend, is the location of the mythical "dakwa," a gigantic fishlike monster that lurked in the deep pools, plucking men from the bank and devouring them beneath the river's murky water. The basis for this legend, like so many others, remains a mystery, but this section of river still claims the lives of unwary boaters. Names like Surprise Ledge, Frank Bell Rapids, the Maze, and Needle Rock foretell the treacherous nature of the section that may have inspired the legend.

Hot Springs is the last town on the river in North Carolina. Formerly Warm Springs, it was a lavish health spa and tourist resort of national fame during the 1800s. Guests from near and far made regular pilgrimages to the beautiful Warm Springs Hotel to partake of the purported medicinal benefits of the area's mineral waters. A visitor to the hotel experienced southern grandeur in its finest form. The accommodations were exquisite and the leisure activities included golf, tennis, billiards, riding, and bowling.

What does the future hold for the French Broad? Thanks to an awakening awareness of the value of the river, the future looks bright. Ashe-

ville is making plans to use the river as a source of drinking water in the not-too-distant future. Municipal and industrial wastewater treatment facilities have been constructed, and the river is once again being used for recreation. Whitewater rafting and canoeing have developed, and the river provides some of the best musky fishing in the nation.

Each year the Land-Of-Sky Regional Council, a governmental agency, coordinates citizens, business, civic, and governmental organizations in sponsoring activities such as river cleanup float trips, shopping mall displays, and seminars that emphasize the importance of keeping the river clean and celebrate French Broad River Week. A volunteer citizen's group, the French Broad River Foundation, has members from all four counties through which the river flows in North Carolina and others, who have banded together to continue the river cleanup. Siltation, garbage, and plastic milk jugs are still a problem, but now local citizens take offense when "outsiders" criticize the French Broad.

What is a river? It is a reflection of ourselves. If we have a selfish, short-sighted approach to our environment and exploit it at every opportunity, we will visualize the river as a tramp and treat it accordingly. But if we are good stewards of our natural resources and use them in a way that does not diminish their value for future generations, then we will see the river as a lady, to be respected and valued for the richness she provides in our lives.

Discovering Stone Mountain

TERRY SHANKLE

"Well, where is it?" I wondered as Joe Mickey and I drove along State Road 1002 following the new signs to Stone Mountain State Park. Joe was pointing out landmarks as we rode. I could see the green, cabin-studded ridges of the Blue Ridge Mountains rising toward summer storm clouds. I could see clear streams, dense vegetation, and land as steep as a mule's face.

What I couldn't see was the mountain that gave the park its name, and since we were right on the edge of Stone Mountain Park I was puzzled. A mountain ought to be its own billboard, I was thinking, something seen for miles away such as Mount Mitchell, or Grandfather Mountain, or Pilot Mountain.

I remembered the Forsyth County den mother whose innocent and slightly mistaken question had provoked this trip. "You people have such a beautiful park up there at Stone Mountain," she had said. "My family loves to camp there. But why have you kept it such a secret?" I had quickly reminded her that the park was operated by the Division of Parks and Recreation, not by the

North Carolina Wildlife Resources Commission. But her question seemed strangely appropriate now. If Stone Mountain was a secret, no wonder—you couldn't see the blamed thing!

We turned at the eastern park entrance at Elk Spur Church and drove farther. I was traveling with Wildlife Commission biologist Joe Mickey because he assists the park in managing the trout fishing streams that lie within its boundaries. He also gives programs on the park's trout fishing opportunities to groups of campers during the summer. He pointed out the new construction that was underway at the park as we drove along a newly built segment of road ready for paving. "They've been doing a lot of building up here recently," he was saying. "They've got a new maintenance building, a campground with a modern washhouse under construction, and a new parking lot near the base of Stone Mountain."

I couldn't stand it any longer. "Where's the mountain?" I blurted.

"We're getting there," Joe said. He turned up a narrow winding

road that quickly brought back memories of the dirt roads in Yancey County where I was a wildlife enforcement officer for six years. "We've already driven completely around the north side of the mountain but the trees obscure any view from down here on the creek."

Within minutes Joe and I had parked at a small parking area near some picnic tables, walked one of several marked trails that took off in various directions, and entered a small, picturesque meadow complete with a house and barn that had obviously been a farm in the recent past. There, towering 600 feet high, was the granite dome known as Stone Mountain.

"Well," I said, "That's worth waiting for."

That's what a lot of people have been saying since Stone Mountain was established as a park in 1968. The park had several movers and shakers who recognized the potential of the site, and corporate angels who donated much of the land. Doris Potter, Claude Billings, and Alfred Houston were impressed early on by the beauty of Stone

Ken Taylor

Mountain, and they pushed for a park. But in the late 1960s it and much of the adjoining acreage was owned by the North Carolina Granite Corporation of Mount Airy. After meetings with Billings, the president and vice-president of North Carolina Granite Corporation, John P. Frank and Frank Smith, agreed to present to their board of directors a plan that would donate Stone Mountain to the state to be used as the focal point of a new state park. The donation was approved and 418 acres including the mountain became the seed of

Stone Mountain State Park. Later the corporation sold an additional 1,068 acres for the park.

By 1970 over 2,100 acres of land had been obtained for Stone Mountain State Park, and 9,000 additional acres have been purchased since then. Federal grants funded much of the land acquisition, while Philip Hanes, Jr., of Winston-Salem gave generous donations of land to the project. The park has been essentially put together with very little state money.

Today, bounded on the north by the Blue Ridge Parkway and on the

The exposed dome of granite gives Stone Mountain its name. Over 11,000 acres of trails, streams, camping, and challenging climbing await the visitor to this state park just north of Elkin.

Photographs by Terry Shankle

At the base of the 600-foot-high mountain is the old homeplace (above) of James Hutchinson, the park's first ranger, whose family donated the cabin to the park. Moonscape effect (top, right) appears at the summit of Buzzard's Rock, where wet-weather springs have carved potholes and craters in the tough granite.

west by the Thurmond Chatham Game Lands, the more than 11,000 acres of Stone Mountain State Park offer opportunities for outdoor activities of all kinds. Camping, fishing, rock climbing, hiking, and picnicking are available, and interpretive programs are available during the summer months. Stone Mountain may once have been a secret known only to a few, but it's fast becoming one of the jewels of the state park system.

Joe and I were interested in exploring one or two of the trout streams, but before we did we wandered the southern base of the mountain where we found rock climbers practicing their techniques on the tremendous boulders that were once part of the mountain. Now shaded by large trees, the boulders offer a cool place to practice during the heat of summer.

Rock climbing on the 600-foot granite dome is probably the most popular feature at Stone Mountain. The sheer rock face offers experienced rock climbers one of the most challenging experiences to be had

on the East Coast. Ascent routes with such names as Fantastic, Great White Way, Mercury's Lead, No Alternative, The Great Arch, and Grand Funk Railroad have become widely known as providing some of the best "friction climbing" anywhere. Friction climbing is a method of ascending a smooth and steep rock face by searching for small cracks or hollows that will serve as footholds. Climbers are secured by ropes, but they get to the top by balancing their weight on all fours.

Stone Mountain's granite dome was first climbed in 1965 by Fess Green and Bill Chatfield using a south face ascent. Since then, thirteen routes have been established on the south face and all are equipped with climbing bolts and hangers anchored in the rock at strategic points to aid the climbers. Most of the climbing bolts were placed in the rock under the guidance of Mike Fishchesser, who is affiliated with the North Carolina Outward Bound School in Morganton. Mike is also responsible for the display of rock-climbing equipment located in the meadow at the southern base of the mountain.

Climbing on the more rugged north face is not encouraged. It is also not wise to start climbs three hours before the park closes. This regulation is necessary because climbers must be off the mountain by closing time. Climbing should be done only on the established routes and by experienced climbers using proper equipment. Also, the mountain is closed to climbing when the rock is wet. Observance of these safety rules has kept accidents to a minimum in nearly twenty years of climbing.

There is no charge for climbing at Stone Mountain and, in fact, rock climbing is officially still on a trial basis, according to park rangers. Climbing was stopped at one point in 1973 but, after a demonstration of proper climbing techniques for then State Parks Superintendent Tom Ellis, climbing was resumed.

A climbing log, documenting many of the first climbs on Stone Mountain, may be read at the park office. The log encourages climbers to add their stories of climbing Stone Mountain so that others, particularly new climbers, can learn from their experiences.

For those who prefer slightly flatter terrain for their outdoor excitement, there are several well-marked hiking trails that wind through the park. One of them, three and half miles in length, goes across Stone Mountain and, because of slope variations, is best traveled from west to east. Other trails, of various lengths, wind to the top of other granite exposures with names like Cedar Rock, Wolf Rock, Buzzard Rock, and Hitching Rock.

The summits of these "rocks" of-

John Widman

A rock climber tries an ascent up the sheer rock face of Stone Mountain. The steep, sloping granite is one of the premiere challenges in the Southeast for climbers.

Jane Rohling

Hikers pass the chimney of an old farmstead (left), evidence of the widespread farming that once took place around Stone Mountain. Over seventeen miles of designated trout waters (right) lie within the park boundaries.

fer spectacular views of the surrounding countryside. They also present the curious observer a graphic lesson in the effects of the elements on solid rock that take place over millions of years. Small potholes and craters dot the flatter areas, creating a moonscape appearance. Wet-weather springs continue to carve troughs in the granite while lichens cling tenaciously to the weathering gray rock.

Three waterfalls are located on Big Sandy Creek, and are only accessible by trail. Beauty Falls, or Upper Falls as it is often called, is a spectacular site where Big Sandy slides down a nearly vertical granite face over 200 feet high. Farther down Big Sandy, you encounter Middle Falls and Lower Falls.

Caution should always be taken on any of the hiking trails and near the waterfalls. They are often steep and rocky, with slick areas caused by running or splashing water. Proper hiking footwear is advised

and steeper rocky ledges avoided. Hikers on high places should also be constantly aware that others might be below them and never throw or dislodge rocks that might tumble down the slope.

As Joe and I continued our trip through the park it was apparent that, amidst all the improvements that were being made, Stone Mountain State Park retained the rural "feel" of the area. Abandoned farms complete with houses and outbuildings were scattered throughout the park. "Three of the park's four permanent full-time rangers live in houses that have come into park ownership when the adjoining land was purchased and added to the park," Joe said. Several rock chimneys stood as silent reminders of the rugged people who made a living farming and logging the area during past generations.

Trout fishing is the next biggest attraction at the park after rock climbing. Over seventeen miles of designated trout waters lie within the park boundaries, and over the years Joe Mickey has spent many hours assisting the park with the management of the trout fishing.

"Garden Creek, Widow Creek, and the parts of Big Sandy Creek that are inside the park are designated as 'Native Trout Water' where only single hook artificial lures may be used," Joe said as we stopped to ask a fisherman about his success that day. "There are special creel and size limits, and anglers should check regulations before going. Rainbow and brown trout dominate the lower parts of the streams while brook trout inhabit the higher, cooler stretches of water." The fisherman had three rainbow trout that, to Joe, were obviously stocked fish.

"The East Prong of the Roaring River, the stream we're beside now, runs beside much of the park road," Joe continued. "It is a stocked stream. For this reason the East Prong is heavily fished, particularly during the early part of the season which runs from early April each year through February of the next year.

"One trout stream in Stone Mountain State Park is being managed as a fish-for-fun stream and special regulations apply. Bullhead Creek and its upper tributary Rich Mountain Creek are divided into eight sections and fishermen can only fish their assigned stretch of water. The project has proven quite popular with fly-fishing enthusiasts and is a great place to teach or practice fly-fishing techniques," Joe concluded.

We ate supper that night at a picnic table under a large apple tree in front of the park office. When we left we could see the area fill with deer. They munched on the early falling apples. Besides the abundant and visible deer herd, other wildlife species can be seen at Stone Mountain. A colony of beavers has created several ponds inside the park on the lower part of the East Prong of the Roaring River, creating excellent habitat for many birds and animals including wood ducks. Buzzards are often seen circling the rocky peaks while at lower altitudes hawks circle the abandoned fields searching for food.

One strange sight sometimes seen by hikers around Stone Mountain is a small herd of goats. Once part of a herd owned by James Hutchinson, the goats run wild around the Hutchinson homeplace which still stands at the southern base of the mountain. After the family left the area, the goats took up on the rocky dome and a few descendants still can be observed at times walking the steep slopes.

As Joe and I left Stone Mountain State Park that summer's night, I thought back on the entire afternoon. I remembered the rock climbers, trout fishermen, hikers, photographers, campers, picnickers, and sightseers. It was obvious that Stone Mountain was no longer a secret. Perhaps someday soon that Cub Scout den mother from Forsyth County will plead with me to keep quiet about Stone Mountain. "It's a secret," I can hear her saying, "And we want to keep it that way!"

Fishing for Ice Age Trout

As I begin, it appears that I'll finish writing this around midnight. In a day of wrapping up odds and ends before a vacation, it was one of the odds that didn't get ended. Shortly before daylight in the morning, my son Scott and I will drop this off at the office and head west. Five hours later I'll take off my watch and put it in the glove compartment. Then, I'll turn up the single-lane dirt road that climbs over what the locals call the staircase. When we drop into the valley on the far side, we'll be home.

I've been coming to these remote mountains for about twenty-five years to fish for trout, explore the ancient trails, and taste a sense of history. In some parts of these hills, you can move in and out of the last century by simply taking the right road, entering an old church, or buying a Cheerwine in a village grocery.

The tiny cabin I stay in was built out of timbers strewn down the gorge by the 1916 flood. The furniture—a bed, chair, and table—was made by an old man who built what he and his neighbors needed with a water-driven saw. If you needed a bedroom suite, you brought him a picture out of Sears & Roebuck and he'd start looking for the right tree to cut. Resting on the rafters of his shop was a handsome walnut coffin he made for himself years before he died—kept his "likker" in it, they said, although I find it hard to believe he kept any whiskey around long enough to store it. He died in the 1960s, and his abandoned house finally fell in a few years ago. Last year, Scott and I found what was left of his "A" Model rusting away in a thick clump of rhododendron. Today, it's hard to imagine how he ever got it up the steep two-mile trail to the Forest Service road.

I guess I don't need to tell you that I love this part of the state, and I have spent my share of spare time fishing its trout streams. Years ago, in that first flush of discovery when the soul is possessed by salmonids, my fellow anglers and I would leave Raleigh in the middle of the night, arrive at dawn, and fish until dark, then drive five hours back home and work the next day. There was literally no price we wouldn't pay for an hour on a trout stream, and that kind of obsession is so rich and wonderful that you feel obliged to try to share it with your children.

Of course, you can't really transfer an obsession, and especially not from parent to child. There is a natural barrier that seems to ensure that few, if any, offspring will acquire the identical interests of their fathers and mothers. Indeed, children are far more likely to gravitate to an opposite extreme, driven perhaps only to express their own identity. Given that general rule, you'd probably expect any offspring of mine to be a mathematician living in a metropolitan penthouse and reading only fashion magazines and *TV Guide*. Okay, so I exaggerate a little.

Actually, in a selfish way, I've been luckier than most. My kids have their own obsessions—which is as it should be—but they also like to share mine.

So it is that this afternoon Scott and I will park the car, string up our fly rods, and stick peanut butter and jelly sandwiches in our vests. Then, we'll begin to walk. The first mile along this particular creek has a fading trail, but, above the falls, the trail peters out and you have to stay in the creek or climb high up the steep banks to the ridge line above the thick laurel "hells" to find enough room to walk.

We'll worry about the lack of a trail later. Meanwhile, we'll begin to fish this tiny tributary above the falls and stay in the creek until it's little more than a trickle. We may catch twenty to thirty trout apiece, but it's unlikely that any will be longer than about eight inches.

These are brook trout, remnants of the ice ages, and the only native gamefish in these remote headwaters. Both the brown and rainbow trout are latecomers, first stocked in North Carolina streams in the late 1800s. Indeed, even the native brookie is a char rather than trout.

That alone makes them special, but there is more to it than that. These trout can exist only in the purest environment where water temperatures average 55 to 65 degrees Fahrenheit. Today, such conditions exist largely in the small headwaters of some—not all—streams. Thus, to me the brook trout is yet another link with this region's history—clinging somewhat precariously to an existence that seems too fragile to last.

For us, fishing this kind of water is at least as much ritual as it is pure fun. The fish are tiny jewels of dark mottled green with pale blue spots touched lightly in the center with scarlet. Their fins are flags of black, red, and white. Getting to these fish is the only difficult part. Catching them is easy, and they're also good to eat, although we never keep any.

In a wistful way, all of this is connected. It is the pleasure of fishing with a son, a sharing of history, and the visceral gratification of using a skill. But it is also the satisfaction of knowing that an appreciation for all of this is being passed to at least one more generation. It is, after all, the only protection any of us can afford to the things we have cared about.

If our children do not have an opportunity to learn the value of such things, they will have no

Jim Dean

incentive to protect them and pass them on to their own children. It may be the best inheritance we can leave, and, having said that, I'm on my way west. In five hours, we'll be catching brookies and passing the torch.—*Jim Dean*

Rambling the Uwharries

JANE ROHLING

In the heart of the Carolina Piedmont lie the skeletal remains of one of the oldest mountain ranges on the Eastern Seaboard. The eroded remnants of these ancient mountains now barely reach 1,000 feet into the sky, but they most likely towered a great deal higher. If these aged mountains could talk, they would unveil 500 million years of history, reaching back to their violent volcanic origin, when the sea floor ruptured and spewed forth wave after wave of molten lava, until new islands rose above the waters. In time the earth became still, and the wind and water began the tedious task of wearing down what the volcanoes had built up.

The worn remains of these ancient mountains are known as the Uwharries today. Most people believe the name was given to the area by one of the many Indian tribes that lived here, but its meaning is not known. In 1701 John Lawson forded a river called "Heighwaree" near present-day Asheboro, a good source for millstones, he said. In the middle 1700s, European settlers used these stones to help them build

Slate was once mined in the Uwharries and used to make flagstones, roofing materials, and gravestones.

Jane Rohling

their new lives. Many of their descendants remain in Randolph, Montgomery, and Stanly counties to this day, along with a rich heritage of dams, gristmills, covered bridges, old homeplaces, and family graveyards. The crumbling remains of the great Carolina gold rush also lie in these mountains.

In March 1983 a new chapter was written in the story of these mountains that has already spanned eons. The U.S. Forest Service announced

an administration proposal to sell about 6,000,000 acres of national forest land. Included on the giant auction block were 41,879 acres of the Uwharrie National Forest—nearly 90 percent of the state's newest national forest, established in 1961. The news spread in North Carolina like fire in a dry season, spurring immediate opposition from almost every segment of the population. Quietly the proposal sank out of sight. Today most believe the Uwharrie National Forest is safe from large-scale dismemberment.

I became curious about the Uwharries as these events unfolded, and traveled through these ancient mountains, talking to the friendly people who live there and learning about the cultural and natural history of the area. I'd like to share my Uwharrie rambles with you, and urge you to experience these mountains for yourself.

April 10, 1983. My first guide in the Uwharries was Bill Donnan, an artist for the State Zoo in nearby Asheboro. Photographer Kay Frazier was also along. The three of us spent a beautiful April day hiking

Jane Rohling

Barnes Creek flows beneath Jumping-Off Rock. Hikers will enjoy the scenery of this Piedmont national forest while exploring sections of the more than 50 miles of trails.

and photographing spring in the mountains.

Most of the day was spent hiking a little of the Uwharrie Trail on Dark Mountain, beginning at the parking area on State Road (SR) 1306 between Flint Ridge and Ophir in north-central Montgomery County. The Uwharrie Trail, which has been designated as a National Recreation Trail, is a marked footpath that follows the crests and ridges of the Uwharries for about thirty-four miles. It was pioneered in 1968 in Randolph County by Scoutmaster Joe Moffitt and some Asheboro Boy Scouts, but the U.S. Forest Service and many other interested groups have contributed to its development and maintenance.

Driving through the Uwharries it's sometimes hard to tell where the mountains are, but as soon as you start hiking the steep, rocky trail on Dark Mountain you'll know you've found them. The view from the top of Dark Mountain overlooks acres of forests dotted with an occasional small farmhouse or bright green

field. It may not be breathtaking but it certainly is peaceful.

After following the ridgeline for a while we descended the south side of the mountain, cut cross-country through a valley dotted with wildflowers, and began an upward climb again. Suddenly, huge monoliths of stone loomed up before us, jutting straight up out of the hillside. Now I knew why Bill liked this place so well—the rocks in front of us could have served as models for giant rocks he sculpts for the natural habitats at the State Zoo. They are rocks of the Carolina Slate Belt called rhyolite, a very hard, erosion-resistant material that caps nearly all of the higher mountains of the Uwharrie Range, creating formations geologists refer to as "monadnocks."

Leaving the stone giants behind, we returned to SR 1306 just east of our starting point by way of a gravel logging road, which ends near the bridge over Barnes Creek. Jumping-off Rock is just a little farther east and on the other side of SR 1306. The view from Jumping-off Rock

looking over Barnes Creek is beautiful—both from the top looking down and from the bottom looking up, but I wouldn't recommend jumping off!

September 10–11, 1983. On a pleasant early fall day, Kay Frazier and I set out for the Uwharries accompanied by my two dogs. This time our destination was the Birkhead Mountains Wilderness Area, 5,586 roadless acres in the northern part of the Uwharrie National Forest. According to Julie Moore, a botanist with the state's Natural Heritage Program, the Birkhead Mountains are very important ecologically as an extensive preserve of mature upland hardwood forests, representative of minimally disturbed natural Piedmont habitats.

A hike into the Birkhead section from the south begins near the once-flourishing community of Strieby. We cheerfully started up the trail but quickly decided that early September is still too hot for backpacking. When we reached the North Prong of Hannah's Creek, we

North Carolina Division of Parks and Recreation

Five hundred million years of wind and weather have eroded these ancient mountains into the soft swells of landscape known today as the Uwharries.

waded into the stream and sat down in the cooling water.

Joe Moffitt's book, *An Afternoon Hike into the Past*, is filled with Uwharrie folklore, and he tells a story of two brothers who died from snakebites on Hannah's Creek. Legend has it that the friendly ghost

of one of the brothers roams the mountains still, warning hikers and hunters when poisonous snakes are near. Another story tells of an old prospector who found gold in the area and in his excitement headed for the nearest booze hall to celebrate. Unfortunately, when he got

head plantation, 3.3 miles from our starting point, we were beginning to feel the weight of our overstuffed packs. Hiking this section of the trail from south to north involves a lot more uphill hiking than down—a fact we grumbled about Saturday but thanked the Lord for Sunday.

A little farther up the trail, at Fairview on the southern crest of Cooler's Knob, a side trail leads to Rush's Mine and Fern Valley, but we were too tired by then to investigate. According to an Indian legend, the ghosts of five braves and a mysterious white deer roam this valley.

Fairview is listed as a campsite in Nicholas Hancock's *Guide to the Uwharrie Trails*, but "unless you have an affinity for sleeping on rock and steep terrain" Hancock doesn't recommend staying here. We agreed and pushed our weary feet to the next site. Camp #1-B, also called the Joe Moffitt Camp, is located 5.3 miles from our starting point in a valley just off the main trail. And a welcome site it was! After a cool drink of spring water, a gourmet meal, and some quiet conversation by the fire, we settled in for the night under clear skies and a canopy of gently swaying trees. Kay was asleep in no time, but before I drifted off I was treated to the eerie sound of two or three screech owls calling to each other from the surrounding hills.

May 26, 1984. My next ramble was to Coggins Mine, a little west of Dark Mountain in northwestern Montgomery County. I was greeted by "Catfish" Spivey and his wife, whose father came to work in Coggins Mine in 1916. Now they watch over the property for its owners. They said it would be all right for me to go in and take a few pictures, but as I left they said, "You know

about snakes, don't you?" I had worn my boots that day as a precaution, but I was hoping the friendly ghost that warns people when snakes are near was on duty.

Several mines were worked along the Uwharrie River late in the nineteenth century, and the Coggins Mine, now a ghost town, was once the site of bustling activity. It was the most important mine in the state from 1915 until it was closed in 1926.

In 1799 a Cabarrus County farmer's boy found a seventeen-pound gold nugget, the first significant record of gold found in America. The boy's father showed the rock to a silversmith who said it was of no value, so it was used in the family's home as a doorstop for three years before its true value was realized. The discovery touched off the first gold rush in America. In his book about the Carolina gold rush, Bruce Roberts says, "The miners went up and down the streams of the Piedmont area with the speed of boll weevils crossing a cotton field, and multiplying just as fast." Most of the excitement of those gold rush years has long since left the Uwharries, but the legends live on, and there are a few places you can still go to pan for gold, although a matchhead-sized nugget is more likely to be found than a seventeen-pound doorstop. The Cotton Patch Mine, located about two miles east of New London in Stanly County, is open to the public for panning.

The present owners of the mine, Royal and Pat Dean, bought it last November. They moved down here from a Chicago suburb, where their friends presented them with a farewell gift of a "gold" brick (made of painted lead) stamped, "All that glitters is not gold." Like that first

over his drunk, he couldn't remember where his strike was, except that it was in a ledge of rock on Hannah's Creek, just north of an old dam. The mother lode has never been found, so keep your gold pan handy and your eyes open.

By the time we reached the Birk-

Photographs by Jane Rohling

Coggins Mine (top, left) is now a ghost town, but in the early twentieth century it produced gold, lead, and zinc. Town Creek Indian Mound (top, right) is an important archaeological site excavated in this century. The house (above) was the residence of Dr. Francis J. Kron, first medical doctor in Stanly County. It is now part of Morrow Mountain State Park.

Carolina gold nugget almost two hundred years ago, it will be used as a doorstop.

May 28, 1984. In late May I visited the Town Creek Indian Mound, on a bluff overlooking the Little River near the Montgomery County–Richmond County line. At this site lived a group of Indians related to the Creek Nation of Alabama and Georgia who had immigrated into the area between A.D. 1450 and 1500, driving out the former Siouan inhabitants. The Pee Dee Indians, as the Creeks became known, stayed in the area for only two hundred years before mysteriously disappearing, leaving behind a ceremonial center that was used by all the clans of the tribe.

Scientific study of the Town Creek Indian Mound began in 1936, and archaeologists have exposed much of the once obscure culture of the Creek Indians. The mound has been excavated and rebuilt, and the major temple, minor temple or priests' dwelling, and one of the thatched-roof burial huts have been reconstructed. The site is now a State Historic Site, open to the public at scheduled hours.

By the time I was ready to leave Town Creek, a light drizzle had turned into a downpour and threatening sounds of thunder could be heard to the west. I had planned to canoe the Uwharrie River that afternoon, but decided to change my plans and do my rambling by car. From Town Creek I headed northwest on N.C. 73, and a few miles beyond Pee Dee I turned north.

A short distance up SR 1150, I discovered an abandoned slate quarry along the banks of Cedar Creek, part of the Volcanic-Sedimentary Sequence of the Carolina Slate Belt. Many millions of years ago, volcanic ash settled into muddy sediments in the bottom of a calm, shallow inland sea, forming bands of light and dark silt and clay materials, which later consolidated under tremendous pressure to form shale and slate. The harder, blue-gray slate has been used extensively in the Uwharrie area for building flagstones and roofing slate—and for gravestones.

Traveling north on N.C. 109, you will pass a sign for the Uwharrie Wildlife Area, which is managed primarily for deer by the U.S. Forest Service and the North Carolina Wildlife Resources Commission. It is a popular area for hunting, fishing, camping, hiking, and motorcycle riding. Continuing northward on N.C. 109, you are treated to a scenic vista. Several peaks of the ancient Uwharries can be seen to the east across an open field.

It wasn't getting any earlier, and I still wanted to make it to the Morrow Mountain State Park, so I got back in the car and headed north and then west, then south around Badin Lake, devouring an ice cream bar for dinner on the way. Driving up Morrow Mountain I finally had the feeling I was really in the mountains. The road is steep and winding and even has a hairpin turn. This is among the highest peaks in the Uwharrie range, reaching 938 feet above sea level and offering fine vistas in several directions. The top of the mountain is littered with millions of slivers of rhyolite, left by the Indians who mined the rock here for tools and weapons.

The park offers a variety of visitor attractions and services, including interpretive facilities, family and group camping, picnicking, boat rentals, a swimming pool, and hiking and bridle trails. One of the park's most notable features is the reconstructed homeplace of Francis J. Kron, the first educated medical doctor in Stanly County. He practiced here from 1834 until his death in 1883, often traveling all day on horseback to treat one patient and charging only one dollar per call plus mileage. As his own health declined with age, the doctor continued to treat patients. He made sick calls in his wagon, lying on a feather mattress, with a servant doing the driving.

In addition to practicing medicine, Dr. Kron conducted many horticultural experiments, and the Kron homeplace was a showplace of many types of flowers, fruit trees, vines, and shrubs. A very large old magnolia tree and several tall cedars grace the property today, along with a variety of fruit and nut trees.

On this Memorial Day evening, one hundred years after Dr. Kron's passing, I was alone with the memory of one of the most highly regarded settlers of Stanly County. The sweet smell of flowers filled the air and the call of a pileated woodpecker occasionally broke the silence. Dr. Kron must have enjoyed many peaceful evenings like this sitting on his front porch. The only thing missing was the distant sound of water tumbling over the great falls of the Yadkin River which the Doctor could hear from a mile away—the river was impounded after the doctor died.

The days I have spent rambling around the Uwharries have been filled with a sense of appreciation for the rich natural and cultural history of these tired old mountains. There's a lot more to see, a lot more to learn, and I plan to return often. There's something here for everyone to enjoy and plenty of people working hard to preserve this part of North Carolina's heritage for the generations that follow us.

A Kinship in Stone

It was an impulsive act. The August sun was falling into the tops of the distant trees, and the last light bathed the fields in a warm glow. At the crest of the hill, I pulled off the dirt path, opened the car door, and stepped out of the artificial cool into 90-degree heat. These rolling fields have not changed in the more than forty years I have known them. I have hunted quail here with a grandfather and father, and more recently with a son.

With no particular goal, I walked between the tall tobacco plants kicking up grasshoppers that soared ahead toward a large field of corn that seemed to fold along the contours like some giant yellow quilt. Off to my right, a quarter of a mile beyond a path, I could see an abandoned house shrouded in vines, its dark windows overlooking a good stand of soybeans that rimmed a small pond. In every direction, the view was familiar. My grandfather, dead since 1968, could walk the same row today and see nothing different. I think that would please him.

As I turned back toward the car, and paused for a last look, I noticed a triangular shape next to my foot. I reached down, half expecting it to be a clod of dry dirt. But no, it was a bit more substantial, an ancient spear point of carefully crafted stone with delicate side notches and serrated edges that came to a sharp point. It was so nearly dark by then that, in order to see the shape better, I held it between my thumb and forefinger and raised it to the dying light. It was an act I recognized immediately as being symbolic—as symbolic as it was accidental.

Here I stood in a tobacco field in 1985, the first human being to pick up this bit of stone in something like seven thousand years. For me, it was a moment of almost overpowering kinship between all humans who have visited, used, profited from, and perhaps loved this particular small plot of land. There seemed little difference between a grandfather dead nearly twenty years and an Indian dead thousands of years. Or me, or those who would follow. I also realized why it was important to walk into the familiarity of that field and take pleasure in such continuity wherever I might find it.

That short incident came to mind again over a month later in what, at first, seemed an unlikely place. I had traveled east to the town of Columbia, capital of Tyrrell County. With a population of something like 1,000, it is the largest town in the county (I think the second largest is Gum Neck). I first saw Columbia when it had few paved streets, and the hotel (now gone) charged two dollars per night. To get there you had to pass a succession of junked cars marked "Eat At Carley's Cafe" for twenty miles in either direction on U.S. 64.

Columbia was my kind of town, and Tyrrell County was a sportsman's dream from Fort Landing, the Frying Pan, and Gum Neck on the Alligator west through the pocosin and swamps to the eastern shore of Phelps Lake. Even with the passage of years and the coming of superfarms, peat mining, and a lot of other changes, the area still retains a lot of its wild appeal.

While I was visiting, we sailed out of Columbia down the Scuppernong River into Albemarle Sound. I was pleased to see that the shoreline of this handsome, blackwater river still looked like the kind of place where you'd want to watch your step. In the middle of the sound, the wind fell out completely as it invariably does when I go sailing. Indeed, the entire sound as far as you could see in any direction was slick calm ("slick cam," as they still say in certain areas along the coast).

We turned loose the sheets, let the boat drift, and jumped over the side. Around us in the water were tiny stingless jellyfish which some people call "phosphors." They brushed lightly against our legs as we drifted on boat cushions. What reminded me of the spear point was the sudden realization as I floated there that I could not see exactly where sky met water in the distance. Indeed, unless I turned to look at the boat or my companions, I could not see anything man-made whatsoever. Here was one of the few places left in North Carolina where an Indian who had lived thousands of years ago might look around and see nothing unfamiliar.

For more than a month, I had thought of that spear point as a gift from the past, a symbol of kinship, and a reminder that we are only temporary keepers of the land and water. Now, all at once, it also seemed like a warning.—*Jim Dean*

Jim Dean

Two Days in John Green's Swamp

L A W R E N C E   S.   E A R L E Y

Up Driving Creek

We had been pushing hard up Driving Creek, deep in Brunswick County's Green Swamp, when the canoe ran headup against a half-submerged log. It was a nice juniper log with the smooth cut of the saw visible at one end. It must have been snorkeling in the creek for the last fifty years or so, ever since the last of the big stands of juniper were logged out of this area.

It stopped us now on this warm March afternoon. There were three of us in the canoe—Manley Fuller, Sharon Grubbs, and myself. Our plan had been to push up Driving Creek to the source, a place known as "the soups." There were alligators there, we had heard. I wasn't as keen as Manley about this venture. Manley is used to alligators, having done his master's research on the alligator population at Lake Ellis, and having "wet his feet," as he put it, on Costa Rican crocodiles last summer. Alligators make me nervous. So do water moccasins. The last thing any human being had said to us that afternoon was, "Now, watch out for

moccasins. In this warm weather you're sure to run into them." That we had made it this far without one falling into the boat was an oversight I felt sure would soon be corrected.

"Guess we'll have to turn back," I said hopefully. Manley was delicately toeing the obstacle. It was not budging and I was glad.

We were approximately 135 miles southeast of Raleigh, 25 miles southwest of Wilmington, and 5 miles north of Supply. By our Green Swamp compass we were, as the crow flies, 7 miles southeast of Big Curve, 5 miles southwest of Big Bay Ridge, and 3 miles south of Honey Island. We were also about 2 feet from a thorny tangle of bay forest, titi (pronounced "tie tie"), and catbrier that had scratched our arms, snatched our hats, and punctured our good humors for the better part of an hour and a half. Above us a wrathful sky was boiling.

The swamp could use the rain, I thought. Two years before, on a broiling June day, I had seen the Green Swamp for the first time and frankly I was disappointed. I had ex-

pected something primeval and haunting, like the Okefenokee Swamp with its acres of standing water and cypress trees. What I saw was parched scrub land and pine plantations, more like desert than swamp. Nevertheless, the Green Swamp is considered one of the most valuable natural areas in North Carolina, with the best remaining examples in the Carolinas of pine savannahs, bay forests, and pocosin. Longtime residents will tell you that it's one of the most game-rich areas in the state, with good populations of bear, bobcat, deer, and raccoon. It's got every one of the fourteen carnivorous plants found in the state, and it's also got some stands of the rare Atlantic white cedar, or juniper as it's commonly called. A lot of people treasure the Green Swamp, including the folks at the North Carolina Nature Conservancy who have acquired 13,850 acres for a nature preserve.

Manley Fuller was stomping the juniper log with abandon even as thunder sounded. Suddenly the log broke from its underwater snag and bobbed gently in the black water.

The Green Swamp shelters all fourteen of North Carolina's insectivorous plants, including the yellow pitcher plant.

"All right!" cried Manley.

"What's our plan if it starts to lightning?" I piped.

"We'll make out. It's so thick in here the rain'll never get to us."

"But we're in an aluminum canoe!"

"Then we'll just get out of the canoe." And he shot me a glance that said as clearly as words, "You've got a very unhealthy imagination."

He grabbed a handful of sweet bay and yanked the canoe over the log. As we pushed forward, deeper into the Green Swamp, I listened to the thunder and then, on my right, through the tangled pocosin . . . did I conjure it up? . . . I seemed to see a writhing row of water moccasins, their cottony mouths gaping open like faces in a boys' choir.

An unhealthy imagination? Me?

John Green's Field

As a man of science, Ebenezer Emmons's imagination was nothing if not healthy and progressive. And yet in the 1850s, as the nineteenth-century geologist studied the Green Swamp and other eastern North Carolina wetlands, it's likely that his idea of "swamp" was similar to the idea of "wilderness" that had been current ever since the first European settlements in America. Quaking at the edge of the great North American forest, seventeenth-century Massachusetts Puritans described the dark miles of woods as a "howling wilderness," a "hideous wilderness." In much the same way, people recoiled from swamps. "Dismal" swamps, they were called, and not only the one that retains that name today. Unproductive and useless, swamps were wastelands, the source of a deadly vapor which was

thought to cause fever and death. It would be several decades and a continent away before the mosquito was correctly identified as the cause of malaria.

Thus when Ebenezer Emmons saw the 140 square miles of Green Swamp, he coolly took note of its vast forests of cypress and gum, the Atlantic white cedar, the longleaf pines, and the beech, maple, ash, and poplars. Without benefit of an aerial view, he correctly surmised the swamp's round shape. Although he didn't comment on it, he probably understood that part of the swamp was drained by the Waccamaw River, while the southern half sloped gently toward the Cape Fear River.

And having considered the forests and other vegetation, he imaginatively swept them off the map. The soil, he wrote in his report, was superb! "The soil was found to be much richer than I anticipated. . . . The earthy matter is as fine as that of the Onslow or Hyde county lands. . . . Hence the cost of drainage should be incurred, and these valuable lands reclaimed."

In place of the cypress-gum forests, he saw crops of corn. Cash-paying cotton or wheat grew where the longleaf pines waved in the summer breezes. The squatters who had made baskets on the sandy islands in the interior of the swamp became industrious farmers, and floating over the scene was a pale blue haze of progressive nineteenth-century chimney smoke.

Such was Emmons's vision, and such was the vision of men several generations before him. For the forest that the geologist saw in the 1850s had remained essentially unchanged since 1795, when three tracts of land totaling over 170,000

acres of the 200,000-acre Green Swamp were deeded to three men for the scant price of $7,100. What Benjamin Rowell, William Collins, and Stephen Williams had in mind with so much land is not known, but agriculture was then on the march up the Cape Fear River and no doubt this figured in the plans of these men.

Though practically impenetrable much of the year, the Green Swamp was well known to many travelers. It had been called "John Green's Field" at first, after an early settler, then "John Green's Swamp," "Green's Swamp," and finally "Green Swamp." Lake Waccamaw, on the northern border of the swamp, was an especial favorite of travelers. In 1734 the botanist John Bartram visited the lake, "as I had heard so much about it." Pushing inland from a Cape Fear River plantation, he swatted "large musquetoes" as he crossed pine barrens and swamp to get to the lake, which he found "the pleasantest place that ever I saw in my life." When his son, William, visited in 1773, he, too, was impressed, finding "the situation delightful."

It was a point of view that the Indian inhabitants would have shared, for archaeological evidence shows that the land was continually inhabited for several thousand years. And why not? It was thick with bear and deer and wild turkey. John Bartram remarked on the tameness of the deer, which looked on him as if they had never seen another human being.

And it had good soil, according to Ebenezer Emmons. Drain it, he said, and we'd put this unproductive swamp to work.

Easier said than done. What kind of machinery then invented could tackle 200,000 acres of swampland, much of it underwater? What kind of men would take on such a job with such evident dangers? In spite of little nips at its flanks, by the end of the nineteenth century the Green Swamp was just as massive and unsavory an obstacle to settlement and communication as it was at the century's beginning. The swampland forests that John Bartram had seen in 1734 and that Ebenezer Emmons had noted in 1860 were still pretty much intact.

Then in 1907 the Waccamaw Lumber Company lay siege to the Green Swamp. It railed in great steam skidders and it built a giant sawmill in Bolton. It laid 18 miles of rail between Bolton and Makatoka, and shorter spurs into the swamp off the main line. They might have called it the "Floating Railroad." Workers cut 8- or 10-inch wide gum logs for crossties, and lay them close together over the wet ground. Waist-high in water and moccasins, gangs of loggers used two-man saws and axes to fell the giant cypress and gum. They skidded out the longleaf pines. They took the maples, the beech, the ash, and the poplar. Flatcars hauled the wood to Bolton, and at night hauled the men to Makatoka where the logging camps were. For thirty-four years they cut virgin timber. When the Waccamaw Lumber Company sold 138,000 acres of the Green Swamp to Riegel Paper Corporation in the 1930s, the forest that Ebenezer Emmons had seen was gone.

By 1914 drainage operations had begun on the cutover land. In one district of 28,000 acres between Lake Waccamaw and Livingston Creek, 44 miles of canals were carved into the quaking soil. Dredgers, 30 feet long and 12 feet wide, driven by coal-fired steam boilers, dug deep into the swamplands. By the late 1930s much of the northern reaches of the swamp had been drained and were being farmed.

It had taken nearly eighty years, but Ebenezer Emmons's vision had almost been realized. The Green Swamp was nearly gone.

Pocosin and Savannah

Manley Fuller has been trying to get me wet for the better part of two days. Yesterday we had grappled with shrub-choked Driving Creek, pulling ourselves along with fistfuls of vegetation until the creek had finally surrendered to the bay shrubs. Earlier today we had waded through muck in order to get into Layman's Pond, a sinkhole in the southern portion of the Green Swamp. I had returned to the car for my hip boots, obeying my undying conviction that there's no need to get your feet wet unless you can't help it. Of course by the time I returned and waded out to the pretty little cypress pond there were Manley and Sharon in the crook of a cypress tree, wet to their waists and smiling a little too smugly for my taste.

And now, midafternoon, with the storm clouds banished by a hot sun, we are about to push off into the pine savannahs—the most fascinating part of the Green Swamp tract that the Nature Conservancy owns. Separating Big Island Savannah, Shoestring Island Savannah and Bean Patch Island Savannah are long fingers of low-lying pocosin, and the rain has made them knee-deep in spots. My hip boots are back in the car again. And Manley is standing by the trail, with that familiar smile on his face. "Well," he is saying in his North Carolina drawl, "we're going to get wet."

I give him a wink. "You're a hard man," I say, and Manley turns and leads the way.

On aerial maps, the 13,850-acre tract acquired by the Nature Conservancy shows up as a broad swath of vegetation. Strikingly absent from this part are the parallel silver scratches that strike east and west on the swamplands to the north—drainage canals. The Nature Conservancy's land, which we are entering here, is practically unaltered, although canals to the north, fire lanes, and Route 211 have changed some of the original drainage patterns. This intact micro-version of the original Green Swamp features three major kinds of plant communities—bay forest, pocosin, and savannah. We ran into the bay forest yesterday as we tested Driving Creek. The pocosin that we're slogging through now consists of thickly growing evergreen shrubs overlying peaty soil. But the savannahs are the most interesting of the plant communities in the Green Swamp, and they are rapidly disappearing from the southeastern landscape. They crop up in the swamp as islands, sandy ridges that drain slowly.

As we break out of the pocosin, my boots streaming and my toes squirting water inside, I take a good look at Big Island Savannah. It's a broad, open area with irregularly spaced longleaf pines thrusting into the sky. A recent fire has swept the understory clear of everything but innumerable clumps of spring-green wiregrass a few inches above the blackened soil. There are scorched pine stumps about six feet high across the broad savannah. Longleaf pine seedlings have bronzed needles. In another two months the floor will be covered with flowers. But now, in early March, the savannahs are merely bright and airy and open, and I can understand why they were once used as pastures.

Although the savannahs have been studied carefully, there is a lot still to be learned about how they work and why certain kinds of things grow there. Elevation and hydroperiod, or the amount of time the vegetation spends in water, have something to do with it. We take a dogleg to the left and angle south where the savannah is being swallowed up by thick pocosin underbrush. Our feet swish through thick golden whorls of unburnt wire grass.

It's hard to tell, but the burned savannah we have been walking on is a ridge. From just about any angle, the savannah looks uniformly flat all around, but there is a slight elevation toward the middle—about one foot's worth—and that seems to make all the difference. At that "lofty" height longleaf pine grows. It will grow there because the savannah is wet in winter and dry in summer, and the longleaf can withstand both extremes. But now as we move toward the edge of the savannah, the vegetation changes. We pass through toothache grass, broomsedge with its wedge-shaped seed tufts. "Look what's happening," observes Manley ahead of me in the afternoon's orange light. "The ground is getting wetter. The longleaf is giving way to pond pines. There's titi, and fetterbrush, too—typical pocosin vegetation." Not twenty-five paces from the higher and drier savannah we're in a wetland.

We begin to find relatively strange adaptations to the wet conditions. "Look—pitcher plants," says Manley. "*Sarracenia flava.*" We have to bend down to see the dried stalks of last summer's pitchers, their tubular leaves still standing straight. These carnivorous plants are thought to have adapted to the nutrient-poor soil by taking nutrients from the bodies of insects that are lured inside their pitchers. There are all kinds of carnivorous plants along the wetter portions of savannahs. All four species of pitcher plant are found in these locations, and some hybrids. So are abundant numbers of Venus's flytraps, two kinds of sundews, two butterworts, and five species of bladderwort—all fourteen carnivorous plant species found in southeastern North Carolina.

The peculiar combination of soil and hydroperiod also produces an extraordinary diversity of other flowering plants. In summer the savannahs bloom with grass pinks, rose pogonias, rosebud orchid, and white-fringed and yellow-fringed orchids. There are milkworts, meadow-beauties, sabatias, snakeroots, trilesas, and goldenrods. Botanists have found over fifty plants in one square meter of savannah, an astonishing figure!

We're now mucking through the lowest point of the pocosin barrier between the savannahs. "You can see why they call these savannahs islands," Manley says as we break out of the pocosin and into the open pastureland once more. "This is Shoestring Island. Across from us there's another pocosin, then it opens up once more to another savannah, Bean Patch Island. Savannah, pocosin, savannah, pocosin—all because of elevation and soil."

And fire. The key to the savannahs is fire. Regular fires keep the understory low and maintain the open, airy effect. Without fires the woody shrubs like dangleberry, wax myrtle, and bitter gallberry would muscle in and take over. The orchids and wildflowers would lose light and disappear. The savannah would turn into a forest dominated by longleaf pines and evergreen shrubs. A woody shrub has no defense against a fire, but wildflowers keep their stems underground and thus they can survive a fire. The pond pine releases its seed only after a fire scorches it, apparently nature's way of ensuring that the seed is dropped into a fertile ash bed with little competition rather than into water where it might not germinate. The seedling of a longleaf pine keeps its bud armored within a thick coat of needles. Fires are essential to the botanical diversity of the savannahs.

We pass several pines that were once used for turpentining. One hundred years ago we might have seen large barrels sitting amidst the wire grass. From May through September, men would gouge V-shaped streaks into the wood. The raw sap would flow down these streaks and into a "box," or a small hollow cut into the wood below. Several times a season the sap would be dipped into the barrels and carted off. We stop by one of the old trees and notice that the deep scar is nearly closed. "Here's a turpentine tree that's about ready to close up," Manley says. "It's good to know they can heal themselves." We see several mounds in this savannah, evidence of the tar kilns that once were constructed here.

The trail to Bean Patch Island slithers through 100 yards of knee-deep muck. I know Manley is enjoying himself. He's far ahead of us. I try to keep pace with Sharon, although I'm extra cautious with cameras strung around my neck.

When we finally emerge Manley is holding out a tiny snake for our inspection. "I found it under the bark

Scattered longleaf pines grow atop sandy savannah islands throughout the Green Swamp. Settlers once tapped the plentiful longleaf for turpentine, much of which was carted to the Waccamaw River and shipped to Georgetown, South Carolina.

of that dead pine," he says, nodding to a fallen log not far away. A baby ring neck snake. "Bark is a real good place to find snakes. Look at the nice yellow belly on this snake!" We push our way through high wire grass. Manley finds a Carolina anole in a tree and spies a gaunt cypress on the far side of the savannah. "Look at that big sucker over there!"

The Green Swamp is rich in wild-life. The longleaf pines in the savan-nahs provide good nesting sites for the endangered red cockaded wood-peckers. While you're looking for its nest holes you might hear the rattle of a canebrake rattlesnake; the wire grass is good habitat for this reptile. Some of the last of North Carolina's truly native white-tailed deer are found in the Green Swamp. Most were killed out of the state near the turn of the century and northern

deer were brought in to boost the dwindling native populations, and have since spread and interbred to dominate the statewide herds. You might still find a native whitetail with a southern drawl here, how-ever. Perhaps that's what we saw earlier today, dead in a ditch by the side of Route 211. Nearly fifty black vultures were sitting in a pine tree nearby, and they flew heavily into the air when we approached. Cautious field workers have avoided making claims that the American alligator is found in the Green Swamp, although they are fairly sure it is. Manley, Sharon, and I know at least two alligators who live in the swamp because we saw them in a drainage ditch north of Driving Creek.

"Here's the trail," Manley is saying.

"Bear? Where is it?" asks Sharon, lagging behind a little and not hearing. She is disappointed when Manley repeats his original statement. "I was hoping we'd see a bear," she says.

The mention of bear reminds me of my conversation with Joe Hufham of Delco not long before. Hufham is a longtime resident of the Green Swamp area and an energetic chronicler of its folk history. In articles for the Whiteville *News-Reporter* and in several books, he's shared stories from a lifetime of logging, trapping, and hunting in the swamp. He told me a story about the time he met a 350-pound bear in the Green Swamp.

"This happened when I was teaching school. I was walking the railroad track out there near Big Ridge, and it was raining. I had on my suitclothes, thick underwear, and a big overcoat, and everything was soaking wet. I was tired. And all of a sudden I heard something whistle. I sort of turned my head back. Not a thing coming.

"It was raining hard. The drops looked like sheets of sleet dropping. I turned my head back and exactly the length of one rail ahead of me stood a three-hundred-and-fifty-pound bear. I knew I couldn't outrun him because a bear can outrun a dog, for a short distance anyway. And something came to me: just

stand still. So I stood there. And the bear challenged me. He had his hind feet and his front feet on the rail and he was shaking his head. My heart was beating so hard I could hear it. He finally got tired of looking at me—he must have looked straight at me for three minutes—and he went on across.

"As tired as I was I didn't want that bear to catch me unarmed again. So I picked up a log that was as big as a crosstie. I picked it up and put it over my shoulder. And I carried that thing to Big Ridge, about three hundred yards, I reckon, before I threw it down. My idea of that was to look bigger, but if he actually come up to me, to throw it on him."

Hufham has had other close calls in the swamp, one time with a cougar. Of course there's no proof that the native species of cougar still exists in the swamp, but like other places in North Carolina cougar sightings are still reported in the Green Swamp. "I heard it said that prior to the coming of the skidders and the locomotives there was many panthers in there killing up many deer in Columbus and Brunswick counties. The logging companies paid such a big bounty they killed them all out. Panthers and wolves."

Wolves? "Now I did know a very old woman—and she's been dead years and years—and she said that they used to hear wolves howling at night."

Hufham remembers stories about Confederate deserters hiding out in the swamp. "There was a camp of them out there in the woods," he said. "They were called 'Scalawags,' and some called them 'Buffaloes.' They had got hold of some Federal uniforms—I reckon they got 'em off of some dead soldiers. And when-

ever Sherman was coming through here they disguised themselves as Federal soldiers. And when Sherman was pillaging and burning, these fellers would ride out, you know, and get all the valuables and stuff just like Sherman's crowd, and they'd go back to the Green Swamp."

The Green Swamp is rich in stories like that. Stories of smart bears and alligators that hunt raccoons from the bottom of pits, like sanddoodles.

But on this unseasonably warm March afternoon, with the warm light of sunset staining the pocosin toward the west, we do not see any black bears or Confederate ghosts. The snakes are still lethargic and the tough men who worked up to their waists in Green Swamp muck are long gone. We are three visitors from Raleigh making our acquaintances with a distinguished bit of North Carolina landscape. Manley is ecstatic as we head back the way we came. "Tell you what," he says, "whenever I feel bad I just oughta come down to the Green Swamp. I just can't get enough of this place!"

Editors' Note: In 1974, the Department of the Interior designated a 24,800-acre portion of the Green Swamp as a National Natural Landmark. Three years later, Federal Paper Board Company, Inc., which had acquired much of the swamp from Riegel Paper Corporation, donated 13,850 acres of the Landmark property to the North Carolina Nature Conservancy "to be held in perpetuity for the people of North Carolina." In December 1986, Federal Paper Board donated an additional 1,872 acres to the Conservancy. The highlight of the donation was 92 acres of longleaf pine–wire grass savannah called Big Island Savannah.

Mattamuskeet Memories

JIM DEAN

Along U.S. 264, the miles click off as you head past Pantego and Belhaven, crossing the dark cypress and marsh-rimmed creeks and skirting the edges of massive black fields that stretch flat to the horizon. By the time you have passed the workboats moored in the backwaters of Pungo River and Rose Bay and swung north of Swanquarter towards Mattamuskeet, you can already sense that this land has a permanence about it. Approached down the 75-mile swamp-bordered stretch of U.S. 264 in the opposite direction from Manns Harbor, or down N.C. 94 from Columbia, the feeling of delicious isolation is even greater.

This land between Albemarle and Pamlico clings stubbornly to its wild origins, and the lake that lies in the belly of Hyde County has done more than its share of clinging. Mattamuskeet is the largest of several sizable natural lakes in this unique "peninsula." Indeed, at approximately 18 miles long and 6 miles wide and at 40,000 acres, it is the largest natural lake in the state, although it averages only about 2½ feet deep.

The old pump station at Mattamuskeet housed the Corliss engine steam pumps that drained the lake in the 1920s before the project was abandoned. The station later served as a hunting lodge until 1972.

Larry Ditto

Mattamuskeet's origin has been debated for centuries—some say a meteor created it. But the most likely explanation is found in Indian legend which recalls a severe drought and a fire that burned for thirteen moons. Given the vast deposits of peat that lie in the lake bed and surrounding land, such a fire is certainly likely, and it could have left a similar shallow depression. Furthermore, in the years following a fire until waters ultimately filled this giant hole, the area might literally have been a dust bowl. Perhaps it is not ironic that the Indian name for this place translates as "dry dust."

Some of the earliest white settlers in this region saw far more than a lake here. To them, the potentially rich farmland beneath the shallow waters held great promise. As early as 1789, a board was appointed to study ways to drain the lake, and, in 1835, the North Carolina legislature authorized drainage even though no funds were appropriated. The state tried again in 1909 with a $500,000 bond issue, and canals were dug and a pump station erected, but heavy rains thwarted the attempt.

After two private efforts met similar fates, an eighty-one-year-old multimillionaire, August Hecksher, took over the project in 1925 and installed four centrifugal Corliss engine steam pumps in the station. Capable of pumping 250,000 gallons of water per minute, all canals in the lake bottom could be pumped dry in a day. Encouraged, Hecksher laid out the town of New Holland, built highways and a railroad line, and put fifty-one tractors into the drained lake to plant rice, buckwheat, popcorn, lespedeza, barley, celery, asparagus, rye, oats, flax, potatoes, and the largest acreage of soybeans in the world.

At first, conditions seemed perfect, but Hecksher did not reckon

Swans rest on the shimmering mirror of Mattamuskeet at sunrise (opposite page). The 40,000-acre lake in Hyde County is a haven for an astonishing number of waterfowl. Picturesque canals are common around the lake and in the surrounding area (above).

Larry Ditto

A snowy egret takes wing gracefully from cover along the shoreline of the lake.

on Mattamuskeet's relentless capability for self-preservation. Rains, wind tides, and a pumping system that proved unreliable were Hecksher's undoing. True, there were bumper crops, but almost invariably the harvesting machinery became mired, and, what the water didn't rot, the insects ate. In 1933 Hecksher called it quits, and a year later the federal government purchased the lake and allowed it to refill.

With the establishment of the Mattamuskeet National Wildlife Refuge in 1934 on the 40,000-acre lake and 10,000 surrounding acres of land, the area rapidly became a waterfowl haven and a sportsman's paradise. The shallow lake formed a huge natural waterfowl impoundment that attracted increasingly vast numbers of ducks and geese which fed not only on the rich freshwater grasses in the lake, but also flew into the surrounding fields to feed on corn.

It was the Canada geese, however, that brought Mattamuskeet a decade of international fame as the goose-hunting capital of the world. During the first winter after the lake refilled, some 12,000 Canadas migrated to the lake, but, by 1937, that total had climbed to 48,000 wintering geese. In 1939, the U.S. Fish and Wildlife Service entered into a cooperative agreement with the North Carolina Department of Conservation and Development to operate controlled hunts in 36 blinds on portions of the refuge. Later, the North Carolina Wildlife Resources Commission conducted these hunts. The old pump station was reopened as a hunting lodge. Numbers of wintering geese oscillated from a low of 25,000 geese to as many as 90,000 through the next dozen or so years, but, in 1958, the population hit

105,000. During the peak years from 1958 until 1964, the wintering population ranged up to as many as 131,000; although it began to drop in the mid-1960s, it remained high. Mattamuskeet's heyday, however, ended rather abruptly in 1968 when the number of visiting geese dropped from 70,000 to 21,000.

Many experts speculate that this decline was almost certain to happen, and that this was an unnaturally high cycle for such a relatively small area. At any rate, with the wintering Canada population hovering at around 20,000 geese per year, the last public hunts were held during the 1972–73 season, and the lodge closed. In the past dozen years, the average number of Canadas wintering on the lake has been about 16,000 (17,000 wintered there in 1985, but only 12,000 were on the lake the previous year).

Hunting pressure both on the lake and on private fields and impoundments around the lake apparently played only a small role in the declining numbers of geese that visited the area. Waterfowl biologists cite three other reasons. During the late 1960s, farmers in the DelMarVa Peninsula farther north were rapidly converting traditional vegetable crops to corn and soybeans, providing a massive resource of food for geese hundreds of miles closer to their breeding grounds. Meanwhile, farmers in Hyde County, and elsewhere in eastern North Carolina, were switching to early maturing corn crops that were being harvested long before the arrival of the geese each fall. Huge flocks of Canadas en route to North Carolina began to "shortstop" in the DelMarVa Peninsula and winter there. Meanwhile, at Mattamuskeet, the habitat at the

Larry Ditto

lake was maturing naturally, and cattails, shrubs, and even trees began to replace the fertile marshes and grasses that had provided so much food in the refuge itself. Ironically, though the number of wintering geese declined at Mattamuskeet and elsewhere throughout the South, the total population of Canadas in the Atlantic Flyway actually increased and has remained at near-record peaks despite heavy hunting pressure in the new wintering grounds farther north.

For a hunter or waterfowl lover who knew Mattamuskeet during its heyday, a winter visit today to the former goose-hunting capital of the world is a wistful experience. Two years ago, I returned with my son to

Sunlight filters through early morning fog, painting an almost impressionistic scene at one of the many farmhouses in this eastern North Carolina region.

Photographs by Larry Ditto

Mattamuskeet to hunt one of the private impoundments still operated outside the refuge. It was a good hunt, and the area looked pretty much the same. We drove across the eight-mile causeway that splits the lake as I had done with my grandfather, father, and brothers so many years ago, and we visited the old pump station where we had stayed. But something was missing, and it wasn't hard to figure out what it was.

As I stood beside the old pump station, I realized that I could not hear any geese. In fact, except for one lonely V of Canadas in the distant sky over the causeway, I had not even seen any, and that realization brought back a flood of memories. Twenty years earlier, there had been

no escape from the geese. It was total immersion; as soon as you got within twenty miles of Mattamuskeet, you could roll down the windows and hear them honking. In late afternoon against a bloodred sky, there were countless flocks of geese as far as you could see heading back to the lake to roost. Half the night, their honking kept you awake in the lodge. When the bell rang for breakfast at 3:30 the next morning, you joined all the other hunters in the large dining room where you ate eggs, sausage, and oyster fritters and washed them down with coffee—all amidst a muted chorus of honking geese that were stirring for the flight to the fields to feed.

We hunted the lake around Christmas almost every year during the late 1950s and early 1960s as a family outing, and I think our last hunt took place in the declining 1967–68 season just before my grandfather died.

The best of it was in the company of an elderly guide named Lemmie Cahoon. Through a stroke of pure luck, we drew his blind—Number 29—two years running. He may have been the best of the bunch; he was surely among the most knowledgeable. Even at his advanced age, it was clear that he loved waterfowling. I still have an image of him calling ducks as we crouched low in the blind, while his yellow lab watched the incoming birds intently through a hole in the side of the blind which had been provided just for that purpose.

Despite the decline of Mattamuskeet as a goose capital, there is still much there for the waterfowler and wildlife enthusiast—even the angler. Over the years, the spring and summer months have provided good bass and panfishing. Crappie and catfishing are still excellent, and, although the bass fishing may have declined a bit in recent years as the old canals in the lake's bottom have silted in, it is still good in some parts of the lakes and in the many canals that border the lake. Mattamuskeet provides a special treat for the angler who likes his fishing in traditional doses. You can wade the shallows around the cypress with a fly rod and popping bugs during the spring spawning season, and float the canals or fish the deeper holes with a small boat. Because the lake is so shallow, it does not attract many big, swift bass boats.

Nor has the waterfowl hunting gone to pot. Indeed, some of it may be better than ever. In 1972, when it became apparent that one of the problems was the maturing of the marshes, refuge personnel began to build waterfowl impoundments around the lake, but still within the refuge. These areas, along with the lake itself, attract an excellent wintering population of ducks and swans. Since 1973, the duck population increased to such an extent that a small portion of the refuge—some 4,000 acres—was reopened to limited hunting with the 1979–80 season.

Hunting can also be good outside the refuge on a variety of impoundments and field blinds provided by private outfitters who can offer a package deal that includes lodging, meals, guide, and sometimes a night-before oyster roast.

Even though the Canada geese are largely gone except for a remnant of the southern flock that still seeks out its old stomping grounds, Mattamuskeet retains its charm. Driving through this largely unchanged rural part of eastern North Carolina on a cold winter afternoon, the old excitement is there even if the sky is not filled with honkers. Mattamuskeet works its magic and you don't have to be freezing in a blind at dawn to share it. And some who remember still cling to the hope that someday more geese will return, even though most realize that 100,000 Canadas would be too much to expect even for such an ideal spot. Times have changed at Mattamuskeet over the years, but the day may return when times change at DelMarVa. If, indeed, the geese ever do come back, it could be just like old times—a bloodred sky filled with geese and honking that never seems to end.

Tundra swans roost at sundown on Lake Mattamuskeet in the company of Canada geese and a variety of ducks (opposite, top). Although the wintering population of Canada geese has fallen at the lake because the geese now winter farther north, the swan and duck populations have increased. Raccoons (opposite, bottom) are only one of many species of wildlife that make their homes in and around the lake.

Saving Nags Head Woods

MICHAEL GODFREY

Squinting into the milky haze at 5,500 feet over Albemarle Sound, I hand Massengale a chart. Can he see a shoreline off to our right? Yes. Good. Thanks. Preoccupied, he folds the chart, wrong of course, and flips it absently into the back seat. While I retrieve it the aircraft begins to bank right, the nose drops, and the airspeed whistles. Massengale looks at his white knuckles as if surprised to see them on the wheel, more surprised to see them instinctively bring us back to level flight.

The pilot is inwardly pleased. Nothing annoys quite like a passenger consumed with his own concerns and unaware that he is in mortal peril. Let 'em participate!

"What do you see?"

"Nothing."

Tom Massengale is a former director of the North Carolina Nature Conservancy. He organized the chapter in 1977. Nationally, the Conservancy had preserved 2.6 million acres of America's critical natural habitats by 1986, many of which would by now otherwise view the sun through an asphalt filter. The

Lawrence S. Earley

North Carolina chapter has been one of the most successful.

"How now, Merriweather? See anything?"

A white strand somehow separates itself from the haze. It cuts the windscreen just below the second screw in the divider. That would be the beach at Nags Head. The milky business below it is Roanoke Sound; that above it, the Atlantic Ocean. Massengale sees it now.

"There's the Woods!" He jams his finger into the plexiglass, shakes it, and starts gathering up real estate plats, apple cores, and briefcases.

The nose angles downward and the airspeed whistles again. We can see a dark band on the sound side of the Outer Banks. At each end of it is a white knob. The knob at the north end is Run Hill. Jockey's Ridge anchors the south end. The lush, five-mile corridor of greenery connecting them is Nags Head Woods. It is a Nature Conservancy preserve, though the work of preservation is far from complete. This is the nineteenth time we've made this flight in the past two years, another move in the chess match to secure one of

Lawrence S. Earley

This freshwater pool fringed by sweet gums (above) is one of several natural habitats in Nags Head Woods. Others include sand dunes, hardwood forest, and salt marsh. Many varieties of duckweed (opposite page) exist in the dozens of freshwater ponds in the woods.

North Carolina's most important natural areas.

For those who like their aesthetics quantified—and there's no other way to raise money to preserve a tract or to convince the government that it's worthy of being named a National Natural Landmark—there is a hefty document by Henrietta List and Tom Atkinson that catalogs the goodies. Nags Head Woods contains:

· thirty-three of the thirty-seven woody communities on the Outer Banks, in most cases the best examples remaining;

· the southernmost occurrence of woolly beach heather (*Hudsonia tomentosa*);

· the northern limit for the green orchid (*Habenaria repens*);

· the only pools in North Carolina containing all genera of duckweed:

Ken Taylor

The many freshwater ponds in Nags Head Woods are the keys to its survival. Though they are all interconnected, each pond hosts different plants.

Wolffia, Wolfiella, Lemna, and *Spirodela;*

· at least seventeen species that are on the Cape Hatteras National Seashore Park list of rare and endangered plants;

· unusually large specimens of American holly, dogwood, hop hornbeam, live oak, and pignut hickory.

Now we're getting to the point. What is Nags Head Woods, anyway? Some kind of condominium development bulldozed out of the dune scrub?

The fact is Nags Head Woods is a *real* woods. It's not a tangle of maritime shrubs and salt-stunted runts. It's a forest of tall pines, oaks, and hickories. There are also hollies and beeches—huge ones you'd expect

Michael Godfrey

Ken Taylor

Serene in winter (left), Nags Head Woods grows atop stabilized sand dunes. Pignut hickories, southern red oaks, American beeches, sweet gums, musclewoods, and red maples send their roots deep into the sand. Red-winged blackbird (above) is a summer resident of the salt marshes.

in an Appalachian cove. But this woods is not in Appalachia. It's at the seashore. In flora and fauna, Nags Head Woods is the most diverse forest on the Atlantic seacoast.

The dunes begin on the west side of Route 158 By-pass, behind the beach at Nags Head. They are dry, hot, and only loosely vegetated. There are stunted wads of greenery that, had fate been kinder in distributing the seeds, would have been trees—pines and oaks. Here the sand impoverishes them; the salt spray knocks them flat.

A quarter mile inland from the surf the oaks and pines begin to look like trees, though they don't act their age. A forty-year-old pine may be only three inches across. The sand underfoot is knit by the rare woolly beach heather, a pioneer on northern dunes. Its spreading, cedarlike clumps lace into the sand at scattered locations between Cape Cod, Massachusetts, and Atlantic Street, Nags Head, North Carolina.

The dunes steepen abruptly. Each becomes a little mountain 50 or 60

feet high with a slope of up to 70 degrees (for reference, 90 degrees is vertical). There is no pattern to them, no ranks marching as before a prevailing wind. The sand is heaped at random and steeper of slope than seems prudent.

It's hard not to notice also that the dunes are forested. We stand amid tall, straight pines, oaks, and hickories. Nearer Roanoke Sound there are beeches two and three feet in diameter towering in the coves of sand just as they would on the Blue Ridge Scarp. Our sense of place is tricked by this dislocation, this importation of a cove forest cathedral to the seashore. It's not like a whole system of values is threatened, though, for this exact ecology occurs nowhere else on earth.

Freshwater pools nestle between the dunes. There are dozens of them varying in size from wet-weather puddles to ten-acre Fresh Pond, until recently the only source of water for the towns of Nags Head and Kill Devil Hills. The depth may be a few inches or many feet; the bottoms are

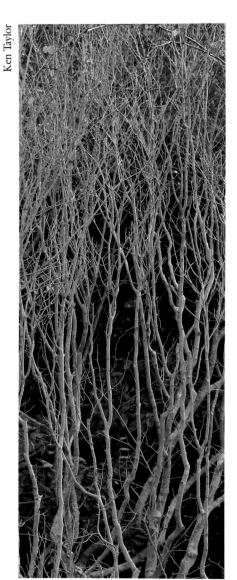

Ken Taylor

Winter northeasters push the sand dunes two to five feet per year in a southwesterly direction, in time covering all but the crowns of trees.

of organic muck underlain by sand. Some of the ponds are vegetatively sterile. Others host some of the world's most unusual plant communities. They may be ringed with littoral zones of submerged and emergent greenery like the water violet and *Hydrocotyle ranunculoides*, a coastal rarity with no common name. Here is a pond carpeted in a green iridescence of watermeal, mosquito fern (a real fern, aquatic, free-floating, fingernail-sized), the duckweeds *Wolffiella floridana* and *Spirodela polyrrhiza*, and the yellow-flowered aquatic carnivore *Utricularia biflora*. In broad perspective these ponds boil and seethe with a broth of plants, frogs, fish, herons, turtles, muskrats, snakes, otters— numerous beings that gurgle, make bubbles, squawk, and plop off logs. A palmful skimmed from the surface sparkles with minute greenery and vibrating invertebrates.

There are also snakes, and some like the cottonmouth moccasin and Eastern diamondback rattler are poisonous. Visitors should be watchful, especially in the warmer months.

There is another feature more striking even than the trees or the steep dunes. The Woods are *cool*— mercifully shaded and 15 degrees cooler than outside.

"Why, Henrietta?" I once asked the resident expert on Nags Head Woods.

She is Henrietta List, a self-taught naturalist who helped bring the Woods to the Nature Conservancy's attention, awakened the Outer Banks to the treasure hidden in the dunes, and with her husband, Jim, is curator and ranger-in-residence of the Nags Head Woods Ecological Preserve. Henrietta's knowledge of the Woods is encyclopedic—from the state's largest live oak to the

toads, ticks, and cottonmouths. She had counted the deer herd, scuffed up the bobcat scats, led the Boy Scouts in hell-for-leather charges into old trash heaps and on broad sweeps against the scattered droppings of *Swinus americanus*, posted the signs on the preserve's boundaries, dealt with the vandals, welcomed the visitors, and interpreted their surroundings.

"Why the trees?" she mused. "Why the pools, the cool air? There's a lens of fresh water under the dunes. Where the depressions between the dunes are deep enough, the water is visible. It moistens the roots and nourishes the trees so that they don't know they're growing in a desert. The trees take up water through their roots and release it through their leaves as vapor. Evaporating, the water absorbs heat and cools the air."

Henrietta talked about the oasis effect and about the conflict in the currents offshore. The Virginia Coastal Drift brings cooler water from the North. It accounts for the goosebumps on the swimmers at Nags Head and for the moderate climate there. The warmer Gulf Stream flows up the coast from the south, depositing subtropical maritime species along the way—the cabbage palm at Cape Fear, the American alligator at Cape Lookout, the yellow-lipped snake, the cotton mouse, the green anole, the squirrel treefrog, and a galaxy of plants including the longleaf pine and the green orchid in the vicinity of Nags Head. Realms of life coming from the North and from the South meet at an oasis. The result is an explosive diversity unequaled on the Atlantic coastline.

"The irregular dunes and steep slopes?" she asked. "Who knows!

Lawrence S. Earley

Ken Taylor

Theories abound. Maybe the inlet that opens once or twice a century south of Jockey's Ridge salted up the sound, killed the forest, destabilized the sand and let the southwest winds play with it."

We circle the huge active dune at Run Hill, checking the wind sock.

"You land this thing, Massengale. I'm going to catch a little sleep." Instantly the cockpit is a blur of floating papers and flying apple cores. The whole bucket of land-preservation paraphernalia rolls to a stop beneath the Wright Brothers monument.

A real estate developer who has a project in the middle of Nags Head Woods is here to meet us. The economics of the times suggests he sell out. If somehow the development can be bought or at least put into friendly hands, the thinking goes, the disturbance can be minimized, the development's private trash dump can be deactivated, and control can be gained over the southernmost access to the preserve—an important measure against vandals and firewood thieves. The unmentionable other side of the coin is a

takeover by an insensitive developer who will bisect the Woods and freshwater pond system with a grid of roads and bulldozed lawns, expanding southward.

There are 1,800 acres in the Nags Head Woods designated (but not yet dedicated because of the large number of owners with divergent views) a National Natural Landmark. The Nature Conservancy holds about 300 acres. Henrietta has just cut a deal with the town of Nags Head to manage its 260 adjacent acres as the preserve is managed. Next southward is the development. Then comes a series of private holdings including a still-active farm in some lowland next to the marsh. There are old homesteads, roadways, and graveyards.

Putting the pieces together was seen as an impossibility from the first talks of preservation. Yet today the northern third, the part containing most of the ponds and many of the unique and irreplaceable habitats, is safe because Massengale, List, and Company brought together the resources and the people of goodwill. The developer wants al-

Slowly but surely, Run Hill dune (top, left) is swallowing the forest and the pond. Nags Head Woods has been called an "ecosystem library" because of its diverse species, communities, and habitats. The forests provide habitat for a large variety of mammals, birds, reptiles, and amphibians, including this forest-dweller, the southern leopard frog (above).

most $1 million for his 56 acres, not the "bargain sale" Massengale had hoped for. The developer suspects—hopes fervently—that the Conservancy has rich friends. Promising at first, his scheme was burdened with the requirement to operate a sewage treatment plant and it has become a nightmare.

We stop by the Woods for a stroll on the way back to the airport. Henrietta talks about Nags Head Woods becoming one of the most visited sanctuaries in America, rivaling the great Audubon preserves at Four-Hole Swamp in South Carolina and Corkscrew Swamp in Florida as a center of learning, research, and interpretation.

Clouding Henrietta's dream is a debt of $200,000 on what has already been acquired. She and Tom are pleased with what has been accomplished but aware that the remainder is vulnerable. Henrietta wants a visitor's center, interpretive facilities, and some means of acquiring the 400 unprotected acres of ponds, marsh, and forest as they become available. And what is to be done with the developer?

"We did have some rich friends," says Tom, "mostly from outside North Carolina. They helped a lot, particularly at a time when the project had little grass-roots support at home. The Conservancy gave it

number one priority nationally and some strong donors came through. The Mary Flagler Cary Charitable Trust gave $600,000, the Goodhill Foundation provided $280,000, the Z. Smith Reynolds Foundation of Winston-Salem gave $100,000, and the Elizabeth City Foundation donated $5,000. An anonymous friend wrote a check for $50,000. With individual donations, the total raised so far is $1.04 million. There has been a trend of generosity on the part of the landowners in the Woods, some of whom donated their land or sold it at bargain prices.

"But time goes on and priorities shift. We have to realize that Nags Head Woods is a North Carolina project. It is this state's most significant natural heritage location and it's up to North Carolina's people to preserve it."

Henrietta leads the way up the near-vertical loose sand. We emerge from boughs of oak puffing and backsliding, gaining the summit of Run Hill lurching on all fours. Our tracks lead out of one of the few forests in North America being eaten by a live dune. On our left the glacier of sand is edging into one of the ponds. Candles of oak and pine, the uppermost twigs of trees 70 feet tall, poke from the dune crest, gasping for CO_2.

"You won't see that many places in the world," says Henrietta quietly.

Grapevines lace the nearly obliterated treetops. Behind us against the sky loom ghostly sentinels of grapevines, their roots in the loam now beneath fathoms of sand.

"Nor that," she notes.

On our right the dune marches into the marshes of Roanoke Sound. An osprey launches from a sand-killed skeleton of oak, plunges into a tidal creek, and lumbers aloft. It pauses midstroke to shake like a beagle and to streamline the fish.

To Henrietta List it is inconceivable that someone—if not everyone—in North Carolina isn't going to step up and do what has to be done about Nags Head Woods.

Editors' Note: By December 1986, the Nags Head Woods Preserve had increased its acreage under ownership to 400 acres, with an additional 300 acres managed under an agreement with the town of Nags Head. The Nags Head Woods Visitors' Center opened in October 1984. Under the state's Nature Preserves Act of 1985, Nags Head Woods was designated as a special area that the state wishes to preserve in perpetuity, the first area in the state to be so named. By the end of 1986, $500,000 had been raised for the preserve in the North Carolina Nature Conservancy's Conserve Carolina capital campaign.

PART FOUR
Hunting and Fishing

"Bucking The Storm—Canvasbacks," courtesy of artist, Owen J. Gromme and Wild Wings

The Perfect Bird Hunt

MIKE GADDIS

"If you could relive just one day of all those you've spent bird huntin', which would it be?"

I had heard the question before. The difference this time was who was being asked. Harold Britt is a bird-hunting legend in the Giddensville part of Sampson County. Most anyone there will tell you that. And it goes further. There was a time when Winchester and Stevens vied for his services to put their best clients into some top-notch North Carolina bird hunting, and a time when he supplied top-flight dogs for their exclusive plantation hunts in Georgia and Florida. Quail hunting has been his life's passion for forty-odd years.

When somebody wants an answer to something like that, there's a lot to sort through. Britt was a while thinking about it.

"There've been several I'll never forget," he began, "but if it had to be just one, it would be the morning in the fifties on Six Runs with my brother, Carroll, and brother-in-law, Frank Sutton. In all the years I've hunted, I've never seen another to match it.

"It had snowed off and on for three days running and stayed windy and cold. The ground was solid covered. But the fourth day broke clear and bright like it does after snow, and it turned warmer. We had been stuck in the house for about as long as we could stand, and that was all the excuse we needed. We loaded up and left about ten or eleven.

"We took three dogs—Ranger, Sport, and Dillon. Dillon was the best dog I ever owned. We turned out in the long narrow field that borders Six Runs Swamp. It was part laid out and part in beans that year. The only way you could hunt it was to walk to the head and then turn around and come back the same way. You couldn't cross the swamp. We hadn't gone a hundred yards before all three dogs were stacked up for keeps. We knocked five birds down on that first covey rise, and, mister, it was on! By the time we made the end of the field, the dogs had pointed three more bevies and we had about five birds apiece.

"As I said, you had to go back the same way and we figured the hunt, as good as it had been, was over. But going back we found four or five more covies. Scenting conditions must have been perfect because I've never seen better dog work. We finished out our twenty-four birds and were back at the truck in less than an hour from the time we left it. So help me, that's the way it happened.

"Those birds were like us. They'd been locked up on the edge of that swamp in all that weather for three days and couldn't feed. They felt plumb light in your hand. When they finally got the chance, they flew out of the swamp and settled into that field like folks at a circus tent revival. That's the only way I can figure it."

I had listened intently, for it was an interesting story. But my attention had wandered a bit too. I was reminded of a similar hunt Sammy Giddens had told me about not long before.

"Nida and I went home to visit the folks with three days to burn," he had said. "We planned to spend a fair part of it bird hunting our old territory. We had looked forward to it for a month. But danged if it didn't start rainin' a solid downpour the first day we got there. It refused to let up right on into the third morning. I looked out the window and the fields stood in water. There was no sign of clearing. The whole world looked pitiful.

"About three o'clock it finally began to taper a bit, though it was still falling a steady drizzle. Beggars and people who have to work can't be choosy. We had to be back Monday, and I wasn't going to be able to face it without getting out for a while. We pulled on the rain gear and started loading up. We had four dogs with us. Two were just beginning to settle in. The other two were seasoned. We hadn't hunted them together before because the pups forgot their manners here and there, and four dogs can be about two too many a lot of times. But they were as stir-crazy as we were and we just couldn't turn any of 'em down.

"By the time we got to the place we wanted to hunt, there was a stiff north wind and it was getting colder fast. It was still raining, too. I really didn't expect to do much. But it wasn't long before we were missing a dog, one of the veterans. We started looking and after a few minutes realized we didn't have a single dog with us! There was a small pocket ahead where the field cut back toward the creek, and an old hog lot. When we made the corner we found the dogs. They were four in line, the young dogs backing the old. You don't get to see four dogs standing that way very often, young or old. You don't forget it when you do. This time was particularly gratifying, seeing the pups come into their own. We killed three or four birds on the rise.

"Not ten minutes later, we had the same thing happen. Except this time it was a turnabout, the older dogs honoring the young'uns. There's a kind of vicarious happiness you get when something like that happens, especially when all the odds say it shouldn't. We ended up with one of the best hunts we've ever had. The birds had been sitting back in the downpour and hadn't fed. When that little change came along, they were out even though it was still rough, relatively speaking."

All this came back the other day during a moment of self-critique, after I'd made a neophyte left when the situation demanded a sage right. I was thinking that after all these years I ought to know the top few things that make for a good quail hunt. I decided at this stage in my bird-hunting career, there were three. Certainly, weather is one of them.

There are days that are just too pretty to spend bird hunting. I mean to say, you'd be better off fishing. An unseasonably warm day in December, dead still with bright sunshine, does little more for bird hunting than make you sweat and wear the dogs out. The same can be said for a balmy day in February that has the spring peepers cranked up. Days like that are beautiful, no denying it. They just aren't beautiful for bird hunting.

The kind of day that makes for an outstanding bird hunt generally lies on either side of a front. If I had a pick, I'd take the last pretty afternoon before the weather began changing. Ideally, there'd be a light, steady breeze and the temperature would be in the upper forties but due to drop. Particularly if the forecast called for ice and snow, nothing would keep me from going. You can count on birds moving and feeding actively, and the conditions favor good dog work. The hunting is pleasant and easy. Close behind though, and occasionally grand, are the days that follow bad weather. It's important to be there just when things begin to turn for the better, even if the improvement is slight and short-lived. They test your fortitude, but there's nothing like being miserable and happy at the same time.

We don't get very many days like this during a season, those that offer dramatic possibilities. So what constitutes a good day otherwise? I've changed my mind about that with the years, given my own experience and that of others. For the last eight seasons, I've spent a lot of time training bird dogs and I keep a log on each day afield with things like the number of coveys, how the dogs did, and what conditions were like. Looking over it, I find that the cold windy days I used to avoid aren't so bad after all. Indeed, the facts argue that they're better as a rule than still days in a period of stable weather.

Sammy expressed it pretty well when he summed up his rainy day hunt. "The days it would seem like you ought to stay home are the days you ought to go."

Good dogs would also have to be one of the three requisites for bird-hunting success. The longer you hunt the more you come to appreciate that. There's a lot to be said for training your own. You learn things about bird behavior in the process that will make you a better hunter. It takes time and effort, but comes with adequate rewards. Beyond basic staunchness on game, the one thing I would train for most is a dog that will handle kindly to a low whistle, or a change in your body attitude. It keeps the hunt quiet and orderly and won't disturb jumpy birds. That's become more important with increased hunting pressure. It takes good rapport with a dog to get this.

There's a strong case to be made also for a dog that's broke to wing and shot. That is, one that's been trained to stop when a bird accidentally gets up and to stay in place when a covey gets up in front of his point and shots are fired. I haven't always felt this way because, like most hunters, I wasn't brought up around dogs finished that well. Bird hunting can get rough-and-tumble in the thickets, and I haven't been sure the wing and shot thing was entirely practical. Working field trail dogs changed that because I have seen the difference it can make in practical terms. A dog only trained for staunchness that bumps a bird on the edge of a widely scattered,

feeding bevy is going to flush them all before he gets through running wildly over the area. A dog steady to wing stops at first flight and stays there. The odds are greatly improved that you will get a shot. A dog that's steady to wing and shot on the covey rise will give you better shooting because the birds aren't chased into one thunderous, momentary explosion. There will be a higher percentage of occasions when the birds will get up in stages, and the lay bird will become more common.

If you buy a dog steady to wing and shot rather than train one yourself, get the trainer to tell you how to keep the dog steady. It will require extra care and attention. The best always does.

When I was a boy, my great uncle, Joel Ashworth, taught me what I would consider the third requisite

for successful bird hunting. It's just that it's taken me forty years to come to terms with it. Maybe I had to slow down a little to become even capable, and I think it's going to be a few years yet before I master it—if I ever do. But he was right: the man who kills birds regularly is a patient shot.

"You've got to take your time on the shot," he'd tell me. I always wondered just how that was possible when it seemed like all the birds were gone about the same time I got the gun up.

For twenty-five years, my objective was to get a shot off when the birds got up. Oh, I'd pick a bird. That wasn't the problem. It's just that I didn't waste any time shooting at it. I did kill some birds, a credit to the reflexes of youth, and I wasn't exactly a slouch as a shot. Some people even thought I was

"Pointers and Covey," David Williams

good. But I'd seen *good* shots, and I had to admit to myself that I wasn't there yet.

At thirty-five years, I began to notice more, and give attention to the fact that birds kept getting up after my gun was empty or that the sight picture on a careening single looked infinitely better a few moments after I pulled the trigger unsuccessfully. And that I usually killed the bird that was obscured on the rise but then presented an open shot about 40 yards out where the shotgun pattern was full.

Now, I'm working hard on putting all this self-realization to practical use. I'm trying formulas like counting five before I pick my shot, and saving a shell back for the lay bird. I am getting better. Try me again in another twenty years.

Maybe it takes a lifetime to really grow into bird hunting—to learn not only more about how to hunt, but also more about why you hunt. For most of us, it's surely not the number of birds we kill, or could kill if we had a mind to.

It's learning that while every day can't be outstanding, each has a little something special in it to make it singularly pleasurable. Perhaps it's nothing more than the first notes of a stirring covey at daybreak and the pleadings of scattered singles in the growing loneliness of dusk. Or the first rays of the morning sun lighting a thousand candles in a heavy frost. Just being afield with somebody you like and not caring a lick

"Bobwhite," David Williams

about when you get back. A crisp double on an unexpected covey rise. The heart and courage of our dogs.

All this introspection had me back near where I started. I was thinking of a day I'd like to go back for.

Don Huffman and I hunted a farm in the eastern part of the state several years ago on a day that started out gray with the somber tones that predict impending weather. We had a pointer and a setter down and the hunt got better as time wore on. Around midafternoon we became aware of an utter stillness, the kind that means only one thing in nature. Maybe you've noticed. Shortly afterward, it began with a few errant flakes and a first slight rustle of sound as frozen particles hit tinder leaves. Thirty minutes later the woods on the opposite

side of the large fields we were hunting were blurred, and here and there accumulations were becoming noticeable on the ground. Snowfall is a lot of things to a lot of people. To me, in the woods, it is a wonderful thing, especially if it also happens to be the first of the year and you're behind two bird dogs.

We'd had a good day and with the birds facing rough weather we decided to call it quits. We were walking toward the truck in an old corn row between dense weeds bordering sparse patches of lespedeza. In the midst of an exuberant conversation about the snow and the hunt I glanced up to see the pointer wheel, wind, road a few feet, and firmly commit himself. His rigid posture and the setting left little room for doubt. The setter bitch came in and backed with the proud, lofty carriage I loved her for.

We let 'em stand a long time.

"Mighty pretty," Don said. He said it for both of us.

On the rise we collected four birds, two neat doubles. I've seen a number of bird-hunting tableaus. They were all pretty. But as a friend has a habit of saying, "Some just remember better than others." That memory of my setter and pointer, lofty and statuesque, holding a bevy amid heavy snowfall, the first of the year, is forever indelible.

It was hard to feel any better than I did riding home that night. Until I remembered that in a few days it would be Christmas.

Three Score and Three with Whitetails

CHARLES ELLIOTT

Deer hunting is like a lot of other things—the more you learn about it, the less you think you know. In my case, this comes under the category of statistics. I've been after a world-record buck since I was twelve years old (not the same buck) and that was some sixty-three years ago. I'm still after that record buck, but must admit that my many attempts have more or less added up to what a lady friend told me about her golf game. "The closest I've ever come to a hole-in-one," she said, "was a six." And that's about my score on trophy racks.

My first effort was with a deer-hunting party that included forty hunters and thirty dogs. That was about the only way southern deer hunting was done back in those days, and usually the only sure way of bagging a buck or doe. Most of the antlered clan survived by living in thickets or swamp jungles so dense that a hunter could hardly see as far as the front sight on his gun. The only chance of getting deer out was to put standers around the edge and run the dogs through, and even then only a small percentage of the deer left their jungle.

Leonard Lee Rue III

I could handle a shotgun on doves and rabbits and such, so I was given a stand by myself with instructions not to leave it and go wandering around since a load of buckshot might fail to identify me in the dense brush.

I'd never had such an exciting morning. I heard the dogs from the minute they struck scent and for four hours I listened to them chase

back and forth in that stretch of swamp. Every time a bird shook a bush or the wind moved a leaf, I expected that world-record buck to step out and stand in front of me as big and as grand as the Hartford Elk. I know I swallowed my heart fifty times and my gizzard once. Twice I thought I saw a deer, but couldn't be positive and someone kept me from pulling the trigger.

It was—and still is—a typical southern deer-hunting party. At noon the hunters were picked up by trucks and hauled to where barbecue and Brunswick stew were being served, along with loud tales of the morning's exploits—and nobody listening to anybody else. I had nothing to brag about, so I concentrated on the barbecue and got my share of that. I couldn't decide which I liked best, the hunting or the eating.

For many years I continued to enjoy these party hunts, as much for the fellowship as for the hunting. They always produced a few deer to be divided among the standers, but not in sufficient numbers to deplete the herd. Even now, with more whitetails, dog-hunting deer is still legal in much of the eastern half of

North Carolina. And it should continue, for it is the only way by which the surplus deer in many of these places can be harvested. The cover is simply too thick for still-hunting.

Many an old codger like me, who stands on or above the three-quarter-century mark, can look back to his younger years and remember wishing for deer that he could still-hunt or stalk in the woods around his home. But those wishes did not begin to come true until North Carolina—and other southern states—set up sound deer programs of introducing whitetails into areas where they could be protected until the herd was established.

Except for a few safaris to the far western states for mule deer and Texas for whitetails, it wasn't until the 1940s that I began perching on tree limbs to watch a trail or made like a specter through the woods in the hope of flushing a buck out of its bed. That was when I began to learn how amazingly smart and frightfully stupid an old buck can often be in almost the same breath. I've seen bucks pull stunts that I didn't believe and hesitate to recall them even now. To these, if you insist, I'll take a dying man's oath—but only when the time comes.

If you have more than a passing acquaintance with a veteran buck, you know how well equipped he is in the ear-eye-and-nose department. A real old buck, already past the trophy age, is imbued with some sort of sixth or seventh sense that tells him you are close by with a shooting iron, even though you are downwind, camouflaged to the eyebrows and holding your breath.

On the other side of the coin, he sometimes conducts himself as though he'd suddenly gone deaf, dumb, and blind. Several times I've met deer on the trail in the rain. I've had them stand and stare at me as if they resented sharing the woods with me in that kind of weather. I have never shot a buck under those circumstances—it would be like walking into the back pasture and blowing a hole through one of grandpa's calves.

A number of times whitetails have almost stepped on me when I was turkey hunting. I can't fault them much there, because they don't expect fireworks in the spring, and, if a turkey hunter doesn't look and act like a stump, he might as well go home and pitch horseshoes with the kids. I had a young buck browse close enough to get poked in the ribs with my gun barrel. Two steps farther on he caught my scent and, from the way he got out of there, I must have been a bit on the rancid side.

Normally, however, a buck or doe is quick to take advantage of every smidgen of carelessness demonstrated by a gunner. One of the most delightful mornings I ever experienced in deer woods was when I sat on a mountainside and watched an average four-pointer work his way through waiting hunters strung out like a miniature Maginot Line.

From my grandstand seat on the opposite ridge, I picked out several gunners with my glasses. They had stands along a well-used game trail that climbed into a low gap. One was chain-smoking cigarettes, as though he expected the smoke to keep him warm. Any moment I anticipated that the white cloud around his stand would bring the revenuers in search for a still. Another Daniel Boone had leaned his rifle against a tree and was walking in circles, flapping his arms across his belly to help his circulation. The nimrod on the hill above him was asleep, with his head resting well forward against his blaze-orange coat.

After about an hour a buck appeared, working his way toward the gap. He wasn't on the game trail, as they expected, but above it. The first hunter sat with his back to a tree, his rifle gripped and ready, watching down the game trail. The deer slipped through a laurel thicket above him, so close that the guy could have hit him with a slingshot.

The buck seemed unexcited and in no hurry, as if he knew where every shooter was located. He worked his way around the cigarette addict, pausing for a few minutes to watch the smoke before he tiptoed on. He paused even longer behind the flapping hunter as if amused by the antics. Then he almost walked over the sleeping nimrod and, from his little dance step when he stopped, I got the impression that he hadn't even seen the man.

Some sixth sense must have warned the hunter. He stirred and opened his eyes, then jerked his head so violently that it knocked flakes of bark off the tree behind him. From this point he went into a series of convulsions that had all the appearance of an epileptic fit, stabbing first at his knees, then at the ground, and then suddenly remembering that he had leaned his rifle against a tree.

The buck didn't wait to see any more. He wheeled and showed his flag. The hunter rolled from a sitting position to his knees and grabbed for the gun. His hand collided with the stock and sent the firearm spinning into the leaves. While he wrestled with his rifle on the ground the buck made tracks, and I saw the flash of his white tail as he went through the gap.

I once waited on a buck that was walking straight toward me through the open woods. I figured that he hadn't seen me and that I had plenty of time to let him get close enough to cut his throat and save a bullet.

Less than 100 yards away he walked into a shallow drain that crossed the woods in front of me. I didn't move until he was out of sight in the depression, then quickly shifted my rifle and propped my elbows on my knees to hold the gun steady without strain as long as necessary.

After five minutes I began to suspect that the buck would not step out at the spot on which I had my gun sights trained. After ten minutes I was sure of it when a rifle cracked about 300 yards behind me.

I got up and examined the depression into which the buck had disappeared. It did not seem deep enough to conceal a full grown deer standing on its feet. Then I walked to where I'd heard the shot. A fellow hunter was dressing his kill, and I didn't need but one look to tell it was the same buck that had slipped past me.

"I was just standing here," the hunter said, "and he walked right up. Never got one so easy-like."

The fellow was a pretty good woodsman, so he went back with me to help figure what had gone wrong between the buck and me. Apparently the deer had seen me when I lifted my rifle. While I was glued to the spot where he was supposed to reappear, he crept up the depression and went out the upper end that was partially shielded by a pair of large tree trunks.

My woodsman friend pointed out a couple of places where he said the deer had walked on its knees, but I wasn't experienced enough as a tracker to verify this, though I did wonder how he'd kept his hind end out of sight.

"It makes you wonder," the hunter mused, "how a deer can be so smart and so dumb in the same half hour. I reckon he was so pleased with himself for putting the double whammy on you, that he just didn't see me standing in the road."

And there you have it. It's what helps make hunting whitetails such a fascinating way to spend your time in the woods, and gives a fellow a smug feeling that maybe not all of his first two-thirds of a century have been wasted.

William Lea

The Expendable Bobwhite

If, by some quirk of fate, bobwhite quail in this hemisphere were suddenly wiped out by disease or some other disaster, I suspect there are a few bird hunters who would continue to feed and train bird dogs and hunt their favorite fields and covers until their souls were finally gathered to that great pea field in the sky.

An odd thought—a hunter with no quarry? Perhaps not. Most bird hunters would tell you the traditions of the sport are more compelling than the kill. Of course, every quail hunter would be heartsick if he thought his beloved "buds" were actually endangered. Indeed, if a referendum were held, he'd vote to plow under the Research Triangle and every major city in the state and replant with soybeans and wildlife food patches (where are the true statesmen when we need them?).

Still, many quail hunters would readily admit that the most expendable part of their sport might be the bird itself. I was again reminded of this just before Christmas last year on a hunt that took place near Wilmington. Despite the fact that bobwhites made barely a cameo appearance, it was probably the most pleasant hunt of the season. I'm not sure I can tell you why.

Part of it had to do with the flat fields cut with hedgerows and ditches—classic quail country. Longleaf pine with a low understory of gallberry, catbrier, and switch cane bordered the fields. We found many quail roosts in the grass. We also hunted with the knowledge that, on a memorable day a year previously, the dog we followed had found eleven coveys in these fields.

We didn't expect that sort of action this time around because the temperature rose to 80 degrees by midafternoon, forcing us to take a breather for a cold soda in a country store. Yet, just before dusk, the pointer found one covey that flushed wild into the pines. After that, we called it quits and spent the evening eating a bushel of oysters.

I'll admit it doesn't sound very exciting. Still, while we were hunting, I realized what it is about quail hunting that is so appealing. Even when the birds are playing hard to get, the sport has a wonderful, timeless familiarity. To put it another way, the quail hunter doesn't need—or want—to own the newest gun each year, and he doesn't have to read a bunch of articles to learn the latest tactics. We were carrying guns owned by our grandfathers, wearing clothes we've had for decades, and walking in fields that have been feeding crops of bobwhites since they were cleared in colonial times. As hunters, we had been as carefully linebred as the dog that bounced through the straw ahead of us. For us, it could as easily have been 1884 as 1984, and that is a feeling I have come to appreciate.

I think this may also explain why there are so few quail hunting articles in national outdoor magazines. What can you write about a sport that has steadfastly resisted change since the days of Nash Buckingham? And in a pursuit so marvelously hidebound, what possible difference could it make that we didn't bring home a limit of birds? I don't suppose anyone but a fellow quail hunter could understand.

There is, however, a darker side that deserves mention. We in North Carolina have been fortunate that there is still a lot of good quail habitat. For the sportsman who bothers to look, it's still possible to find good places and landowners who are glad to let you hunt. That's no longer true everywhere in the nation, and, even here, the situation has been undergoing an increasingly rapid change, especially since the 1950s. Farming practices have changed, small farms have been gobbled up by larger farms, urban sprawl has spread rapidly, and more and more land has been posted. There's not a quail hunter alive who can't point to a parking lot or housing development sitting on what was once prime bird cover.

I could tell you that we ought to resist unwise development and set aside some areas for the future, but you know that. I could also suggest that we take special care not to abuse our privileges to hunt on private land, but I suspect the people who need to learn that lesson aren't reading this. In short, the problems are apparent, but the solutions are not.

Indeed, it's this uncertainty about the future of quail hunting that makes it so special today. Perhaps this uneasiness is merely the year-end blues—a sudden taste of mortality—but a bird hunt has always been like a visit with an old and dear friend. One can't help but wonder how much longer either can last.—*Jim Dean*

Leonard Lee Rue III

Brackish Water Bass

JOEL ARRINGTON

The push pole that Currituck guides use to shove their heavy juniper skiffs is a fascinating and perhaps unique fishing tool. It is fashioned by local craftsmen from lengths of ash that have been cut and dried, then smoothed with a draw knife into remarkably flexible poles. Push poles are used by the few remaining guides who still take clients fishing in wooden boats throughout Currituck Sound and nearby waters. Years ago, I bought one from the late guide and boatwright Blanton Saunders for fifty cents a foot.

It is round for most of its length, then flattens into a narrow paddle at the bottom. These days you sometimes see a metal expanding foot attached to offer greater resistance in soft bottom, but usually not, and therefore the wooden tip is worn to a dull point. The design permits shoving, and it allows the pole to be used as a lever to force one end of the boat over, changing direction quickly. But the best reason for a bladelike end is that it can be rotated to knife through the water easily as you drag the pole back after a shove, saving time and energy.

Push poles are also deadly instruments against cottonmouths that make the mistake of swimming within a pole's length of a guide. Blanton, ever since one bit him years ago, waged a zealous holy war against the cottonmouth population of Currituck Sound. He would have you believe they could leap from the water into his boat, and would if given half a chance, so he would whack them urgently when they came within reach of his twelve-footer.

The new generation of guides at Currituck uses contemporary bass boats with pedestal seats, carpet, and electric trolling motors. They have no use for a push pole. I must admit my back likes the comfortable seats, and the additional speed permits ranging much farther over the vast acreage of Currituck Sound, but when in the more modern craft I miss the old-time charm of a juniper boat rubbed fuzzy at the gunwhale by a push pole.

Currituck Sound is the most famous of many brackish water, large-mouth bass areas in coastal North Carolina. Tributaries of Albemarle Sound, the waters of Kitty Hawk and Colington bays in eastern Albemarle Sound are well known. But the western margin of Pamlico Sound, including tributaries at the mouths of the Pamlico and Neuse rivers, also offer good fishing opportunity and are far less crowded. Alligator River and its tributaries, as well as East Lake and South Lake, which are embayments off southern Albemarle Sound, are also good bass fishing waters, especially in the spring. You will not likely find a guide to help you south of Dare County, but there are public boat ramps everywhere.

Fishing conditions obtaining to brackish water bass are the most constantly in flux. Change is the name of the game, and the most successful anglers are often those whose arrival coincides with favorable conditions. The highly skilled and determined among us will take a few fish practically any time and during good conditions will take more and bigger bass than those of us who take a more casual approach to fishing. But for the most part, all anglers are at the mercy of the

Even small bass like this one unzipping the surface of Currituck Sound are feisty when you catch them in brackish water. Brackish water bass, however, do not usually grow as large as those further inland.

Because many brackish water hotspots are weedy, many artificial lures won't work; however, a weedless spoon or plastic worm will take some nice bass (above). Weed beds and marsh lines like this one at Currituck (right) are good spots.

Photographs by Joel Arrington

weather on big water where you find brackish bass.

Wind is the major factor. In North Carolina, favorable water temperatures for bass prevail except in deepest winter and during the hottest weeks of summer. But wind direction and velocity, probably more than barometric pressure, air or water temperature, time of year, or time of day, determine what kind of fishing you will have.

In Currituck Sound and generally throughout the northeastern sections of the state, you want southerly winds. Between late May and September the prevailing wind is southwesterly. Wind from this direction pushes water into Currituck and holds back what otherwise would flow into Albemarle Sound, causing the water level to rise, flooding marsh shores. Bass are likely to feed actively along shorelines, especially in early morning.

From October through mid-May, the prevailing wind is northeasterly, pushing water out of Currituck and lowering water levels. Bass are likely to desert the emerging shorelines for deep water and dense weed beds toward the center of the sound, and to stop feeding. They can sometimes be tempted with natural baits dropped into holes in these weed beds, and elsewhere in deep water with plastic worms and bait, but rarely in shallow water.

During peak seasons—spring and fall—the wind is highly changeable. It will blow northeast for a few days, lay out for about nine minutes, it seems, then blow hard from the south for a day or two. Many trips are blown out altogether. If you can arrange to stay for a while, conditions are sure to change and fishing will get better. Sometimes everything seems perfect but fishing is poor. I guess nobody knows why.

Fairly frequently, however, coastal bass become so outrageously cooperative that the rankest amateur can catch and release dozens of fish. Even the bigger fish become active and a few bass weighing over seven pounds are caught.

The maximum size of brackish largemouths is considerably less than that of bass from the interior. Nevertheless, in Currituck Sound five-pounders are fairly commonplace and fish exceeding seven pounds are caught probably weekly in spring and fall. In northern Currituck Sound around Knotts Island and up into Back Bay, several ten-pounders are caught every year. Fish that size are rare farther south. Chowan River bass tend to run larger than those of more brackish water to the east, and some trophies exceeding seven pounds are taken from the mouths of tributaries along the western edge of Pamlico Sound.

It is not the size of bass that distinguishes brackish water fishing from the rest, but the number you may catch when conditions are favorable. Persistent anglers routinely release several times the daily limit. Many anglers believe that action is ample compensation for small size.

Fishing technique for brackish bass has both remained the same and changed over the years. A piece of crab or live minnow offered with a cane pole is as effective now as at the turn of the century, and quite a few anglers still work the weed beds and duck blinds that way. In Currituck Sound you still see flyrodders—now probably more than ever—laying bugs up against a marsh shore. What has changed is the increased application to brackish bass of plug and spin techniques developed in the last ten to fifteen years largely as a result of swelling interest in bass fishing nationally. The upshot has

been tournaments on all levels and proliferation of both local and national bass clubs. Manufacturers responded with a diversity of products whose development came largely out of competitive fishing and the expanding market of new bass anglers.

Plastic worms in their many and varied configurations crawled over submerged cover catch many brackish bass. To fish heavy milfoil grass, you can rig one without a weight and flip it into little clearings. Any basser worth his Red Man has enough spinner baits to decorate a Christmas tree. Some of the most vicious surface strikes I have seen from bass have been on buzz baits, which are surface spinner baits.

The contemporary brackish bass fisherman is prepared to use either fly, spin, or plug, depending on conditions and personal preference. He has probably two fly rods. One, a number eight, is for light winds. He may have a number nine or ten for days when it blows over fifteen miles per hour and he wants to put up with it to fish a fly. Most, however, will switch to casting or spinning lures when it blows.

No doubt the most popular subsurface lure in brackish water is the Johnson Silver Minnow. It may be silver or gold and tipped with pork rind or, more often these days, a plastic worm. The best choice overall for big brackish bass is unquestionably a live minnow, but the best artificial lure is the spoon. Since spoons carry big hooks, you must fish them on fairly stout tackle. It is difficult—often impossible—to stick a big hook into a bass's bony mouth with a whippy rod and light line. Spin or plug rods should be at least medium weight, with lines testing, in my opinion, at least twelve pounds. Fish should be hit hard on the strike. Several times I have had spoons fall out of a fish's mouth in the boat because the hook never penetrated, and I have lost no telling how many fish for the same reason just trying to fish too light.

Spinner baits are effective because they, too, are fairly weedless, and plastic worms can be rigged to be weedless. There is so much grass in brackish water that weedless lures are often the only practical way to fish. Currituck Sound and the entire northeastern corner of the state are heavily infested with Eurasian water milfoil, an exotic that was imported for aquariums and has gotten out of hand, as so many exotics have. It is filamentous and pervasive, fouling all lures to some degree and even outboards of under about 50 horsepower. You constantly have to lift and clear an outboard and pick strings of moss from your lures between casts. Careful anglers, however, may use gang-hooked plugs in clear water near structure. It takes patience. I have seen waders hip-deep in weed beds casting Mepps spinners with treble hooks. They could catch fish because the tide was up enough to submerge the grass tips and, by casting into the wind and pulling the lures back along the bend of the grass filaments, they avoided most hangups.

But largely because of the grass, ultralight tackle is not practical. Even the most weedless lures catch on the milfoil and it takes a rod of a certain stiffness to pull them off. Milfoil seems to be dying back a little. It is not nearly the problem it was ten years ago, but there is still plenty of it.

Because coastal waters are shallow and—where they are fresh enough—hold good populations of hungry bass, and because there are so many miles of shoreline, fly fishing is popular. At times, a fly seems to be the very best way to catch fish. You can work every inch of holding water thoroughly with a fly and do it more efficiently than with a top-water casting or spinning lure. And sometimes bass just seem to want bugs.

They also like streamers. The Marsh Hare originated in Chesapeake Bay and was brought to Currituck by Joe Brooks. My version is a rather crude palmering of hackle down a weedless number 1 or 1/0 bass hook. There are calf shoulders and a pair of hackle tips for a tail. It sinks, but slowly, and tends to come to the surface when stripped in. Nearly all takes are just below the surface so that you get a big boil and the satisfaction of a surface strike. I have had good luck with all white, brown, and especially red-yellow. This lure, as all streamers, enters the water more quietly than any bug and therefore does not spook fish so badly out of thin, calm water.

Much of the time, though, I fish hardbodied or deerhair poppers. Hair is better in very calm water, but when the wind gets up a little you almost have to use a balsa, cork, or other hard popper to get that sharp "blub" that seems to attract fish. The Gerbubble Bug is one of the old-time poppers used on brackish water. It is balsa or cork with feathers sandwiched between top and bottom.

But practically any popper on number 1 to 1/0 hooks will do a good job for you in brackish water, provided it is weedless and has a wide gap between the hook point and the popper. Commercially made bugs often need to have their hooks opened a bit with pliers. Thin wire weed guards work well enough, but the best are made of monofilament loops. All streamers and bugs fished in North Carolina's brackish water should have weed guards.

There are several lodges along Currituck Sound's western shore that cater to fishermen in season and still a few guides who early in the morning meet clients who camp or stay in rental rooms in beach motels or cottages.

If you own a suitable boat, you may obtain a chart and fish brackish water safely if you keep a weather eye. Guides are a great help, especially if you don't have a boat or know where to fish. About the only problem with guides is that they usually do not start early enough and they bring you in way before dusk. Special arrangements can sometimes be made to fish early or late, but usually not both.

When the weather is hot, early morning may be the only time fishing is worthwhile, but it's not the only advantage to being on Currituck at dawn. If a cloud bank has not obscured the horizon, the sun rises as a great red globe behind the dunes. Gulls screaming fly across it. On calm mornings, you can hear moaning seas breaking on the beach not far away across the marsh. In May there are still a few coots working the weed beds behind the Currituck Bank in the lee of a light northeast wind. A muskrat inscribes a V across the smooth water surface and you make your first casts.

Into Big Timber Creek

STEWART HARDISON

The last mountain lion in North Carolina was reportedly killed in the western part of the state in 1900. But even today, rumors circulate among the hill people that the big cats are still "out there." Though these rumors are rarely based on anything more than a far-off scream in the night or a pair of eyes gleaming in a car's headlights or sometimes a mysteriously mauled coon dog, they will not die. And while I doubt whether a conclusive shred of evidence will ever be found, the rumors live for me. Admittedly this belief is an act of faith; it makes little sense to think a mountain lion could be prowling the almost suburbanized mountains of North Carolina.

But however irrational this belief is—call it hope even—I still persist in believing. For the mountain lion, like a hawk sailing high in a thermal, is one of those curious fragments of the natural world that can loom in a man's mind and become the very essence, symbol, of what is wild. And, as the idea of wilderness becomes increasingly elusive, this symbol, or any particular natural symbol, becomes more and more important.

These symbols help fill the growing void in that part of a man's heart that is reserved for what is wild. That is why I believe in a mountain lion that rationally can't exist, and that is one reason why I enjoy fishing for trout. For the trout, to me, is one of those symbols. Only it is a symbol that I can see, experience. And when I'm on a remote stream and see a wild trout holding in a clear swirl of current, his every spot distinct and his spread fins the color of sunlight and reflected pebbles, then I have the heartening feeling that nature, at least somewhere, is having her say.

Aside from actually catching a trout and the sometimes intricate ritual involved in doing it, I believe that what fires a trouter's heart the most is the place he fishes. And when I think of trout fishing in North Carolina, I think of a place called Big Timber Creek. Shortly, I will try to tell you something about that place, but for now I must confess to you that I have fictionalized its name. Admittedly, I do this partly out of angler's greed. But there is another reason, too. And this is the fact that Big Timber

Creek, like any good trout stream, is a fragile watercourse of living things. Should this watercourse be exposed to a sudden and dramatic increase in fishing or other recreational pressure, these living things and the aesthetics entwined with them could be irretrievably damaged. I want no part in that.

Like numerous other North Carolina trout streams, Big Timber Creek's entire watershed lies within the boundaries of a national forest. Even so, it is easy to get to; gravel roads follow the ridgecrests above it, and one even spurs off to give access to its headwaters. Also, the heavily traveled Blue Ridge Parkway curves around a mountain above the upper end of its valley. There is even a pull-off so that tourists may park their cars and view the panorama at leisure. But few cars stop. Evidently, it's just another hazy, green gorge and by the time a vacationing family has traveled a couple of hundred miles of parkway they are sick of pretty scenery anyway.

Yet despite its easy access and close proximity to a major recreational highway, Big Timber Creek remains lost to all but a few. Fortunately, it lacks the kind of epic grandeur—towering mountain peaks, misty waterfalls, sheer cliffs of oblivion, and so forth—that attracts people in hordes. So, curiously, whatever it might lack in geological scale it gains in green seclusion.

When I go in for trout, I prefer to walk in, following a switchback trail that leads in some four miles below the one access road. It's become a kind of prelude, this trek down the ridge, and I enjoy the building anticipation in hearing the faint roar of water grow louder as the trail descends, constantly turning back on itself as it winds through tunnels of overhanging laurel and across mushy spring pools and in and out of timbered hollows. Because of the dense timber, you're upon the stream suddenly. It's not large, but open enough for pleasurable fly casting.

When I hit the stream, I always head up (an instinct as normal to anglers as salmon) and walk half a mile to a spot where the stream splits around a grassy island and riffles, in two channels, into a wide pool. It's beautiful water—a green glide of smooth current down either side and a submerged bar of pebbles and sand in the middle. It is also forgiving water, a good place to cast out the hindering anticipation that is chronic in the first few minutes of fishing. For if a trout doesn't take in the near run, it's a simple matter to lay a line across a bar and fish the opposite run. Usually one or the other will produce a fish.

This particular day is no exception. After greasing my fly, a number 18 Adams, I work line into the air with a quick series of false casts, then shoot a long curl upstream into the near run of current. Before the fly can ride a yard, it's taken in a

quick slurp and a fat rainbow, a nine-incher with scarlet-pink sides, bores against the rod. After netting him, I release him. Browns predominate, but there are also rainbows and, in the highest headwaters, brook trout or "speckles" as the mountain people call them.

Moving upstream, I come to a long narrow run that sweeps in tight against the laureled bank. It is deeply shaded and I can see feeding activity. Wading in very slowly, I make one exploratory cast. Nothing. So I strip in line and wait, studying the water for a possible clue. Up and down the trout are dimpling the surface with their rings, but I can see no insects. Midges, I suspect, and dig in my vest for a one-pound test tippet.

Unlike eastern waters, there is comparatively little aquatic insect life on a southern Appalachian stream. The trout, for the most part, feed on various terrestrial insects and assorted stream food—minnows, crayfish, snails, and salamanders. Consequently, fly selection is seldom a fussy matter. But not so now and, after tying on the platinum fine tippet, I open my midge box. Through the acetate lids covering the different compartments, I see several dozen flies in sizes 20 to 24. Scarcely larger than dust motes, they're marvels of fly-tying art. I select a number 22 Quill Gordon and after a painstaking half-blood knot begin false casting.

When I can feel the curl of line pulling in the air, I take a careful step forward for better positioning. But it's a mistake. For no sooner have I lifted my foot than a trout shoots off, only ten feet from me, and churns directly up the run leaving a V-shaped wake. The feeding stops. Now there's nothing to do

but wait. I light a cigarette (very carefully) and smoke it down before the first rise appears again. Feeling too eager, I decide to give the trout some more time, knowing that one more such performance will put them down for good.

Then, to my surprise and horror, I see another trout, this one scarcely six feet from my boot. I know he's seen me because he's holding perfectly still in the shallow current. It's the same as when the bird sees the stalking cat and the cat knows he's been seen and they play a game of psych-out. Only it's me and the trout. So I stand motionless, fearful that the slightest move on my part will launch him on a panic dash up the run. He's a nice brown, perhaps thirteen inches, and I can see his every spot and the quiverous spread of his fins—beautiful but a bother. Then, get this, he eases upstream to a rock a few feet away, turns on his side, and wiggles under the rock. I am dumbstruck. I know trout have the uncanny ability to hide in a trickle of water. But half eel?

With the pool crier out of my way I start to work out line. When twenty feet is in the air, I lay it on the water. Even at that distance the tiny fly is invisible. I will have to react to any rise in the general vicinity of my tippet. But no strike. So I pick up the line, lengthen it in the air, and lay it back down half a dozen feet upstream. I keep doing this until I'm forty feet out, about the limit I'm willing to go for fear of hanging on my backcast. And still no strike, though the trout continue to rise. Fortunately my casting has not put them down.

The tension builds and I go from the gray Quill Gordon to a gray-brown Adams and then to a brown Dark Cahill, repeating the casting cycle with each. And each fly fails to draw a rise. Finally, my one-pound tippet whittled to a few inches, I tie on a cream-colored Light Cahill. My first cast draws a rise, but I miss. Quickly, before my concentration breaks, I roll the line back out, make two savage false casts to lengthen it, and shoot for the head of the run. My line is on the water for a second or two when there is a dimple above it. Gently, I raise the rod and feel the sharp, delicious surge of a hooked trout.

Because of my light tippet, it's ten minutes before he lies curled in the net, a brown of about fifteen inches, his heavy sides measled with pea-sized red and black spots. I release him in a gentle current and watch him hold over the pebbly bottom, gathering strength with each pump of his gills. Finally, he moves away.

I change to a larger pattern and fish casually, eventually coming to a tight, deep pool of fast water where there is a large, blocklike rock jutting from the bank. It is perfect to sit on and, deciding I need a break, I do. Here, the rhododendron and alders spread over the stream and, though it's nearly noon, the sun does not blaze, but filters through their foliage in soft splinters of yellow light. I lay my rod on the rock and light a cigarette, feeling satisfied.

Almost at my feet, a small rainbow flashes up for a bug and disap-

A large, streambred brown trout is not only a trophy for the angler but a symbol of all that is wild and wary, even though the species is not native to this continent.

pears into the deep current. I watch for him or another, but no trout shows and I'm left studying the myriad whorls of current that race through the run. They change colors as the weak sunlight refracts through—deep blue then green then sunlight-brown and back to blue with the flickering quickness of a strobe light. It's mesmeric, psychedelic even, and I have to look away into the shaded forest to refocus my eyes.

But then, like the elusive depth of turbulent water, the blue gloom of the alder jungle becomes infectious, transfixing and random; past images experienced on Big Timber Creek

begin to leap out—the eerily human print of a bear track in sand, spring snow sifting through the laurel, a silent rattler coiling back on itself, a puzzled doe snorting for my scent.

I look around at the woods and water and rocks, knowing I'm not in wilderness but nevertheless awed at the intimation of wildness. This intimation is so deep and elusive, it can only be absorbed as the rattler absorbs the weak sunlight that filters through the forest canopy: with unblinking eyes. And for a moment I feel that this, here and now, is the way it was when the continent was green. Back when.

Calendar Art and the Sacrificial Bass

The trouble with an obsession is that reality rarely seems to live up to the dream. Take bass fishing, for example. In the mind of the obsessed fisherman, the quintessence of the sport is probably best exemplified by calendar art out of the 1940s or 1950s. You know the kind of painting I'm talking about. Here is a handsome gentleman, graying a bit in the mustache, but still robust and fully capable of handling the oars of the skiff he's sitting in. Clutched rakishly in his teeth is a pipe, and on his head is a jaunty fedora bespangled with lures and flies.

Of course, you only notice this after you have looked past the gigantic largemouth bass that is leaping in a shower of spray amidst a tangle of lily pads. Naturally, there's a Lucky 13 (always in frog finish) poking out of its mouth like a stogie. The sky is blue, the angler is smiling, the rod is bent, and all's right with the world.

That image—or something similar—is what drives those of us who have bitten hard on the treble hooks of bass fishing. There is, by the way, a myth that only fish are ever hooked. Anglers can also taste the steel, and, unlike some bass, once solidly hooked they are never set free again.

All winter, the bass fisherman works on his tackle, buys new gear, reads books on *Micropterus salmonides*, and dreams his dreams. This past winter, I seemed to have a particularly bad case of cabin fever and I spent many evenings "getting ready." I rearranged tackle boxes, replaced line, sharpened hooks, repainted old lures. It's been

years since I awaited the arrival of spring with such delicious tension, and I was ready to sally forth at the first opportunity. This year, life would duplicate art—calendar art, at least.

I suppose you know what happened. For over two months, everything went wrong. Plans fell through, equipment failed, partners reneged, work conflicted, and the weeks sailed by. Worse than that, the occasional trips I managed were unsatisfactory. Instead of lunkers leaping in lily pads, I had to be content with an occasional yearling yanked out of some stagnant waterhole.

"What's the point?" a nonfishing friend responded when I complained about my frustration. "Why do you torture yourself? You devote all that imagination and energy to fish—not to mention money and time—and you readily admit that you haven't had a single truly successful trip this spring. I think you're crazy."

Well, yes. And until that late Sunday afternoon in May, I'll admit that I was beginning to think there might be more personal satisfaction in something like, say, golf. Sooner or later you're going to get the ball in the hole. No such certainty exists in fishing.

But, as I said, there was that Sunday afternoon when I decided to visit a small, one-acre pond that I hadn't fished in a while. The pond is nearly forty years old, and it certainly looks fishy with all the old stumps, arrowroot, and cattails that threaten to choke it. Of course, the fishier a pond looks, the poorer the fishing is as a rule. But what the heck, I figured, I could at least enjoy the fading hours of a fine day in the company of red-winged blackbirds and frogs. I've done worse.

I won't bore you with all the details, just most of them. I decided to fish with a flyrod and deerhair bug simply because, if I'm not going to catch fish, I'd rather be skunked on my own terms. At least it's fun to cast and work a bug.

Imagine my surprise at catching a bass. Then another, and another. The fourth one weighed three pounds, certainly a satisfying fish on a fly rod. Finally, at dusk, I made a long cast toward a stump and twitched the bug. The strike was immediate and furious, and I was looking at five pounds of largemouth cartwheeling over the dark water. The bass jumped clear of the water three times, twice ran the line into the backing, and generally towed me around the pond. The whole thing seemed to occur in slow motion, and I was distinctly aware of the way the slanting light reflected off the droplets of water and shone through the transparent fins each time the bass jumped.

When I finally landed the fish, I debated whether to take a picture of it, but somehow it seemed more appropriate simply to commit this one to memory. I weighed the fish, held it in the water for a few minutes, then turned it loose.

Behavioral scientists would call this episode reinforcement, like feeding a laboratory rat to reward it for some simple act. Once conditioned, it takes only an occasional feeding to keep a rat performing. I'll buy that.—*Jim Dean*

Largemouth bass, Frank Stick, "An Artist's Catch"

Two Different Ducks

JOEL ARRINGTON

It is calm on Core Sound, the surface so flat it reflects wheeling seabirds and my companion's pipe smoke that hangs about the stake blind. Warm sunlight casts shadows of disconsolate decoys on the bottom as we view the still day from our aerie. Outboards drone far away; gulls laugh hysterically.

A bluebird day.

From our elevated box, we are nettled by hundreds of pintails and a few black ducks sitting placidly on the shallow water 400 yards away. The pintails whistle softly, seemingly to mock our puny efforts. A pair of mergansers feeds around our blind, looking like muskrats as they swim with heads submerged. When I peer over the edge of the box, one sees me and swims away. Soon the other follows and at a distance they resume diving. Watching them is our only amusement on a slow day. Clearly hunting prospects are poor.

There is little the hunter can do in such conditions to increase his chances, but there is plenty of time to consider the error of his duck-hunting ways. We were looking at perhaps thirty mixed redhead, pin-

Tim Hergenrader

tail, and Canada goose decoys, a paltry stool indeed considering that we hoped to decoy redheads, and especially considering the sleepy raft of genuine waterfowl nearby—competition with our decoys for the occasional duck that returns from some distant feeding spot.

I think we ended up with a merganser and a single redhead that slipped in unannounced that day— probably more than we deserved. We were in the right place, it could be argued, but at the wrong time and with woefully inadequate decoys. Still, it was an opportunity to consider what had gone wrong this and so many other times.

The only thing that qualifies me to write about duck hunting is that I

have done it poorly so much. Nevertheless, by random chance, and thanks to guides and expert companions, I have gotten it right occasionally and probably killed a duck or two that wouldn't have come to us otherwise. I do not have all the answers, but I do know this: there is a right way and a wrong way to hunt ducks. True, there is more than one right way, and sometimes you do it right and still fail because luck plays such a large part. But you can increase your odds by employing tried-and-true methods. These tactics, together with persistence and hard work, will pay off over many seasons, if not right away.

You must hunt diving ducks differently from puddle ducks because the two waterfowl tribes behave differently and prefer different habitats. Of course, there are places where you may pursue both divers and puddle ducks. The big reefs behind Hatteras and Ocracoke in Pamlico Sound are examples, attracting such dabblers as black ducks and pintails, such divers as redheads and canvasbacks; and ringneck or goldeneye can slip in unannounced whenever

Joel Arrington

you are trying to decoy mallards and wood ducks in some pond or small impoundment.

But as a rule, you employ different strategies and tactics for divers than for puddlers, also called dabblers. With minor exceptions, divers are big-water birds of large flocks. They fly faster than dabblers, run along the water before becoming airborne, and may swim underwater to feed. Their wings are shorter and set farther back on their bodies than those of puddle ducks. Dabblers merely tip over to feed in shallow water and spring directly into the air from the water. Puddle ducks also fly more slowly and precisely and may be found on smaller water bodies and in wooded swamps, although they too like big, open water. Divers are more likely to be at-

tracted to large decoy spreads, likely to ignore small ones. Puddlers will come to just a few decoys, but they are generally more wary than divers.

The idea in decoy placement is to get them to look natural while at the same time attracting waterfowl to a point where you can shoot them. You do it out of experience and hunch. No array of decoys is right in all conditions and locations, and there is much nuance involved. Books have been written about it, and, among hunters, decoy placement is a matter of often fervent opinion and subject to interminable debate.

The basic rules are well known.

Ducks are attracted best to their own kind. You set redhead decoys for redheads, for example, pintails for pintails, and you segregate de-

Along the coast in sounds, bays, and large natural lakes, setting out the decoys is a dawn ritual for waterfowl hunters (above). Your choice of decoys and how you arrange them depends upon whether you are anticipating diving ducks or puddle ducks, or perhaps both. The ringneck (opposite page) belongs to the clan of diving ducks that includes canvasbacks and scaup.

Ken Taylor

Puddle ducks such as mallards can be hunted virtually throughout the state on lakes, beaver ponds and rivers, and it takes fewer decoys to attract them than it does the diving ducks which prefer more open water.

coys within a stool. There are exceptions. Teal, widgeon, pintail, gadwall, and black ducks will come to mallard decoys. Still, if you have both mallard and black duck decoys out, blacks will usually go to the black duck decoys, and mallards to mallards. The degree to which ducks are decoy specific is especially notable in diving duck hunting. In Pamlico Sound near Swan Quarter, we set old squaw imitations between separate rafts of sea duck and scaup decoys. Almost every time, scaup would go to scaup, sea duck to sea duck, old squaw to old squaw.

Ducks are attracted better to oversized decoys. I would rather have twenty large redheads spread widely than thirty realistically sized decoys. Ducks have little sense of proportion, but good vision. Three giant black duck decoys are plenty for a small cove. In nearly every case, the problem is portability. You can only carry so much.

Divers need a lot of open water between decoys to land in. They will fly over their own kind to land, invariably upwind, at the head of the flock, so you need to keep that in mind when setting your decoys. Puddle ducks, on the other hand, will not fly low over decoys, fearing collisions, but will alight behind their own kind or decoys on the water.

You can't have too many diving duck decoys. The only practical limitations are cost, room to carry them, and time to put them out. It's possible to crowd small water with puddle duck decoys, however, because dabblers seem to dislike competition.

Spread decoys in calm weather, bunch them in bad. This is what ducks actually do.

Leave an open spot in the decoys

so that ducks will land within ideal gun range. That depends on the type of gun and shells and what is comfortable to the individual hunter. For decoying ducks, I shoot a 12-gauge, 26-inch barrel bored improved cylinder. With it, I am comfortable shooting at birds from 20 to about 40 yards. If long shots are expected, I shoot a 30-inch, full choke which extends my comfortable range to 50 yards. Experts can shoot ducks farther than that. The important thing is to know where you want the birds and set your decoys to attract them there. Some hunters like to place a decoy or two to mark the far edge of the range. When I did it, ducks always seemed to sit down just outside them while I fumed.

Confidence decoys of species you probably wouldn't shoot or wouldn't expect to attract are recommended. These include seagulls, coots, geese, and swans. Probably Canada goose imitations are most popular for this purpose, and, who knows, you might get lucky and a single goose or small flock will decoy. Guide and expert hunter Bob Hester likes snow goose decoys set off to the side when field hunting for Canadas, black ducks, and mallards around Lake Mattamuskeet. They are visible for miles. Half a dozen coots to the side of your decoy raft and close to shore will give puddle ducks a sense of security. In some areas, seagulls are similarly employed, although I have never used them. Waterfowl biologist and skilled hunter Dick Brame says he once tried a seagull and attracted so many other gulls, he couldn't hunt. The late guide service operator Vern Berg of Kitty Hawk sometimes used exquisitely carved ruddy ducks as confidence decoys.

The wind should be anywhere but in your face. Generally you want a lee shore, but, if the wind is quartering from behind, it's ideal. Ducks land into the wind, of course. Birds will approach with vulnerable breasts and undersides toward the gun. With the wind directly in your face, ducks have to swing over the blind to approach your decoys. Usually they'll see you, and you have tough going-away shots.

Configuration of decoys in a stool is subject to endless theorizing and debate. There is the "pipe stem," the "C," and the "J," among scores of other systems. Bob Hester has systemized his decoy-setting methods that grew out of many years as a guide, and described them in a book that has met with wide acclaim.

There are other ways to hunt ducks than decoying them to your blind. You may float down on singles or small flocks as they feed or rest along the edges of rivers. That would be puddle ducks almost exclusively. A canoe works well, but you have to be very careful not to capsize. Some hunters construct a camo panel up front that quickly falls forward when it's time to shoot. Often two hunters will alternate in the shooting position in the bow, the other steering from the stern. You may scull a low boat up to a raft of divers. It is a technique used farther north, mostly for scaup, but hardly ever in North Carolina.

Hunting in frozen fields and over ice is a separate game altogether. If you are sitting over the only open water in the country, you are in a good spot to kill ducks. But you will not get a shot at the many birds that approach if you overcrowd a hole in the ice with too many decoys.

The degree of confidence hunters have in calling varies over the coun-

Michael Godfrey

The black duck is considered the wariest of the puddle ducks, and is often mistaken for a female mallard. In recent years, biologists have become concerned that interbreeding between black ducks and mallards could further reduce the numbers of purebred black ducks.

try. In the bottoms of Mississippi and Arkansas and Louisiana, calling to mallards is highly efficacious, everybody believes it works, and everybody calls. Where mallards and other puddlers inhabit inland swamps and river bottoms in North Carolina, it works just as well. But in my experience, calling of ducks over open water is not particularly effective. Sometimes they come when you call, sometimes not. Sometimes they'll come when you don't call. Most guides I have hunted with blow widgeon and pintail whistles, mallard calls, and calls for divers, but I think they blow them for the customers rather than for the ducks. No doubt poor calling is worse than none at all. I have seen some very effective calling of Canada geese in North Carolina,

but little or none for ducks, but maybe I haven't been traveling in the right circles. Incidentally, I blow calls whether it works or not.

Where you set up a blind falls more under the heading of strategy than tactics, and it is the most important aspect of duck hunting. The immutable rule is "hunt where they use." Only neophytes believe they can set up just anywhere and kill ducks. In inland reservoirs, rivers, marshes, or open sounds—everywhere—ducks have established flight patterns. They feed at spot A, rest at B. In the early morning they fly across point C; in late evening you may expect them to fly to their habitual roosting spot. It is the hunter's first task to discover these patterns, because to hunt elsewhere will be a slow pick indeed.

One of my biggest problems, particularly on slow days, has been inattention. There is no telling how many ducks, or their descendants, are alive today because I was not watching when they made a single surprise turn over the decoys and went on. I once peered at my decoys through a crack in a blind at Bodie Island and saw one scratch its head. When I jumped, so did the teal and it made its escape. It's hard to stay alert when there is a lot of time between flights, but, remember, the price of ducks is eternal vigilance (and a lot of dollars).

Ed Zern used to say "you can never beat luck with brains," and it's true. I would rather be lucky than smart, but, in duck hunting at least, you can be just as lucky when you are hunting smart as when you are not. In the long run, a combination of good fortune and good tactics will put more excitement in your hunting day and more ducks on the table.

Gigging and Swatting

CURTIS WOOTEN

Lights from the small skiff threw a six-foot circle of brilliance into the night, penetrating the shallow water and illuminating the sandy bottom. Eerie shadows danced across the marsh. A man, his face and torso lit by the yellow glow, eased his craft along, scanning the channel bottom intently, a ten-foot flounder gig in one hand. Pinfish, gar, and minnows frolicked in the light; shrimp and crabs edged their way into the shadows. He ignored them all.

He raised his gig as the outline of a flounder materialized, and then he relaxed. It was only the flounder's imprint in the sand. The fish that camouflages itself by fluttering its fins on the bottom and kicking up a protective blanket of sand had moved.

A few minutes later another outline appeared, a flounder this time. The man raised the gig, calculated the difference between the actual and observed position of the fish—caused by the refraction of the water's surface—and with a quick jab pinned the three-pound fish to the bottom. After a brief struggle, the flounder was lifted into the boat.

Flounder gigging is a sport with obvious table benefits for many North Carolinians. It takes place nightly in the spring, summer, and fall in the estuaries and tidal waters of the Carolina coast. It is called "strike fishing" along the lower portion of the Pamlico River, but on Harkers Island and portions of the Outer Banks where Elizabethan English still flavors the language, old-timers refer to it as "bloind stobbin"—blind stabbing to us inlanders. South of Wilmington it is sometimes called "proggin" or "jobbin."

These terms probably relate more to the nineteenth-century daylight flounder "gigging" than they do to the nighttime efforts that are common today. In the 1800s friends and neighbors would fetch their pitchforks from the barn and convene at the edge of the sound or tidal creek at low tide. There they would enter the water and work their way through tidal pools, three or four abreast, blindly stabbing the bottom in front of them. When a flounder was "forked," the fisherman would reach down and, lifting the fish on the tines of the pitchfork, flip it into a burlap bag carried over the shoulder or floated behind. Flounder were apparently more plentiful then, for the technique is said to have been rather productive. It is still used occasionally today.

Two thousand years ago, Romans speared fish at night using an artificial light and a gig. The Greeks knew about the method before them. It's likely that long before the first Englishman set foot at Manteo Indians were spearing flounder and other fish using the light from pine knot torches.

By the late 1800s coastal fishermen had refined the system to some extent by rigging a cast-iron pot so that it could be swung over the side of their boats. The pot was filled with "lightwood," the rosin-rich heartwood of the longleaf pine, and set afire to provide light for a night's fishing. It was a dedicated lot that used this method. Lightwood gives off a tremendous amount of smoke, and fishermen would come in after a night on the water black with soot and more than a bit bleary-eyed.

Curtis Wooten

For awhile in the late 1800s and early 1900s kerosene lanterns were used, but they weren't much better than pine knots. The dim yellow light didn't penetrate the water's surface enough to see well.

It was the development of the gas lantern, with its intense white light, that brought flounder gigging into its own. Since the late 1940s and possibly earlier, recreational fishermen have been wading the shallow sandbars near inlets in the summer and fall, lanterns in hand, spearing flounder bedded there. Others, including some commercial fishermen, attached one or two lanterns to the bow of small, flatbottomed skiffs, and poled their way along the edge of the Intracoastal Waterway and tidal creeks that threaded their way through the marsh.

I first flounder gigged in the early 1960s with such a skiff and lantern. At the time both could be rented at Davis's at Sneads Ferry for two dollars a night. An evening's fun hasn't been so inexpensive since.

In the mid-1950s, some unknown inventor came up with the idea of encasing a 12-volt light bulb in a waterproof marine globe and attaching it to a fully charged battery to provide light for gigging. A good battery would burn a 50- or 75-watt bulb for the better part of a night and, since both the bulb and globe could be placed under water, much less light was lost to reflection from the water's surface. Visibility improved markedly—as did flounder-gigging success. The use of lightweight portable electric generators soon followed, providing an even better source of electricity.

One sultry night in late August back in the mid-1960s, I recall watching what I thought was a well-lighted research vessel motor slowly along the edge of the Intracoastal Waterway toward me. It turned out to be just a fellow flounder gigger, poling a skiff equipped with a generator that powered a string of four 200-watt lights immersed below the bow of his boat and two more along each side. The waterway bottom within a 15-foot radius of the boat was lit in a fashion that would have made Jacques Cousteau proud.

I have since fished from a generator-equipped boat and found the additional light helpful, but the noise bothered me and such gear is expensive.

The marsh is tranquil at night. Frogs, night herons, gulls, and other marsh creatures produce a symphony of calls, sounds that are lost when a generator is used. Floundering becomes less of an outdoor experience and more of an exercise in picking up as many fish as possible. There's nothing wrong with that, I suppose, but, for me, the promise of a few fish for the table and the experience of a night on the marsh is enough to keep me coming back. Sheer numbers of fish are unimportant.

The principle behind flounder gigging is simple. As the tides change, flounder move into shallow water—often only a few inches deep—where they settle and wait to ambush small fish that swim past. Flounder are found in the shallows during the daytime, but can see the approach of a would-be gigger and "run" before he gets within reach. At night, however, they move into even shallower water and the flounder gigger, using darkness as a cover and a bright light which blinds or mesmerizes the fish, can easily get close enough to plant a gig.

Techniques and equipment vary, but here are a few of the secrets.

Flounder giggers fall into two schools—those who gig while wading and those who gig from a boat. Waders generally work the large sandbars around inlets and along the shore of brackish rivers and the Intracoastal Waterway on warm summer nights. A growing number work the ocean surf in November. Some still use a handheld gas lantern as a light source, while others opt for the brighter light of a high-intensity spotlight or standard 12-volt lightbulb encased in a waterproof marine globe. The power source is generally a battery which is either floated behind on an inner tube to which a plywood bottom has been strapped, or carried in a backpack. Backpackers use a small battery of the type used in a lawn mower or motorcycle.

Wading can be productive, but it has a few disadvantages. The deep water and mud restrict the areas that can be fished in this way, and oyster shells, broken glass, and rusty nails are hazards to look out for. People who gig while wading generally wear old shoes or boots and use a spear, with a stringer attached to it, rather than the standard barbed gig. Flounder that are speared are simply pulled up the spear shaft onto the stringer and dragged along behind.

Gigging flounder in the surf, principally in November, can be productive, but the backpack light rig is the only one that works well there. Light from a handheld lantern is reflected by surf foam, and a battery towed in an inner tube is often flipped by waves. East-west beaches offer the best surf gigging after several days of light northerly winds calm the waves. Chest waders make the cool November waters more comfortable.

A 12- or 14-foot aluminum johnboat is the most popular choice of those who gig from a boat. They are light, yet stable enough to stand up in, and large enough to carry the necessary gear and a small outboard. Almost all have some type of bow cap or platform from which the gigger poles the boat and gigs and to which the lighting frame is attached. Other equipment may include a box designed to help remove flounder from the gig, one or more 12-volt batteries or a portable generator, and a cooler with ice, cold drinks, and snacks. I usually throw in a crab net. If flounder are scarce, crabs provide a welcome diversion and prevent me from going home empty-handed. Some giggers use electric motors to propel their boat and install swivel seats on the bow cap, but most stand and pole.

The gig itself generally is a standard 3- or 5-prong model which can be found in most coastal hardware stores. It is generally attached to a 10- to 12-foot section of wooden closet rod which can generally be found at the same stores.

Although flounder can be found anywhere in the salt and brackish waters of the coastal region at any time of the year, they are a migratory fish. Consequently, flounder gigging is better at some locations at certain times of the year than others.

Flounder spawn in 50 to 100 feet of water off our coast in December. The adults and young slowly begin to make their way back into the estuaries in March. By April the water temperature has warmed to the point that flounder can be found in the shallows. By then the air temperature is fairly comfortable for giggers. April, May, and June generally offer good gigging around inlets, as fish move from the ocean back into the estuaries. As summer progresses, larger fish move farther up tidal creeks and rivers into brackish water, getting fat on the abundant food supply found there. It is in midsummer that gigging is best along the lower Pamlico, Neuse, and Cape Fear rivers.

When the water temperature begins to drop, generally in early September, flounder begin a quick, six-week migration back to the ocean, concentrating for a period near dozens of inlets found between Manteo and Calabash. This is when serious flounder giggers get going.

The ideal night for flounder gigging is a moonless, windless night after a period of low rainfall in September, October, or early November. The water is generally clear then and there's less plankton in the water, improving visibility. Windless nights are more common.

Wind is a problem for two reasons. It creates ripples on the water surface which make visibility difficult, and the waves it creates beat against the shore, stirring up silt and muddying the water.

The times just at dark and right before dawn are usually best for gigging because more flounder seem to move into the shallows to feed then. The best tide is a rising one shortly after dead low tide.

At high tide look for flounder near the bank, at low tide in deeper water—generally as deep as you can see.

Moonless nights are best, but, if the moon is out, fish with its light in your face. With the moon at your back, you cast a shadow which generally spooks the flounder before you have a chance to gig it.

Flounder tend to frequent the same areas from year to year; if you fish regularly, eventually you find where these areas are. Sandbars along the Intracoastal Waterway near tidal creeks are almost always productive, as are almost any shallows near drop-offs. It's more productive to hit the hot spots, working your way around every hour or so, rather than just poling around the marsh.

If you're fishing from a boat, keep an eye on the tide. Getting caught up a tidal creek on a falling tide is no fun. You may have to pull a stranded boat over a mud flat or sandbar to get it out. When dawn breaks the flounder begin to run at the approach of a gigger, so it's time to go home—whether you're tired or not.

Twenty years ago catches of 150 to 200 pounds of flounder per night were not uncommon. The flounder population has since declined, probably because of man-made changes in the estuarine environment. A 30- to 50-pound catch for a night is considered good today, but it's not unusual to come home empty-handed. That certainly doesn't discourage most flounder giggers, though. They know that there's far more to this kind of fishing than just catching fish.

A History of Blues

JOEL ARRINGTON

The first big bluefish I ever saw hit trolled spoons in the rain on Wimble Shoals out of Oregon Inlet in May 1969. They weighed about twelve pounds apiece and I was amazed. After years of saltwater fishing in North Carolina, I had never caught a bluefish larger than about three pounds; nor in my ignorance had I even heard of such jumbo blues anywhere. Previously the biggest I had seen were six-pounders some of us had caught on a head-boat out of Montauk, New York, in 1960.

The big bluefish we boated that spring day presaged an angling era on the Outer Banks and in the western Atlantic Ocean generally that has not run its course to this day. We had no way of knowing that big bluefish populations would continue to expand and that the pursuit of them by hoards of new anglers would change the nature of surf fishing on the Outer Banks for the next fifteen years and more.

I should not have been surprised at the size of those fish we caught on Wimble Shoals. If I had been better read on blues, I would have

Angler admires giant bluefish caught when these lunker choppers returned to the Atlantic Coast in the late 1960s after a long absence.

known that the big fish have a history of population surges, sudden disappearances, and long absences, and that a few large blues had been caught by sport fishermen in North Carolina through the 1960s. However, not until 1970 were the runs major and the anglers who experienced them numerous, nor was the publicity about them extensive.

It must have been Outer Banks publicist Aycock Brown who first used the term "blitz" to describe the way hundreds, perhaps thousands, of big blues congregate in the surf zone and trap bait and sometimes

larger fish against the beach. A bluefish blitz has come to be the single most memorable angling experience of many Outer Banks surf fishermen, the holy grail sought by thousands of hopeful pilgrims to the Banks lured by accounts of wild fishing and blood in the water.

The first one I participated in was a dandy.

Actually, it was speckled trout that lured me to Nags Head in November 1970. I learned on arriving that there had been a few scattered bluefish and striped bass caught in recent days north of Kitty Hawk. For some forgotten reason, however, we began the first morning at Oregon Inlet and caught just a few, maybe three, blues in the eighteen-pound class, the biggest I had ever seen and the first from the surf. But action ended quickly and we moved north, looking for birds.

I remember that the weather was ideal, with highs in the sixties and a light northeasterly wind. In fact, the wind had been blowing gently from the northeast for several days and the surf had cleared to emerald green. The beach was littered with

When big blues hit the beaches, especially at Cape Point on Hatteras Island (right), action is often fast and hectic. Big bluefish offer surf fishermen a chance to tangle with a strong fish (below).

Photographs by Joel Arrington

countless thousands of man-o-war jellyfish whose floats popped under our tires. We drove up from the inlet and arrived at the stretch of beach north of Jennette's Pier just as the blues and stripers moved in.

There were only a few at first, with birds working over them— gulls over the bluefish, terns over the stripers. We caught all the blues we wanted and two striped bass in just a little while and sat back in the car to watch the show. Gradually the birds increased and apparently word had been spreading like wildfire, because more and more anglers arrived on the beach. Some walked over the dunes from the road, others drove. By this time, some of the early anglers had accumulated stacks of sandy bluefish on the beach and excited drivers, intent on the now thousands of squalling gulls and scores of wild-eyed anglers, ran over them and kept going as if nothing had happened. Many of these people were men, women, and children who had never caught a big fish in their lives, people from Elizabeth City and Norfolk who had heard about this most amazing thing that was happening on the beach at Nags Head and had picked up freshwater tackle, anything, however inadequate, and rushed to get in on the bonanza. They cast bait and lures of every description, but it made no difference whatever, because the blues hit anything, with no hesitation, and ran off with miles of line as they snapped and cut monofilament right and left. People were screaming and cursing and bleeding from fingers incautiously thrust into fishes' mouths. Soon the riot ended when the tide turned and gradually the fishing tapered off.

Some of these fish weighed

Joel Arrington

A rising sun backlights this bluefish. During the early years of the cycle, blues larger than this were more common, and 20-pounders were by no means unusual.

twenty pounds and a little more. You hear a lot of people say, these days, that they caught some "twenty-pound blues," but they didn't actually weigh them. Fish approaching twenty pounds were rare after 1972, and only recently have a few more than usual been showing up in tournaments. In 1970 and again the following fall, they were commonplace. Recently fall-run blues have averaged about sixteen pounds, spring-run about twelve.

There is no doubt that the resurgence of bluefish in the 1970s accounted in large measure for the vast increases in Outer Banks beach traffic that occurred subsequently and continues today. Red drum and speckled trout could not have attracted the numbers of people that bluefish did because they are too hard to catch. Here, after all, was a big fish that assaulted the beach in great numbers, was fast, strong, ravenous, and utterly undiscriminating between lure types or baits. Why, anyone could catch them. At least that's what people thought, and the idea sold a lot of beach buggies and motel rooms.

But they were only partly right. Despite much publicized blitzes, big bluefish over the years have proven to be not so universally available to sport fishermen and not so easy to catch when they are about. Even veteran anglers make trips to the coast in season and never see a bluefish. Before December 1965, when a mini-blitz occurred on Hatteras Island, big bluefish were last recorded in numbers on the Outer Banks in 1935. Now their renewed presence here and elsewhere in the western Atlantic after thirty years of total absence added a new dimension to surf, pier, and inshore fishing. Without them, North Carolina

coastal angling in the last twenty years would be much the worse.

Bluefish occur in many of the earth's oceans, along the shores of North and South America, Africa, and even in the Pacific. In eastern America, they generally are distributed from Massachusetts to Florida, with smaller fish in the Gulf of Mexico. In years when populations are large, a few range to Nova Scotia and Cuba. There are blues off Venezuela, Brazil, and Uruguay.

Bluefish everywhere, not just in North Carolina, display wild and mysterious fluctuations in abundance over a period of years. Hal Lyman in *Successful Bluefishing* quotes one Zaccheus Macy in his *Account of Nantucket* to the effect that bluefish were abundant for five years around the Massachusetts island when settlers first arrived, then suddenly disappeared in 1764. Big blues have reportedly done this in over two hundred years of fishing records.

Numbers of theories have been put forward to explain these population variations, but none is totally convincing. Lyman offers his own: since bluefish have been present in the western Atlantic during this cycle longer than any other period in recorded history, and since bluefish are known to be susceptible to parasites that proliferate only when the population reaches a certain density, perhaps, he suggests, heavy fishing pressure these days is keeping the population cropped below the critical level at which disease or parasites can spread and wipe out all but a few survivors. Under Lyman's theory, the population crash never occurs and we continue to enjoy good fishing.

It is a good theory, but there are other possibilities, too. In the past,

perhaps the fish have gone somewhere else—to Africa or South America. We don't know, but research goes on.

At one time it was thought, without much evidence, that there was only one race of bluefish in the western Atlantic and that migrations were principally north and south. Tagging studies have revealed, however, that the situation is much more complicated than that. There are at least two, possibly three or more, distinct races. One, called the "southern spring spawners," breeds off the mid-Atlantic coast at the edge of the Gulf Stream. Another, the "northern summer spawners," breeds closer to shore between Chesapeake Bay and Cape Cod. Young of these northern fish move southward in the fall to spend their first winter off the Carolinas, then move into the sounds in the spring. From then on, these fish apparently migrate north in the spring and back again in the fall. Just how far they migrate and how far offshore they move is still largely unknown.

Young of the southern spring spawners move southward offshore and contribute to the Florida winter fishery. Apparently there is yet another race that breeds off Florida.

All this is quite complicated, and may prove to be even more so as additional studies are made. Researchers have concluded that the bluefish are more oceanic than formerly thought, rather than associated with inshore waters, and that movements are less predictable.

For several years, there was a commercial fishery in the winter off Cape Fear, and, whenever weather permitted, sport fishermen could run the thirty-five or so miles from Southport or Carolina Beach Inlet to the fishing grounds near the

At dawn, anglers gather in great numbers at Cape Point when schools of giant bluefish gather in the turbulent crosscurrents to feed.

Frying Pan Shoals navigation tower. Those fish failed to show up in the winter of 1981–82, and only a few have returned since. Similarly, sportfishing success in spring and fall is largely dependent on whether any numbers of blues move close to shore where anglers can get at them, either from pier, surf, or boat. Factors such as currents, turbidity, presence of bait, and temperature are so complex that fishing success is highly unpredictable even though we may know from recent catch records that the fish population level is high.

The largest bluefish recorded as a sportfishing catch is attributed to James Hussey of Tarboro. His fish was caught off Hatteras Island on January 30, 1972, and, at 31 pounds, 12 ounces, no other records even come close. No other listing of the International Game Fish Association even exceeds 25 pounds. Hal Lyman reports an old handline catch of 45 pounds from northern Africa, but the United States has a virtual monopoly on world sportfishing records. The exceptions are a 17-pound, 10-ounce fish from the Canary Islands in 1981 and a 24-pound, 3-ounce fish from the Azores in 1953.

Some of these bigger fish are quite old, as fish go. Growth rates slow down as bluefish reach about six years, so that a 15-pound fish is likely to be about ten years old, a 17½-pounder about fourteen. Bluefish tend to be thick and heavy in the fall, big-headed and rakish in the spring. Some blues caught at Oregon Inlet in the spring of 1983 were exceptions, however, being heavy for their length and weighing, some of them, over 18 pounds.

Such fish are a challenge to catch on light tackle. Wherever anglers can find a concentration of big bluefish in relatively clear water and cast to them with line testing under seventeen pounds, the level of sport increases exponentially. One of these

Photographs by Joel Arrington

The sustained high cycle of big bluefish has probably done more to sell beach buggies (above, left) than any other single factor, but their use has not been without controversy, and there are now restrictions on many beaches. At times, giant blues are caught on shoals in the sounds or inside inlets like this rock jetty behind Cape Lookout (above, right).

locations is Cape Lookout shoals in April and November. Spring bluefish usually come into shallow water near the cape to feed and warm themselves. Sometimes, early in the morning, they can be found on the shoal west of Cape Lookout jetty basking like largemouth bass on a bed. These fish are not easy to entice to a lure, but they can be caught. Light-tackle angler Tom Earnhardt uses a large white popping bug and picks up the lure noisily and casts it repeatedly to goad the fish into striking. Fair weather in the fall produces calm seas and clear water on cape shoals where bluefish may be in packs stalking menhaden, mullet, and other bait. These fish will readily take any surface lure over three inches in length, and they show a preference for a noisy one, like the Arbogast Scudder.

The most interesting bluefish angling I have seen occurs at Oregon Inlet in May and June. Guide Vernon Barrington of Wanchese showed me schools of blues up on the extensive shoals south of the in-

let and stretching along the western side of Hatteras Island. We cast to them with eight-foot spin rods and pencil poppers with great success, and one year even teased some close to our boat with a hookless popper so that Chico Fernandez could get one on fly. He was fishing six-pound test leader and caught an eleven-pound fish.

Although many North Carolina bluefish are caught from boats out to the edge of the Gulf Stream, particularly around wrecks, most are hooked from piers and the surf. The fall run usually begins in October with a few fish caught from the beach north of Kitty Hawk. Oregon Inlet frequently is a hot spot for weeks at a time, and sometime in early November the first fish appear at Cape Hatteras Point. This spot, the hub of surf fishing in the mid-Atlantic, may very well be the most consistent producer of bluefish in the world—if you can stand the crowds. Through the winter, blues may appear whenever there is mild weather at Hatteras Inlet, Ocracoke

Inlet, along the Core Banks, and at Cape Lookout shoals. Less frequently the big fish come to the shore south of Lookout.

In the spring, usually by mid-April, there are jumbos in the surf zone of Core Banks and particularly on Cape Lookout shoals. May and the first two or three weeks of June are tops for Oregon Inlet. In summer only a few stragglers are left around the inlets. However, there are smaller blues weighing up to five or six pounds near inlets all along the coast from spring through fall. Some of the most enjoyable late summer fishing I know is for two- to five-pound blues on eight-pound line and topwater plugs beside marsh islands near Outer Banks inlets. These snappers come into the inlets on falling tide and work upcurrent into the sounds, slashing bait they trap against a bank or shoal. They are spectacular surface strikers and tough fighters.

If the big blues behave true to form, they will suddenly be gone one day, just as they always have. I look on their continued presence as a gift. Although we had more speckled trout before the blues came back, I'm not sure there was a connection. If the great bluefish disappearing act occurs again, I, for one, will miss them.

Fly Fishing for Grouse

I quote herewith this report which appeared in the fall 1985 issue of *The Flyline*, a newsletter published by the North Carolina Council of Trout Unlimited:

Bud Hunter from Hendersonville was fly fishing on the Tuckaseigee River in Jackson County recently and brought his old bird dog, Pal. As Bud was fishing, Pal was in the laurel thickets in search of grouse. One flushed out and flew directly over Bud as he was making a backcast. The bird became tangled in the leader and took 10 yards of line; however, the 6X tippet broke and the grouse took his favorite fly and continued flying downstream.

This report has the ring of truth, and moreover has the potential for revolutionizing the sport of grouse hunting. It has long been recognized that one of the disadvantages to hunting is the inability to come up with any sort of catch-and-release mechanism that could prove workable. Discounting those sportsmen who have solved this problem by simply missing all their shots, there has heretofore been no way to collect a bag limit and also release it no worse for wear. Or to put it in the jargon of professional wildlife enforcement officers, once a critter has been "reduced to possession," there is no way to "enlarge it to freedom."

But suppose you could combine the best elements of fishing with those of hunting and come up with a workable combination? That's what it appears that Bud and Pal have done. There remain, however, some unanswered questions. If it is apparent that a 6X leader is too light, then what test leader would hold an adult grouse? Obviously,

1X would be unsporting, but what about 4X or 5X? Would bamboo flyrods be suitable, or should the grouse angler choose a graphite or boron rod? It would seem that a glass rod might be a violation of propriety, and certainly no sporting grouse angler would stoop to a casting or spinning rod.

Furthermore, our reporter is typically obscure in naming the fly pattern that proved successful in this instance, saying only that the grouse took Bud's "favorite fly." Was it a grouse and teal pattern, a soft-hackled partridge, or something else?

This brings up another point. Would grouse anglers be restricted to the use of artificial imitations, or might there be certain covers set aside where it was permissible to use natural bait? If so, I foresee a controversy since it is all too clear that mortality will be higher for grouse that gulp a succulent natural fox grape threaded on a Mustad, as opposed to being lightly hooked in the beak by a carefully wrought imitation grape made of hair from a purple deer. Would grouse anglers claim that a bird on a hand-tied fly is worth two on a bush bait? Would it be considered unsporting to hook a grouse on the ground, or must one cast only to rising birds? Would there be a great hue and cry to stock fingerling grouse in areas where populations ebbed? These are not mere questions of proper regulation and management, but seek the higher ground of ethical behavior.

I can't settle these matters here, but this whole business reminds me of an incident I witnessed some years ago when I dropped in to visit a friend one afternoon. He was out in the woodlot behind the house stalking those little striped lizards called skinks. He wanted to photograph them, but they were not in the mood. They were also a good bit quicker than he was, but, alas, not quite as clever. Using a ten-foot surf rod, he had run monofilament through the guides so that a small loop protruded from the tip. Although the skinks would not let him approach any closer than about eight feet, they were not alarmed by the rod and he was able to creep within reaching distance and slip the almost invisible loop over their heads. Then by pulling on the monofilament, he could close the loop around their necks and "reduce them to possession."

He was so fascinated by this advance in technology and the sporting qualities of the capture, he had totally forgotten why he had ever wanted to catch them in the first place. When I arrived, he had already captured half a dozen, gently releasing them, and was concentrating on only the most wary skinks.

"I think I'm on to something here," he whispered excitedly so as not to alarm his prey. "With the proper exposure, this could become a national sport. Chapters of Skinks Unlimited would be formed, and members would hold annual fundraising banquets and auction paintings of skinks. I've already determined that a proper skink rod would be about twelve feet long and have a very delicate tip action. Graphite, because of its light weight, would be ideal. Skillful skinkers could play them on cobwebby 8X leaders."

I must have seemed a bit dubious because he paused a moment, apparently lost in thought. "Of course, they don't jump much," he added as he unjointed his surf rod and leaned it against the woodshed.

We walked back to the house and sat on the porch. "You don't think the world is ready for this, do you?" he asked. "Well," I answered, choosing my words carefully, "most of mankind's great thinkers have been ahead of their time."

—*Jim Dean*

Ten to One

ROD AMUNDSON

It was after five-thirty, and some of the boys were beginning to gather around the pot-bellied stove in Guppy's General Merchandise Emporium, Guppy's Crossroads.

Luke Guppy, owner of the store, is not especially old-fashioned; he believes in supplying his customers with everyday needs. The needs range from mule collars to ladies' undies, and are often displayed in close proximity.

I came in to get a cup of Luke's potent coffee, a barbecue sandwich with chopped onions, and a bowl of Mrs. Guppy's delicious homemade chili, which she confided one time is seasoned with wild onions.

As usual there was an argument going on, and as usual it had to do with who had the best bird dog—Luke's old buddy and neighbor, Elmo Cooter, or Clete Elmore.

"Elmo," said Clete, "I know why you named that dangfool mutt of yours 'Ram.' He'll ram into a covey of birds half a mile ahead of you. I seen him point a rabbit one time!"

Elmo squirted a stream of tobacco juice that sizzled on the stove, shifted the cud to the other side of his mouth, and said, "Clete, ol' Ram has forgotten more about bird hunting than that mangy mongrel of your'n will ever learn. You oughta seen him last Saturday. It was gittin' on toward sundown, and I knowed he was on point. But the brush was so thick I couldn't see him and he didn't come when I called. I went home, ate supper, and come back out with a flashlight to look for him. It was pitch dark, and when I found him he was still on point and that covey of birds was sittin' in a circle, sound asleep."

"That ain't nothing," said Clete. "My little ol' Bitsey has got the best pedigree of any setter in this part of the country. Let me tell you 'bout her granddaddy, Pokey. We called him Pokey because he was a slow poke, but he was steady and wouldn't never break a point.

"Bout five years ago me and cousin Goatsford hunted him last day of the bird season. It was gittin' dark, like you said, and we couldn't locate him. Went back the next mornin', and the next, and the next and finally give up. Next summer we was cleanin' brush along the trail to the soybean field and we found him. Nothin' but his bones and his collar hangin' 'round his neck. The birds was gone, but ol' Pokey was still on point!"

There were a few guffaws and some shuffling of feet among the hangers-on, and no one said anything for a while. Luke's shoulders were quivering like he was laughing inside. Finally Elmo spoke up again.

"Clete," he said, "If you think that dang mongrel of your'n is so cotton pickin' good, why don't we jus' go out an' see who has got the best dog?"

"Shucks, Elmo," Clete responded. "Ol' Bitsey wouldn't be seen in the same field with ol' Ram. She's ten to one better than he ever will be!"

"Ten to one. Ten to ONE? Man, put your money where your mouth is," said Elmo. He laid a five-dollar bill on the counter.

Clete looked at the five, looked around at the now silent group, and pulled out his billfold. "I ain't got fifty on me, but I'll write you a check."

"That's good enough for me," Elmo said, and the deal was closed.

Luke picked up the check and the bill, placed both in a wrinkled envelope, and put them in the cash register.

"A bet is a bet," Luke said, "but when we goin' to see who wins?"

Clete and Elmo looked at each other and agreed that, since the next day was Saturday, nine in the morning would be fine. There was considerable argument as to who would be the judge, and it was finally agreed that since I was from another county I would be the referee. When Luke told me a night's lodging, supper, and breakfast would be on the house, I agreed.

I slept late, then ate a leisurely breakfast of country ham and scrambled eggs. It was still foggy and misting a little at eight-thirty—a perfect day for quail hunting and good bird dogs.

There was a long argument as to where this mini–field trial should be held. Luke contended that the contest would be more even if the dogs were turned loose on land they had never hunted on before. After all, both probably knew where all the coveys were on their home grounds. So it was finally decided the hunt would be held on Uncle Lem Crowder's place several miles down the road. There was a general exodus in that direction.

By the time we reached the first field the sun came out. Bitsey and Ram were pleased, and both dogs began quartering beautifully. Ram made the first point, which Bitsey honored. Then Bitsey pointed and Ram honored. This went on for over an hour. Both retrieved beautifully, and I realized I had a tough contest on my hands.

In the next field, a covey got up after both dogs came to a simultaneous point. Elmo dropped a bird cleanly, but Clete's bird angled off and fell into a farm pond. Ram retrieved Elmo's bird, then headed for the pond. When we reached the pond, old Ram was standing on a ramrod point—at the water near the dam; but there was no sign of the bird. Quail can swim, and dead ones float.

Despite the blue streak of curses Elmo directed at Ram, the dog held his point. Elmo Cooter is well known for his temper and I'm sure he figured his five-dollar bill was a goner, not to mention the ridicule his erring pointer would bring down on him. Clete was lying on the ground, laughing.

Elmo pulled up his gun and shot at Ram's head. Fortunately he missed. There was a shocked silence among the spectators and Ram stayed on point. Then there was a slight swirl in the water at which Ram was pointing, and up came about a twelve-pound largemouth bass. In his mouth was a still-warm bobwhite quail.

Elmo laid down his gun and knelt down beside Ram. He didn't say anything, just patted his head and scratched behind his ears. Clete Elmore stopped laughing.

Thirty-five Acres
Was the World

MIKE GADDIS

The law had been out for a good while on big game like rabbits, squirrels, duck, and quail, but I was hard into a Saturday of sorting and cleaning all available tools of the hunt for another opening day come Tuesday. Laid around for inspection were a Daisy BB gun, two slingshots, magnum and small bore respectively, a hawkbill knife with a broken handle, several tubes of Red Top BBs, a leather pouch weighty with choice creek and roadside ammunition for the slingshots, and a small can of 3-in-1 Oil. If you're wondering about the oil, BB guns commonly developed performance problems associated with barrel friction, and a single drop of the 3-in-1 did wonders to restore the ballistic properties desired. Knowing that kind of thing at the time was of the same magnitude as the knowledge acquired later that you had to compensate a bit for the first shot from a clean rifle barrel.

It was mid-June, school had been out long enough to forget, and the wheat harvest was at hand. I knew because my close surveillance of the crop, sow to reap, was only slightly

less exacting that that of those whose livelihood rested more solidly in its success or failure. By mid-to-late May, the green stalks had begun to show the yellow mottling that led with sunny days and warm nights to the deep gold of maturity during the wedding month. Now the heavy, whiskered heads beckoned, rippling and furling over the earth at the will of the winds.

Of the vast array of adventures awaiting a foot-loose boy of nine in rural Randolph County, circa 1951, combining wheat held stature near the pinnacle. It wasn't the cutting of wheat itself; that was only the means to an end. For the adults, it was mean, sweltering, exhausting work. When conditions were right, it was hot and dry, and the heat demons danced vigorously over the tops of the grain. The dust rose in constant clouds about the man on the combine, busy with bagging the chutes and loading the ramp, and the chaff was an unrelenting irritant to sweaty skin. When the combining was done, the heavy bags had to be loaded on the truck, and later the straw bales.

But I enjoyed the immunity of youth in a season of unbridled spirits. My job was to ride armed on the combine once things got going good, dismount for high-mettled rabbit chases, and generally ward off varmints that had invariably taken residence in the unknown depths of grain stalks.

I have often wondered since if anyone has ever studied the ecology of a Piedmont wheat field; that is, if they're the way they used to be. An idea says it would be self-contained in good measure for there was invertebrate and vertebrate, insect and mammal, vegetarian and carnivore, predator and prey. Most of the native species we knew were well represented. Small bugs and beetles, spiders, grasshoppers by the scores, terrapins, toads, leopard frogs, snakes, indigo buntings, voles, mice, field rats, and rabbits were in abundance, and foxes red and gray were there in one collection, with even an occasional weasel or deer. It was the only time I could ever expect to find the combined fascinations of my boyhood in one place at one time.

My mentor and guardian for the

associated happenings, as well as all other outdoor pursuits of the era, was my maternal uncle, Sidney Walker. A day began predawn. I walked down the hill and double-timed through the deep pines owned by the big owl to my uncle's back steps. The yellow glow of the kitchen beckoned an ever-welcome and faithful haven from the intimidation of night. Over cereal and fruit, a morning ritual, my lead questions always concerned the present reliability of the combine. From my perspective, there could be little tolerance for errant machinery, and the hateful thing was constantly devastating me with broken belts, cracked conveyor slats, broken cross-shear teeth, or some other unexplainable malady in its internals.

Uncle Sid was a craftsman. Whether it involved the intricate woodwork of an antique restoration or building a woodshed, he was meticulous. It carried over into his farming. Most of it was wasted on me at the time, I'm afraid, for it all meant slow. By the time we made the equipment shed, well after day, I had little appreciation for the ordered sequence of the work process, but a lot of understanding about what professional people now call emotional stress.

It was up in the morning, after the dew was off, when we finally got started. The metal flap on the exhaust stack of the big Case sprang open with the initial, blue-fumed belch of engine ignition, and then settled into a tinny dance in time with the combustion rhythm. The old tag-along combine followed disengaged, but protesting, to its final shakedown at fieldside.

Moody Hoover was our combine man, all six-and-a-half towering feet of him. When he swung his lanky frame onto the riding platform, the check was complete and the morning's work could begin. His hail to my uncle was the long-last signal when it seemed the day would surely be sacrificed to unending preparation. Hung with assorted weaponry, I scrambled to my designated perch beside the drop chute.

The forward lurch of the tractor started the shearing blades and, as the first cut of the tawny stalks fell with the reel to the ribbed intake conveyor, the whole machine shook and vibrated itself into life with a deafening roar. Separated from the head, the clean grain cascaded into the burlap bags waiting on the spreaders, and the mouthful that came from the first run was always sweetest. The dust grew in billows, grasshoppers rose in armies, and the air was heavy with anticipation. With all senses alerted, the vigil was on.

Fields were judged largely by size and the character of the crop. The big, dense fields were best as they offered added shelter and harbored more. But you had to cut them in one day, otherwise the still of darkness presented escape opportunity for their inhabitants. It was a personal tragedy when we engaged a big field in midafternoon. The small fields could be cut quickly, which kept you on edge, but you saw less and the rabbits nearly always beat you to the woods.

The thing about cutting wheat was the farther you went, the better it got. The first several turns around a field usually didn't create a lot of excitement because all residents simply migrated toward its center. But, as you kept whittling on the perimeter, the general population became reconciled through an increasing state of alarm to an unavoidable de-parture. From then on the pace of the affair was torrid.

It seemed the snakes were among the earliest refugees. A holler and beckon from the tractor brought me on the run to confront whatever was at hand. I was left to my own means with the shiny black racers, big chicken snakes, musky garters, and gray snakes. These were usually pinned to the ground with a stick behind the head and captured alive to suffer integrated incarceration in a burlap sack for tally and closer inspection at the end of the day. But, the foreboding cat-eyed and pregnant-bodied copperheads commanded the attention of all parties. Barring breakdowns, it was the only time Uncle Sid stopped the tractor.

It was here that the slingshots came into play, for the vipers were given no quarter. They might show up later when you reached for a piece of lumber or bite one of the dogs come early fall. If my eye was good, I'd send them into a writhing demise with a flattened head, in which case my stock and reputation was aided considerably. If I missed, I endured the self-humiliation of seeing Moody or Uncle Sid deal an undignified end to a respected foe with a whippy sapling. But either way, the hapless creature came to bag, to be later removed from its hide. The beautiful hourglass markings of the skin made the prettiest kind of cover for a belt or hatband, demanding no less respect among my peers than that we understood to be afforded the eagle feather by the Plains Indians.

Then came the rabbits. Most of all there were the rabbits, from the fragile young of the year to the grown bucks and does with the big, deep, liquid eyes, capable of expressing fear and hurt but never anger or threat. Watching closely, you could detect them when they first broke the wheat cover in front of the tractor and threw themselves with abandon into a desperate race for the sanctuary of the woods line. All year they had eluded me with their fleetness on fair terrain; but now the loose, layered straw countered the thrusts of those powerful hind legs and vengeance surged sweet. Finding their driving legs suddenly of no advantage, they became terrified when pursued and would eventually dart under a pile of leavings, lulled into false security. It was then that I would stalk and pounce, bringing them struggling to hand. With the unabridged exuberance of a puppy, the joy of the chase unparalleled, I ran them until I lay panting cotton-mouthed and sweaty in the hot summer sun, waiting for my legs to hold me again, to resume once more.

We never harmed the rabbits. They were admired and petted awhile, and then released. With boyhood defiance, I tried to keep some now and then in the face of admonition from my uncle. But I found quickly and harshly that they are tender creatures, far from being endowed with an indomitable will to live. Even more so than most wild things, they languish rapidly into a comatose state when robbed of freedom and will soon die. I had five in a box one time and apparently they became so distraught that they chewed each other's ears to the skull. They were just sitting there in complete depression, no longer beautiful and without dignity. I had to destroy them, and the experience left me with very deep feeling for the importance of freedom a long time before I learned and under-

stood all the personal assurances of the Constitution.

You expected the rabbits, but you could usually count on something unexpected, too. We were making the last few rounds on a secluded field near a slab pile one morning when three young gray foxes ran out from behind the combine. Moody and I both gave chase and one became so confused that it lay down on top of the straw in the open field. I was strong for catching it alive, but Moody immediately began gathering rocks. His daddy had some chickens that fell prey to the foxes now and then, and, like most second-generation farmers of the region, he grew up at war with Reynard. But Moody was excited and the fox would live for another day. He threw five rocks point-blank, only to watch the kit finally get up and bound off untouched, not altogether without my blessing.

Another time we saw two deer leave, and I gave their story to my aunt later with much drama and importance. There was an Eastern diamondback that had caused a stir, because we didn't see rattlesnakes very often. After dragging its carcass around on a stick most of the day, I cut the rattlers off with the hawkbill and kept them handy for commanding immediate attention at strategic moments, particularly in Sunday school with the girls. And, we nearly ran over a five-foot chicken snake that had caught a half-grown rabbit and was in the process of swallowing it. The lower jaw was unhinged and the neck skin was so distended that the white showed between the scales.

When the last swath of stalks no longer stood over the field, and the

fat grain bags lay in pattern, marking the passing of the combine, I gathered up the BB gun, stuffed pockets with Red Top tubes, and disembarked to spend the waning afternoon hours foot hunting in the ground cover. It was a grand safari, wholly my own, while Moody and Uncle Sid, bound with the shackles of responsibility, labored the harvest sacks onto the flatbed Chevy. The straw was alive with field rats and big lubber grasshoppers, and a brisk kick produced either a challenging ground target scurrying for new territory or a fast, crossing wing shot that demanded my best. Lead and follow-through were not strangers when I graduated to the shotgun in the next year or so.

I took most of them fairly but would have to admit succumbing to the temptation of a sitting shot here and there. When you're nine, you're not as old as you are later, and the mellowing of the years hasn't yet introduced as many ethics. I shot the BB gun hot, counted coup unmercifully, and laid out my assorted bag for unabashed display before my elders.

Whiling away the time so, it was rare that I heard my uncle's first summons near sunset, for I was in a land and place beyond his reach. We had endured a lot of geography that year, drilled into us in Mrs. Rice's fourth-grade classroom. I would come to see more of it later, and the dimensions of the world would change forever irretrievably. But right then, for all its reported vastness, it lay totally in my grasp, within the boundaries of a thirty-five-acre Carolina grain field.

A Country Store Gourmet

JIM DEAN

Rare is the hunter or fisherman who can accurately be called a gourmet or epicure. Quite frankly, most of us think that "Chateaubriand for two" is a love nest in a shabby French hotel, or that an "aspic" is something you wear around your neck.

And yet, the outdoorsman has a very special—some would say unusual—appreciation for food. This appreciation, or perversion, inevitably manifests itself away from home. For example, at home I cannot eat a tomato unless I first pick out all the seeds, and the only green vegetable I like is key lime pie. But let me spot a raw, dirt-stained turnip in a field while I'm bird hunting, and I'll wipe it on my pants and devour it with gusto.

If I'm hunting, I'd rather take a lunch break at a country store than have it catered by the finest restaurant on the continent. If I'm on a wilderness trout stream, happiness is a couple of mashed liverwurst and onion sandwiches. I might turn up my nose at a water-spotted wine glass at home, but I'll drink contentedly from a woodland spring

Potted meat smeared on a peanut butter cracker makes the ideal hors d'oeuvre for the weary hunter dining in a country store.

clogged with dead leaves and live salamanders.

Why is that? Who knows really. It seems that food and drink just taste better out there; and no doubt you—like me—have fond memories of such things as oysters roasted on a November beach, or peach cobbler cooked in a dutch oven buried in embers of a dying campfire. Or maybe it's venison tenderloins simmered in butter and sour cream

in a downeast deer camp or mountainous breakfasts served at 4:30 in the morning by the wife of a waterfowl guide.

Most of my fondest outdoor memories have nothing to do with fish caught or game killed. Though it's been years, I still remember the "Great Fairfield Oyster Orgy" that followed a day of goose hunting at Mattamuskeet when my dad made the ill-advised offer to buy me all the oysters I could eat. I had 'em raw, steamed, stewed, and fried, and even managed to get a couple of oyster fritters just barely past my vocal cords before staggering back to the car.

Then there was the time I made chili for my companions Joel Arrington and Tom Earnhardt on a trout-fishing expedition. While they watched with interest—or maybe it was alarm—I tossed a double handful of chili powder and red pepper into the iron pot with the beef, tomatoes, onions, and beans. We left it simmering over a low fire while we scattered out to fish the stream. The whole valley reeked of chili, and

Ken Taylor

No noontime feast in a four-star country store would be complete without a slab of rat cheese and a pickled sausage or pig's foot. Of course, there are stranger things to eat if you have the appetite, and cast-iron innards.

when we returned I raised the lid for a quick sniff and promptly lost most of the hair in my nose. Tom credits my chili with curing a congenital sinus condition.

One cold October day, with a stinging rain riding a stiff northeast wind, I stood alone on the end of an ocean pier plugging for bluefish. After awhile two fishermen joined me and I could see right away that they were better prepared for this kind of fishing by a long shot—not to mention several short ones. After

taking a couple of nips, they set about lighting the only thing that was not already well lit, a small charcoal grill they'd brought.

While one tended the grill, the other began fishing. He launched a wobbly cast into the teeth of the gale. Every time his plug hit the water, a two-pound bluefish would grab it. The cook would split the fish, sling out the innards, and place it skin up on the grill.

My friends graciously offered me grill space for my blues, and a snort

for my health. During the next hour, we caught and ate perhaps a dozen crisp, delicious blues; and my health was so improved that, when I finally judged it prudent to leave, I merely leaned back on the wind and sailed down the pier to a safe port.

An appreciation for oysters, chili, or grilled bluefish is not hard to understand. What is less easy to explain is the sportsman's fascination with the kind of food one finds in country stores. A man of impeccable breeding, exquisite manners, and unquestionable taste will deny his heritage after following a brace of bird dogs all morning and gorge himself on the most incredible array of swill. There is something about a can of sardines or pickled pig's feet that is absolutely irresistible to a hunter or fisherman.

If you have never dined in a four-star country store, you are culturally deprived. There is, of course, no Michelin Guide to assist you in the selection of a superior country store, but I can tell you what to look for.

It has been my experience that the food is better in those country stores where the driveway is paved with old bottle caps, relieved by a single, rusty gas pump. In the dusty windows of the weathered building, you should find at least one very old movie card advertising a double feature starring the likes of Tom Mix, the Durango Kid, or Lash LaRue.

Once inside, it is proper to nod to the maitre d' who will be leaning against the counter in his overalls, picking his teeth with a toothpick. Other diners may already be seated on upended crates around a pot-bellied stove chewing tobacco, pouring peanuts in their soft drinks, and spitting on the hot stove to hear it sizzle.

In order to appreciate the atmosphere, one must not hurry. Pause and breathe deeply, sorting out the various scents of fertilizer, seed, leather, dust, and tired feet. Look around. On the wall, you will find everything from harnesses to hankies, Barlow knives to radiator belts. You may even find something you've always wanted, like a little perfumed

chenille skunk to hang on your rearview mirror to mask the musk of working mutts. My favorite store has a sign on the wall that says:

"We will crank your car and hold your baby, but we sell for cash and don't mean maybe."

Carefully sniff the jars of pickled eggs and pig's feet. I cannot recommend too highly any pickled sausages you might find. Sometimes, if you are truly in Mecca, you will find a keg of salt herring.

On the counter of every country store worthy of the name, there will be a wheel of greasy rat cheese. Buy a slab. Even if you don't like cheese, its ingestion may help offset any unpleasantries occasioned by the rich mixture you will soon savor.

On the shelves will be cans of vienna sausages, salmon and tuna, sardines, hash, and potted meat. Avoid reading the label on the potted meat unless you are uncommonly interested in the final disposition of such items as pork snouts, beef hearts and stomachs, assorted lips, and a variety of less distinguished cuts.

Elsewhere, you will find Nabs, wrapped sandwiches, 12-gauge peppermint sticks, candy bars, cookies in jars, and a vast assortment of cupcakes, raisin cookies, cinnamon buns, and pies.

I have one hunting companion whose favorite country store lunch is a large can of whole, peeled tomatoes and a watery chocolate drink. I personally consider that an ostentatious show of redneck; but if your taste runs to such extremes, you are certainly free to indulge.

My own taste runs heavily to dill

pickles, rat cheese, potted meat scooped out of the can with peanut butter crackers, cold pork 'n beans, magnum orange soft drinks, and coconut candy bars.

Once, while several of us were dining at a country store, my son Scott noted that his can of pork 'n beans contained only a single, small chunk of fatty pork. "That is to be expected," explained our companion, Joe Phillips. "There is never more than one chunk of pork in a can; otherwise, they would call it 'porks 'n beans.'"

As I have said, I cannot explain the almost universal appeal among sportsmen for meals of this nature; but if I had to guess, I would say that it reflects some primeval lust for independence. As a kid, I was constantly being reprimanded for squandering my weekly allowance on similar items in the neighborhood grocery instead of forthrightly facing the daily onslaught of boiled collards, cabbage, rutabagas, and snap beans thought necessary for proper growth.

Perhaps it is the shuddering recollection of those collards that drives me across the bottle caps and through the threshold to the herring keg and the potted meat. I only know that once there, I am in the midst of gastronomic glory; and sometimes, as I sit contentedly on a drink crate watching a cutthroat game of checkers, I feel moved to offer a judgment.

"It was," I might say, "a good pig's foot, but not a great pig's foot."

Purple Gallinule (Jack Dermid)

Epilogue

Wildlife in North Carolina is a monthly magazine published by the North Carolina Wildlife Resources Commission, the agency charged with the regulation of hunting, fishing, and trapping in the state and with the welfare of the state's resources of game, nongame, and endangered and threatened wildlife. The magazine has been in existence for fifty years, although not in the present form or with the same name. Indeed, *Wildlife* predates the Wildlife Commission (founded in 1947) by ten years. First published in November 1937 as *Wildlife Management in North Carolina*, the magazine was a collaboration between the zoology department at North Carolina State College in Raleigh and the North Carolina Department of Conservation and Development. It grew out of an interest to introduce the then new concepts of wildlife management to sportsmen and landowners.

The early magazine reflected the rural character of the state. Edited by Clyde P. Patton for a brief period and by Rod Amundson from 1947 until 1975, the publication soon featured the stunning wildlife photography of Jack Dermid. The 1950s' *Wildlife* blazed the path that the magazine of the 1980s still follows,

promoting ethical hunting and fishing, reporting on the Wildlife Commission's efforts on behalf of sportsmen, and providing management advice for landowners. But as the magazine entered the 1960s, its subject matter broadened to reflect the times. There were stories on environmental degradation, pollution, and habitat loss. The state was growing and its growing pains could be sensed in the magazine of those years.

Under Duane Raver, who became managing editor of *Wildlife in North Carolina* in 1960 and later editor, the look of the magazine changed as well. Color began to appear not only on the cover but also in its interior pages. Raver's wildlife art became a fixture in the magazine. Some familiar staff names in the magazine of the late 1950s, 1960s, and early 1970s were illustrator Win Donat, photographers Jim Lee and Joel Arrington, and writers Bill Hamnett and Luther Partin. There were many others. The subscription price increased from fifty cents a year in the 1950s to one dollar, and, as late as 1977, subscriptions could be bought for only two dollars. In 1978, the price was raised to five dollars a year.

Jim Dean was named editor when

Raver retired in 1979. The magazine maintained its focus on the wise use of the state's wildlife resources. A reader survey indicated that hunting and fishing stories were preferred subjects, with North Carolina history and its sporting heritage also popular. Profiles on the state's wildlife continued to be staples of monthly coverage.

By the 1970s, magazines nationwide were publishing more color and neighboring state wildlife magazines were improving their designs. *Wildlife* took a big step forward in 1978 by hiring its first full-time art director, David Williams, and its first full-time photographer, Ken Taylor. Assistant editor Mark Taylor also joined the staff, followed shortly by associate editor Lawrence S. Earley.

Under Williams's art direction, the magazine underwent a redesign in January 1978, the first of several new looks. Two new departments— "Our Natural Heritage" and "Nature's Ways"—were added, as well as a back-of-the-book section edited by Mark Taylor. The new design and liberal use of color photographs in feature layouts resulted in many design awards in the ensuing years.

The additional editorial staff enabled the magazine to take on more ambitious projects, most notably reportage on environmental problems experienced in various parts of the state. On the masthead of the March 1979 issue was added this statement of mission: "*Wildlife in North Carolina* is the official educational publication of the North Carolina Wildlife Resources Commission, and is dedicated to the sound conservation of the State's wildlife and other interrelated natural resources and the environment we share with them." In response to this broad mission, staff writers began to address complex and controversial topics. During the late 1970s and into the 1980s, stories appeared on the effects of agribusiness on wildlife, on acid rain, and on the plight of the Pigeon and the Pamlico rivers. There were looks at toxic waste, the quality of water, the destruction of bottomland hardwoods, management problems in privately owned forests, and the effects of growth on wildlife habitat.

The magazine is only part of the Wildlife Commission's overall educational effort. The Division of Conservation Education also produces films and slide shows, and distributes these and other audiovisual programs to the public. In addition, seven educational representatives stationed throughout the state arrange media coverage for wildlife-related stories and hold conservation-education workshops for primary and secondary school teachers.

As *Wildlife in North Carolina* passes its golden anniversary, it remains a deeply committed voice on behalf of the conservation of wildlife and other natural resources.

Publication History

"Old Times on Currituck," H. H. Brimley, March 1943.

"Currituck's Historic Sporting Clubs," Lawrence S. Earley, December 1980.

"Ship of Frogs," Jim Dean, February 1983.

"Core Sound Memoir," Julian Hamilton, Jr., November 1985.

"Some North Carolina Decoys and Their Makers," James S. Lewis, Jr., November, December 1977; January, February 1978.

"Traditional Boats of North Carolina," Mark Taylor, July 1984.

"Death of a Turtle," Jim Dean, October 1982.

"Johannes Plott's Famous Hunting Dogs," Curtis Wooten, October 1983.

"I'm a Bear Hunter," Clyde Huntsinger, November 1982.

"Stalking the Old-Time Apples," Doug Elliott, September 1980.

"Cutting the Tree," Jim Dean, December 1985.

"Willie and Me and the Two-Moon 'Turkles,'" Paul Koepke, July 1978.

"Those Incredible Hummingbirds," Jane Rohling, May 1984.

"Magnificent Monarchs," Harry Ellis, April 1984.

"Everything but the Squeal," Jim Dean, November 1982.

"Our Wild Orchids," Doug Elliott, June 1981.

"Discovering the World of Spiders," Harry Ellis, August 1980.

"The Ultimate Survivor," Doug Elliott, November 1980.

"A Quest for Wilderness," George Ellison, January 1980.

"Where the Wind Comes From," Jim Dean, November 1983.

"Following the French Broad," Jay Davies, November 1984.

"Discovering Stone Mountain," Terry Shankle, May 1984.

"Fishing for Ice Age Trout," Jim Dean, July 1986.

"Rambling the Uwharries," Jane Rohling, August 1984.

"A Kinship in Stone," Jim Dean, November 1985.

"Two Days in John Green's Swamp," Lawrence S. Earley, June 1983.

"Mattamuskeet Memories," Jim Dean, January 1986.

"Saving Nags Head Woods," Michael Godfrey, December 1981.

"The Perfect Bird Hunt," Mike Gaddis, December 1983.

"Three Score and Three with Whitetails," Charles Elliott, October 1981.

"The Expendable Bobwhite," Jim Dean, December 1984.

"Brackish Water Bass," Joel Arrington, April 1985.

"Into Big Timber Creek," Stewart Hardison, August 1975.

"Calendar Art and the Sacrificial Bass," Jim Dean, July 1985.

"Two Different Ducks," Joel Arrington, November 1984.

"Gigging and Swatting," Curtis Wooten, September 1983.

"A History of Blues," Joel Arrington, December 1984.

"Fly Fishing for Grouse," Jim Dean, March 1986.

"Ten to One," Rod Amundson, February 1976.

"Thirty-five Acres Was the World," Mike Gaddis, July 1980.

"A Country Store Gourmet," Jim Dean, December 1978.

Contributors

Rod Amundson was editor of *Wildlife in North Carolina* from September 1947 to 1975 and helped develop the magazine into a national award winner. He lives in Raleigh.

Joel Arrington is a free-lance writer/photographer and former outdoor editor of the North Carolina Division of Travel and Tourism. His articles and pictures have appeared frequently in *Wildlife in North Carolina* and other magazines.

Larry Barton is a former editorial cartoonist who became a full-time wildlife painter in 1979. In 1986 his painting was the first-of-state design for New York's duck stamp. He lives in Pfafftown, North Carolina.

Richard E. Bird, a Charlotte radiologist, is an enthusiastic photographer of wildflowers and birds. He has won many state and regional awards for his photography. He teaches nature photography at Central Piedmont Community College.

H. H. Brimley (1861–1946) was the first director of the North Carolina Museum of Natural History. Born in England, he and his brother, C. S. Brimley, were collectors, researchers, and taxidermists for the museum.

Art Carter is senior editor of *Sporting Classics* and former staff photographer for *South Carolina Wildlife* and *Outdoor Life*. His book of photographs, *Southeast Coast*, was recently published by Graphic Arts Center Publishing Company.

Debbie Conger is a former Wildlife Resources Commission photographer.

Jay Davies is an educational field representative for the Wildlife Resources Commission and a former Commission fisheries biologist. He lives in Sylva, North Carolina.

Jim Dean is editor of *Wildlife in North Carolina* and author of many articles in national sporting magazines.

Jack Dermid is a free-lance photographer who lives in Wilmington. From 1950 to 1962 he was chief photographer for *Wildlife in North Carolina*. He taught biology at the University of North Carolina at Wilmington from 1962 until his retirement in 1984.

Larry Ditto is refuge manager for the Lake Mattamuskeet National Wildlife Refuge, and a talented and enthusiastic wildlife photographer.

Ted Dossett is the cinematographer for the Wildlife Resources Commission. He has written and photographed several films, the latest being *Wildlife Horizons*. He is currently producing a film on fishing in North Carolina.

Lawrence S. Earley is associate editor of *Wildlife in North Carolina* and author of *Crisis in Habitat*, published by the Wildlife Resources Commission in 1985.

Charles Elliott has written eighteen or more books on forestry, conservation, and other outdoor subjects. He has been a field editor for *Outdoor Life* since 1950. Now retired, he lives in Covington, Georgia.

Doug Elliott is a writer, photographer, and lecturer who lives part of the year in Burnsville, North Carolina.

Harry Ellis, a writer and photographer from Bakersville, North Carolina, has published articles and photographs in *National Wildlife*, *Audubon*, and *National Geographic*.

George Ellison wrote the biographical introduction to the revised edition of Horace Kephart's *Our Southern Highlanders*, published by the University of Tennessee Press.

Kay Frazier is a former Wildlife Resources Commission photographer.

Mike Gaddis writes frequently for *Wildlife in North Carolina*. A former fisheries biologist, he is a noted amateur bird dog trainer and field trial judge.

Michael Godfrey is a nature writer and photographer from Chapel Hill. He is the author of several books, including *The Sierra Club Naturalist's Guide to the Piedmont* (1980), *Winter Birds of the Carolinas* (1978), and *A Closer Look* (1975). He is currently writing and filming natural history video bird guides.

Owen J. Gromme is a Wisconsin artist whose wildlife paintings have appeared in exhibitions too numerous to mention. The 91-year-old painter's book, *The World of Owen J. Gromme*, was published in 1984.

Stewart Hardison was author of several articles in *Wildlife in North Carolina* while a student at North Carolina State University in the early 1970s.

Tim Hergenrader is a former educational field representative for the Wildlife Resources Commission. He is chief of the Information and Education Division of the Tennessee Wildlife Resources Agency.

Robert Herr's artwork has appeared in *Wildlife in North Carolina* and most recently in the 1987 North Carolina Wildlife Calendar. He lives in Cary, North Carolina.

F. Eugene Hester is past deputy director of the U.S. Fish and Wildlife Service, and an outstanding wildlife photographer. A North Carolina native, he lives in Springfield, Virginia.

Paul Koepke is a retired professor of music theory and composition. His articles on gardening, wildlife, and conservation have appeared in *Organic Gardening* as well as *Wildlife in North Carolina*. His book *Two Moon Pond* was published by John S. Blair of Winston-Salem.

Lefty Kreh is a freelance writer and photographer whose work appears frequently in national outdoor magazines. He lectures widely on fly fishing and outdoor photography.

William S. Lea works with the U.S. Forest Service in Pisgah Forest, North Carolina. His photographs have appeared regularly in *Wildlife in North Carolina* as well as in national outdoor magazines.

James S. Lewis, Jr., who headed Lewis Construction Associates, Inc., of Goldsboro, was an avid and highly respected decoy collector. He died in 1986.

Karl and **Steve Maslowski** are father and son photographers from Cincinnati, Ohio. In addition to their widely published still photographs, they produce motion picture wildlife documentaries.

Robert Peet is associate professor of biology at the University of North Carolina at Chapel Hill. His research interest is plant communities and population ecology. He is currently studying the high levels of diversity in coastal North Carolina ecosystems.

Duane Raver was managing editor and later editor of *Wildlife in North Carolina* from 1960 to 1979, when he retired from the Wildlife Commission. His paintings have appeared in many magazines and books, and he has several times been named the North Carolina Wildlife Federation's wildlife artist of the year.

Jane Rohling is an educational field representative for the Wildlife Resources Commission and lives in Chapel Hill. She is a frequent contributor to *Wildlife in North Carolina*.

Leonard Lee Rue is one of the nation's foremost wildlife photographers whose pictures have appeared in magazines and books too numerous to mention. He is also the author of many books on wildlife, photography, and the outdoors.

Joe Seme's work has appeared in *American Artist* and *Ducks Unlimited* as well as in *Wildlife in North Carolina*. He lives in Linville, North Carolina.

Terry Shankle is an educational field representative for the Wildlife Resources Commission and lives in Denton, North Carolina. His articles and wildlife photographs have appeared frequently in *Wildlife in North Carolina*.

Frank Stick was one of the leading outdoor illustrators in the nation, painting for *Field and Stream*, *Sports Afield*, the *Saturday Evening Post*, and other magazines before his death in 1966. His book, *An Artist's Catch*, was published by the University of North Carolina Press in 1981.

Mark Taylor is assistant editor of *Wildlife in North Carolina* and specializes in environmental articles. A resident of Raleigh for nine years, he is active in Sierra Club activities.

John Widman is a former associate graphic artist for *Wildlife in North Carolina*. Mountain climbing is his passion, and he has pursued his sport in Argentina and New Zealand and on various peaks in North America.

David Williams is art director of *Wildlife in North Carolina*. His natural history illustrations appear every month in that magazine's department "Nature's Ways." He is a member of the North Carolina Nature Artists' Association.

Curtis Wooten is western region representative of North Carolina Ducks Unlimited and former educational field representative for the Wildlife Resources Commission. His articles have appeared frequently in *Wildlife in North Carolina* and other publications.